CW00722947

CONTENTS

DEVON

CHAPTER I.

THE WESTERN FOLK

Ethnology of the Western Folk—The earliest men—The Ivernian race
—The arrival of the Britons—Mixture of races in Ireland—The
Attacottic revolt — The Dumnonii — The Scottic invasion of
Dumnonia—The story of the Slave of the Haft—Athelstan drives
the Britons across the Tamar—Growth of towns—The yeomen
represent the Saxon element—The peasantry the earlier races—
The Devonshire dialect—Courtesy—Use of Christian names—
Love of funerals—Good looks among the girls—Dislike of
"Foreigners"—The Cornish people—Mr. Havelock Ellis on
them—The types—A Cornish girl—Religion—The unpardonable
sin — Folk-music — Difference between that of Devon and Cornwall and that of Somersetshire.

IT is commonly supposed that the bulk of the
Devonshire people are Saxons, and that the
Cornish are almost pure Celts.

In my opinion neither supposition is correct.

Let us see who were the primitive occupants of the
Dumnonian peninsula. In the first place there were
the men who left their rude flint tools in the Brixham
and Kent's caverns, the same people who have deposited such vast accumulations in the lime and chalk
caves and shelters of the Vézère and Dordogne. Their

remains are not so abundant with us as there, because
our conditions are not as favourable for their preservation; and yet in the Drift we do find an enormous
number of their tools, though not *in situ*, with their
hearths, as in France; yet sufficient to show that
either they were very numerous, or what is more
probable, that the time during which they existed
was long.

This people did not melt off the face of the earth
like snow. They remained on it.

We know that they were tall, that they had gentle
faces—the structure of their skulls shows this; and
from the sketches they have left of themselves, we
conclude that they had straight hair, and from their
skeletons we learn that they were tall.

M. Massenat, the most experienced hunter after
their remains, was sitting talking with me one evening at Brives about their relics. He had just received
a volume of the transactions of the Smithsonian
Institute that contained photographs of Esquimaux
implements. He indicated one, and asked me to
translate to him the passage relative to its use.
"Wonderful!" said he. "I have found this tool
repeatedly in our rock-shelters, and have never known
its purport. It is a remarkable fact, that to understand our reindeer hunters of the Vézère we must
question the Esquimaux of the Polar region. I
firmly hold that they were the same race."

A gentle, intelligent, artistic, unwarlike people got
pressed into corners by more energetic, military, and
aggressive races. And, accustomed to the reindeer,
some doubtless migrated North with their favourite

beasts, and in a severer climate became somewhat stunted.

It is possible—I do not say that it is more than possible—that the dark men and women found about Land's End, tall and handsome, found also in the Western Isles of Scotland and in West Ireland, may be the last relics of this infusion of blood.

But next to this doubtful element comes one of which no doubt at all exists. The whole of England, as of France, and as of Spain, was at one time held by a dusky, short-built race, which is variously called Iberian, Ivernian, and Silurian, of which the Basque is the representative so far as that he still speaks a very corrupted form of the original tongue. In France successive waves of Gaul, Visigoth, and Frank have swept over the land and have dominated it. But the fair hair and blue eyes and the clear skin of the conquering races have been submerged by the rising and overflow of the dusky blood of the original population. The Berber, the Kabyle are of the same race; dress one of them in a blue blouse, and put a peaked cap on his head, and he would pass for a French peasant.

The Welsh have everywhere adopted the Cymric tongue, they hug themselves in the belief that they are pure descendants of the ancient Britons, but in fact they are rather Silurians than Celts. Their build, their coloration, are not Celtic. In the fifth century Cambria was invaded from Strathclyde by the sons of Cunedda; fair-haired, white-skinned Britons, they conquered the North and penetrated a certain way South; but the South was already occupied by a body of invading Irish. When pressed by the Saxons, then the retreating Britons poured into Wales; but the substratum of the population was alien in tongue and in blood and in religion.

It was the same in Dumnonia—Devon and Cornwall. It was occupied at some unknown time, perhaps four centuries before Christ, by the Britons, who became lords and masters, but the original people did not disappear, they became their "hewers of wood and drawers of water."

Then came the great scourge of the Saxon invasion. Devon remained as a place of refuge for the Britons who fled before the weapons of these barbarians, till happily the Saxons accepted Christianity, when their methods became less ferocious. They did not exterminate the subject people. But what had more to do with the mitigation of their cruelty than their Christianity, was that they had ceased to be mere wandering hordes, and had become colonists. As such they needed serfs. They were not themselves experienced agriculturalists, and they suffered the original population to remain in the land—the dusky Ivernians as serfs, and the freemen, the conquered Britons, were turned into tenant farmers.

This is precisely what took place in Ireland. The conquering Gadhaels or Milesians, always spoken of as golden-haired, tall and white-skinned, had subdued the former races, the Firbolgs and others, and had welded them into one people whom they called the Aithech Tuatha, i.e. the Rentpaying Tribes; the Classic writers rendered this Attacotti.

In the first two centuries of our era there ensued

an incessant struggle between the tenant farmers and the lords ; the former rose in at least two great revolutions, which shows that they had by no means been exterminated, and whole bodies of them, rather than be crushed into submission and ground down by hard rents, left Ireland, some as mercenaries, others, perhaps, to fall on the coasts of Wales, Devon, and Brittany, and effect settlements there.

When brought into complete subjugation in Ireland, the Gadhelic chiefs planted their *duns* throughout the country in such a manner as to form chains, by which they could communicate with one another at the least token of a revival of discontent; and they distributed the subject tribes throughout the island in such a manner as to keep them under supervision, and to break up their clans. As Professor Sullivan very truly says, " The Irish tenants of to-day are composed of the descendants of Firbolgs and other British and Belgic races; Milesians, . . . Gauls, Norwegians, Anglo-Saxons, Anglo-Normans, and English, each successive dominant race having driven part at least of its predecessors in power into the rent-paying and labouring ranks beneath them, or gradually falling into them themselves, to be there absorbed. This is a fact which should be remembered by those who theorise over the qualities of the ' pure Celts,' whoever they may be."*

The Dumnonii, whose city or fortress was at Exeter, were an important people. They occupied

* Introduction to O'CURRY (E.), *Manners and Customs of the Ancient Irish*, 1873, I. xxiv.

the whole of the peninsula from the river Parret to
Land's End. East of the Tamar was Dyfnaint, the
Deep Vales ; west of it Corneu, the horn of Britain.

The Dumnonii are thought to have invaded and
occupied this territory about four centuries before the
Christian era. The language of the previous dusky
race was agglutinative, like that of the Tartars and
Basques, that is to say, they did not inflect their
substantives. Although there has been a vast influx
of other blood, with fair hair and white complexions,
the earlier type may still be found in both Devon
and Cornwall.

Then came the Roman invasion ; this affected our
Dumnonian peninsula very slightly ; Cornwall hardly
at all. When that came to an end, a large portion
of Britain had fallen under the sway of the Picts,
Saxons, and Scots. By Scots are meant the Irish,
who after their invasion of Alba gave the present
name to Scotland. But it must be distinctly understood that the only Scots known in the first ten or
eleven centuries, to writers on British affairs, were
Irish.

In alliance with the Picts and Saxons, Niall of the
Nine Hostages poured down on Britain and exacted
tribute from the conquered people. In 388 he
carried his arms further and plundered Brittany.
In 396 the Irish supremacy was resisted by Stilicho,
and for a while shaken ; it was reimposed in 400.
In 405, Niall invaded Gaul, and was assassinated
there on the shores of the English Channel.

In 406 Stilicho a second time endeavoured to repel
the Hiberno-Pictic allies, but, unable to do much by

force of arms, entered into terms with them, for Gildas speaks of the Romans as making confederates of Irish. Doubtless Stilicho surrendered to them their hold over and the tribute from the western part of Britain. And now I must tell a funny story connected with the introduction of lap-dogs into Ireland. It comes to us on the authority of Cormac, king-bishop of Cashel, who died in 903, and who wrote a glossary of old Irish words becoming obsolete even in his day.

"The slave of the Haft," says he, "was the name of the first lap-dog that was known in Erin. Cairbre Musc was the man who first brought it there out of Britain. At that time the power of the Gadhaels (Scots or Irish) was great over the Britons; they had divided Albion among them into farms, and each of them had a neighbour and friend among the people." Then he goes on to say how that they established fortresses through the land, and founded one at Glastonbury. "One of those divisions of land is Dun Map Lethan, in the country of the Britons of Cornwall." This lasted to A.D. 380.

Now Cairbre was wont to pass to and fro between Britain and Ireland.

At this time lap-dogs were great rarities, and were highly prized. None had hitherto reached Ireland. And Cairbre was desirous of introducing one there when he went to visit his friends. But the possessors of lap-dogs would on no account part with their treasures.

Now it happened that Cairbre had a valuable knife, with the handle gold-inlaid. One night he rubbed the haft over with bacon fat, and placed it before the kennel of the lap-dog belonging to a friend. The dog gnawed at the handle and sadly disfigured it.

Next morning Cairbre made a great outcry over his precious knife, and showed his British host how that the dog had disfigured it. The Briton apologised, but Cairbre promptly replied, " My good friend, are you aware of the law that 'the transgressor is forfeit for his transgression?' Accordingly I put in a legal claim to the dog." Thus he became its owner, and gave it the name of Mogh-Eimh, or the Slave of the Haft.

The dog was a bitch, and was with young when Cairbre carried her over to Ireland. The news that the wonderful little beast had arrived spread far and wide, and the king of Munster and the chief king, Cormac Mac Airt (227–266) both laid claim to it; the only way in which Cairbre could satisfy them was to give each a pup when his lap-dog had littered. So general was the amazement over the smallness and the beauty of the original dog, that some verses were made on it, which have been preserved to this day.

" Sweet was your drink in the house of Ailil (King of Munster) !
Sweet was your meat in the house of Cormac !
Fair was your bread in the house of Cairbre !
O doggie, Slave of the Hilt ! "

It was probably during the Irish domination that a large portion of North Devon and East Cornwall was colonised from the Emerald Isle.

But to return to the Saxon conquest. When

Athelstan drove the Britons out of Exeter and made the Tamar their limit, it is not to be supposed that he devastated and depopulated Devon; what he did was to destroy the tribal organisation throughout Devon, banish the princes and subjugate the people to Saxon rule.

The Saxon colonists planted themselves in "Stokes" mostly in the valleys. The Celts had never been anything of a town-building people; they had lived scattered over the land in their *treffs* and *boths*, and only the retainers of a chieftain had dwelt around his *dun*.

But with the Saxons, the fact that they lived as a few surrounded by an alien population that in no way loved them, obliged them to huddle together in their "Stokes." Thus towns sprang into existence, and bear Saxon names.

It is probable that the yeomen of the land at the present day represent the Saxon; and most assuredly in the great body of the agricultural labourers, the miners, and artisans, we have mainly a mixture of British and Ivernian blood.

Throughout the Middle Ages, and indeed till this present century, there can have been no easy, if possible, passage out of the labouring community into that of the yeoman class—hardly into that of tenant farmer; whereas the yeomen and the tradesmen, wool merchants and the like, were incessantly feeding the class of *armigeres*, squires; and their descendants supplied the nobility with accretions.

There is, perhaps, in the east of Devon a preponderating element of Saxon, but I have observed in the Seaton and Axminster district so much of the dark hair and eye, that I believe there is less than is supposed, and that there is a very large understratum of the earlier Silurian. Perhaps in North Devon there may be more of the Saxon. West of Okehampton there is really not much difference between the Devonian and the Cornishman, but of this more presently.

It is remarkable that the Devonshire dialect prevails in Cornwall above a diagonal line drawn from Padstow to Saltash, on the Tamar; west of this and below it the dialect is different. This is probably due to the Cornish tongue having been abandoned in the west and south long subsequent to its disappearance in the north-east. But this line also marks the limits of an Irish-Gwentian occupation.

The dialect is fast dying out, but the intonation of the voice will remain long after peculiar words have ceased to be employed.

The "z" has a sound found nowhere else, due to the manner in which the tongue is turned up to the palate for the production of the sound; "ou" and "oo" in such words as "you" and "moon" is precisely that of the French *u* in " lune."

Gender is entirely disregarded; a cow is a "he," who runs dry, and of a cock it is said "her crows in the morn." But then the male rooster is never a cock, but a stag.

The late Mr. Arnold, inspector of schools, was much troubled about the dialect when he came into the county. One day, when examining the school

at Kelly, he found the children whom he was question-
ing very inattentive.

"What is the matter with you?" he asked testily.

"Plaaze, zur, us be a veared of the apple-drayne."

In fact, a wasp was playing in and out among
their heavily oiled locks.

"Apple-drayne!" exclaimed Mr. Arnold. "Good
gracious! You children do not seem to know the
names of common objects. What is that bird yonder
seated on the wall?" And he pointed out of the
window at a cock.

"Plaaze, zur, her's a stag."

"I thought as much. You do not know the difference between a biped and a quadruped."

I was present one day at the examination of a
National School by H.M. Inspector.

"Children," said he, "what form is that?"

"A dodecahedron."

"And that?"

"An isosceles triangle."

"And what is the highest peak in Africa?"

"Kilima Ndjaro."

"Its height?"

"Twenty thousand feet."

"And what are the rivers that drain Siberia?"

"The Obi, the Yenesei, and the Lena."

Now in going to the school I had plucked a little
bunch of speedwell, and I said to the inspector,
"Would you mind inquiring of the children the
name of this plant?"

"What is this plant?" he demanded.

Not a child knew.

"What is the river that flows through your valley?"
Not a child knew.

"What is the name of the highest peak of Dartmoor you see yonder?"

Not a child knew.

And this is the rubbish in place of education that
at great cost is given to our children.

Education they do not get; stuffing they do.

They acquire a number of new words, which they
do not understand and which they persistently mis-
pronounce.

"Aw my! isn't it hot? The prepositions be runin'
all hover me."

"Ay! yü'm no schollard! I be breakin' out wi'
presbeterians."

The "oo" when followed by an "r" has the sound
"o" converted into "oa"; thus "door" becomes
"doar."

"Eau" takes the sound of the modified German
"ü"; thus "beauty" is pronounced "büty."

"Fe" and "g" take "y" to prolong and emphasise
them; thus "fever" becomes "feyver," and "meat"
is pronounced "mayte."

"F" is frequently converted into "v"; "old father"
is "ole vayther." But on the other hand "v" is often
changed to "f," as "view" into "fü."

The vowel "a" is always pronounced long; "landed"
is "lānded," "plant" is "plānt." "H" is frequently
changed into "y"; "heat" is spoken of as "yett,"
"Heathfield" becomes "Yaffel," and "hall" is "yall."

"I" is interjected to give greater force, and "e" is
sounded as "a"; "flesh" is pronounced "flaish."

"S" is pronounced "z," as in examples already given. "O" has an "ou" sound in certain positions, as "going," which is rendered "gou-en." "S" in the third person singular of a verb is "th," as "he grows," "a grawth," "she does" is "her düth."

Here is a form of the future perfect: "I shall 'ave a-bin an' gone vur tü dü it."

There is a decided tendency to soften harsh syllabic conjunctions. Thus Blackbrook is Blacka-brook, and Matford is Mattaford; this is the Celtic interjected *y* and *ty*.

This is hardly a place for giving a list of peculiar words; they may be found in Mrs. Hewett's book, referred to at the end of this chapter, and collected by the committee on Devonshire provincialisms in the *Transactions of the Devonshire Association*.

As a specimen of the dialect I will give a couple of verses of a popular folk song.

> "The gügü es a purty burd,
>   'Er zingeth as er vlieth;
> 'Er bring'th güde tidin's,
>   'Er tell'th naw lies;
> 'Er zucketh swate vlowers
>   Tu kaype 'er voice clear,
> An' whan 'er zingeth gügü
>   Tha zummer drāeth near.

> "Naw āll yu vair maidens
>   Wheriver yü be,
> Your 'earts dü nat 'ang 'em
>   On a zicamore tree.
> The layfe it will wither,
>   The mores (roots) will decay;
> Ah me, I be waistin'
>   An' vaydin' away."

The Devonian and Cornishman will be found by
the visitor to be courteous and hospitable. There
is no roughness of manner where unspoiled by
periodic influx of strangers; he is kindly, tender-
hearted, and somewhat suspicious. There is a lack
of firmness of purpose such as characterises the
Scotchman; and a lively imagination may explain
a slackness in adhesion to the truth. He is prone
to see things as he would like them to be rather
than as they are. On the road passers-by always
salute and have a bit of a yarn, even though personally unacquainted; and to go by in the dark
without a greeting is a serious default in good
manners. A very marked trait especially noticeable
in the Cornish is their independence. Far more intimately than the inhabitants of any other part
of England, they are democrats. This they share
with the Welsh; and, like the Welsh, though
politically they are Radicals, are inherently the most
conservative of people.

It is a peculiarity among them to address one
another by the Christian name, or to speak of a man
by the Christian name along with the surname, should
there be need to distinguish him from another. The
term "Mr." is rarely employed. A gentleman is
"Squire So-and-so," but not a mister; and the trade
is often prefixed to the name, as Millard Horn, or
Pass'n John, or Cap'n Zackie.

There is no form of enjoyment more relished by
a West Country man or woman than a "buryin'."
Business occupations are cast aside when there is
to be a funeral. The pomp and circumstance of woe

exercise an extraordinary fascination on the Western mind, and that which concerns the moribund person at the last is not how to prepare the soul for the great change, but how to contrive to have a " proper grand buryin'." " Get away, you rascal!" was the address of an irate urchin to another, " if you gie' me more o' your saāce you shan't come to my buryin'." " Us 'as enjoyed ourselves bravely," says a mourner, wiping the crumbs from his beard and the whiskey-drops from his lips ; and no greater satisfaction could be given to the mourners than this announcement.

On the other hand a wedding wakes comparatively little interest ; the parents rarely attend.

The looks of Devonshire and Cornish lasses are proverbial. This is not due to complexion alone, which is cream and roses, but to the well-proportioned limbs, the litheness of form, uprightness of carriage, and to the good moulding of the features. The mouth and chin are always well shaped, and the nose is straight ; in shape the faces are a long oval.

I am not sure that West Country women ever forget that they were once comely. An old woman of seventy-five was brought forward to be photographed by an amateur : no words of address could induce her to speak till the operation was completed ; then she put her finger into her mouth : " You wouldn't ha' me took wi' my cheeks falled in ? I just stuffed the *Western Marnin' News* into my mouth to fill 'n out."

Although both in Devon and Cornwall there is great independence and a total absence of that servility of manner which one meets with in other parts of England, it would be a vast mistake to suppose that a West Country man is disrespectful to those who are his superiors—if he has reason to recognise their superiority ; but he does not like a "foreigner," especially one from the North Country. He does not relish his manner, and this causes misunderstanding and mutual dislike.   He is pleased to have as his pass'n, as his squire, as a resident in his neighbourhood, a man whom he knows all about, as to who were his father and his grandfather, as also whence he hails.   A clergyman who comes from a town, or from any other part of England, has to learn to understand the people before they will at all take to him.   " I have been here five years," said a rector one day to me, a man transferred from far, "and I don't understand the people yet, and until I understand them I am quite certain to be miscomprehended by them."

The West Country man must be met and addressed as an equal.   He resents the slightest token of approach *de haut en bas*, but he never presumes ; he is always respectful and knows his place ; he values himself, and demands, and quite rightly, that you shall show that you value him.

The other day a bicyclist was spinning down the road to Moreton Hampstead.   Not knowing quite where he was, and night approaching, he drew up where he saw an old farmer leaning on a gate.

" I say, you Johnnie, where am I ?   I want a bed."

" You 'm fourteen miles from Wonford Asylum," was the quiet response, "and fourteen from Newton

Work'us, and fourteen from Princetown Prison, and I reckon you could find quarters in any o' they—and suitable."

With regard to the Cornish people, I can but reiterate what has already been said relative to the Western folk generally. What differences exist in character are not due to difference of race, but to that of occupation. The bulk of Cornishmen in the middle and west have been associated with mines and with the sea, and this is calculated to give to the character a greater independence, and also to confer a subtle colour, different in kind to that which is produced by agricultural labour. If you take a Yorkshireman from one side of the Calder or Aire, where factory life is prevalent, and one from the other side, where he works in the fields, you will find as great, if not a greater, difference than you will between a Devonshire and a Cornish man. Compare the sailors and miners on one side of the Tamar with those on the other, and you will find no difference at all.

There will always be more independence in miners who travel about the world, who are now in Brazil, then in the African diamond-fields, next at home, than in the agricultural labourer, who never goes further than the nearest market town. The mind is more expanded in the one than in the other; but in race all may be one, though differing in ideas, manners, views, speech.

I venture now to quote freely from an article on Cornishmen that is written by an outsider, and which appeared in a review.

" The dweller in Cornwall comes in time to perceive the constant recurrence of various types of man. Of these, two at least are well marked, very common, and probably of great antiquity and significance. The man of the first type is slender, lithe, graceful, usually rather short; the face is smooth and delicately outlined, without bony prominences, the eyebrows finely pencilled. The character is, on the whole, charming, volatile, vivacious, but not always reliable, and while quick-witted, rarely capable of notable achievement or strenuous endeavour. It is distinctly a feminine type. The other type is large and solid, often with much crispy hair on the face and shaggy eyebrows. The arches over the eyes are well marked and the jaws massive; the bones generally are developed in these persons, though they would scarcely be described as raw-boned; in its extreme form a face of this type has a rugged prognathous character which seems to belong to a lower race."

Usually the profile is fine, with straight noses; and a well-formed mouth, with oval, rather long face is general, the chin and mouth being small. I do not recall at any time meeting with the "rummagy" faces, with no defined shape, and ill-formed noses that one encounters in Scotland.

There is a want of the strength and force such as is encountered in the North; but on the other hand there is remarkable refinement of feature.

I had at one time some masons and workmen engaged upon a structure just in front of my dining-room windows, and a friend from Yorkshire was visiting me. The men working for me were perhaps fine specimens, but nothing really extraordinary for the country. One, a tall, fair-haired, blue-eyed mason, my friend at once designated Lohengrin; and he was the typical knight of the swan—I suspect a pure Celt. Another was not so tall, lithe, dark, and handsome. "King Arthur" was what my friend called him.

The writer, Mr. Havelock Ellis, whom I have already quoted, continues :—

"The women are solid and vigorous in appearance, with fully-developed breasts and hips, in marked contrast with the first type, but resembling women in Central and Western France. Indeed, the people of this type generally recall a certain French type, grave, self-possessed, deliberate in movement, capable and reliable in character. I mention these two types because they seem to me to represent the two oldest races of Cornwall, or, indeed, of England. The first corresponds to the British neolithic man, who held sway in England before the so-called Celts arrived, and who probably belonged to the so-called Iberian race; in pictures of Spanish women of the best period, indeed, and in some parts of modern Spain, we may still see the same type. The second corresponds to the more powerful, and as his remains show, the more cultured and æsthetic Celt, who came from France and Belgium. . . . When these types of individual are combined, the results are often very attractive. We then meet with what is practically a third type: large, dignified, handsome people, distinguished from the Anglo-Saxon not only by their prominent noses and well-formed chins, but also by their unaffected grace and refinement of manner. In many a little out-of-the-world Cornish farm I have met with the men of this type, and admired the distinction of their appearance and bearing, their natural instinctive courtesy, their kindly hospitality. It was surely of such men that Queen Elizabeth thought when she asserted that all Cornishmen are courtiers.

"I do not wish to insist too strongly on these types which

blend into one another, and may even be found in the same family. The Anglo-Saxon stranger, who has yet had no time to distinguish them, and who comes, let us say, from a typically English county like Lancashire, still finds much that is unfamiliar in the people he meets. They strike him as rather a dark race, lithe in movement, and their hands and feet are small. Their hair has a tendency to curl, and their complexions, even those of the men, are often incomparable. The last character is due to the extremely moist climate of Cornwall, swept on both sides by the sea-laden Atlantic. More than by this, however, the stranger accustomed to the heavy, awkward ways of the Anglo-Saxon clodhopper will be struck by the bright, independent intelligence and faculty of speech which he finds here. No disguise can cover the rusticity of the English rustic; on Cornish roads one may often meet a carman whose clear-cut face, bushy moustache, and general bearing might easily add distinction to Pall Mall."

There are parts of Devon and of Cornwall where the dark type prevails. "A black grained man" is descriptive of one belonging to the Veryan district, and dark hair and eyes, and singular beauty are found about the Newlyn and St. Ives districts. The darkest type has been thrust into corners. In a fold of Broadbury Down in Devon, in the village of Germansweek, the type is mainly dark; in that of North Lew, in another lap of the same down, it is light. It has been noticed that a large patch of the dusky race has remained in Bedfordshire.

The existence of the dark eyes and hair and fine profiles has been attempted to be explained by the fable that a Spanish vessel was wrecked now here, now there, from the Armada, and that the sailors remained and married the Cornish women. I believe that this is purely a fable. The same attempt at solution of the existence of the same type in Ireland and in Scotland has been made, because people would not understand that there could be any other explanation of the phenomenon.

I have been much struck in South Wales, on a market day, when observing the people, to see how like they were in build, and colour, and manner, and features to those one might encounter at a fair in Tavistock, Launceston, or Bodmin.

I positively must again quote Mr. Havelock Ellis on the Cornish woman, partly because his description is so charmingly put, but also because it is so incontestably true.

"The special characters of the race are often vividly shown in its women. I am not aware that they have ever played a large part in the world, whether in life or art. But they are memorable enough for their own qualities. Many years ago, as a student in a large London hospital, I had under my care a young girl who came from labour of the lowest and least skilled order. Yet there was an instinctive grace and charm in all her ways and speech which distinguished her utterly from the rough women of her class. I was puzzled then over that delightful anomaly. In after years, recalling her name and her appearance, I knew that she was Cornish, and I am puzzled no longer. I have since seen the same ways, the same soft, winning speech equally unimpaired by hard work and rude living. The Cornish woman possesses an adroitness and self-possession, a modulated readiness of speech, far removed from the awkward heartiness of the Anglo-Saxon woman, the emotional inexpressiveness of the Lancashire lass whose eyes wander around as she seeks for words, perhaps completing her unfinished sentence by a snap of the fingers.   The Cornish woman—at all events while she is young and not submerged by the drudgery of life—exhibits a certain delightful volubility and effervescence.   In this respect she has some affinity with the bewitching and distracting heroines of Thomas Hardy's novels, doubtless because the Wessex folk of the South Coast are akin to the Cornish.   The Cornish girl is inconsistent without hypocrisy ; she is not ashamed of work, but she is very fond of jaunts, and on such occasions she dresses herself, it would be rash to say with more zeal than the Anglo-Saxon maiden, but usually with more success.   She is an assiduous chapel-goer, equally assiduous in flirtations when chapel is over.   The pretty Sunday-school teacher and leader of the local Band of Hope cheerfully confesses as she drinks off the glass of claret you offer her that she is but a poor teetotaller.   The Cornish woman will sometimes have a baby before she is legally married ; it is only an old custom of the county, though less deeply rooted than the corresponding custom in Wales."*

The Cornish are, like the Welsh, intensely religious, but according to their idea religion is emotionalism and has hardly enough to do with morality.

"So Mr. So-and-So is dead," in reference to a local preacher.   "I fear he led a very loose life."

"Ah ! perhaps so, but he was a sweet Christian."

Here is something illustrative at once of West Country religion and dialect. I quote from an amusing paper on the "Recollections of a Parish Worker" in the *Cornish Magazine* (1898) :—

"'How do you like the vicar?' I asked. 'Oh, he's a lovely man,' she answered, 'and a 'ansome praicher—

* *The New Century Review*, April, 1897.

and such a voice! But did 'ee hear how he lost un to-day?
Iss, I thought he would have failed all to-wance, an' that
wad have bin a gashly job. But I prayed for un an' the
Lord guv it back to un again, twice as loud, an' dedn't 'ee
holler! But 'ee dedn't convart me. I converted meself.
Iss a ded. I was a poor wisht bad woman. Never went
to a place of worship. Not for thirty years a hadn't a bin.
One day theer came word that my brother Willum was
hurted to the mine. So I up an' went to un an' theer he
was, all scat abroad an' laid out in scritches. He was in
a purty stank, sure 'nuff. But all my trouble was his poor
sowl. I felt I must get he converted before he passed.
I went where he was to, an' I shut home the door, an'
I hollered an' I rassled an' I prayed to him, an' he nivver
spoke. I got no mouth spaich out of him at awl, but I
screeched and screeched an' prayed until I converted
myself! An' then I be to go to church. Iss, we awl have
to come to it, first an' last, though I used to say for
christenings an' marryin's an' berrin's we must go to church,
but for praichin' an' ennytheng for tha nex' wurld give me
the chapel; still, I waanted to go to church an' laive every-
body knaw I wur proper chaanged. So I pitched to put
up my Senday go-to-mittun bonnet, an' I went. An' when
I got theer aw! my blessed life 'twas Harvest Thanksgivin',
an' when I saw the flowers an' the fruit an' the vegetables
an' the cotton wool I was haived up on end!' And heaved
up on the right end she was."

The table of Commandments is with the Cornish
not precisely that of Moses. It skips, or treats very
lightly, the seventh, but it comprises others not found
in Scripture: "Thou shalt not drink any alcohol,"
and "Thou shalt not dance."

On Old Christmas Day, in my neighbourhood,
a great temperance meeting was held. A noted

speaker on teetotalism was present and harangued. A temperance address is never relished without some horrible example held up to scorn. Well, here it was. "At a certain place called ——, last year, as Christmas drew on, the Guardians met to decide what fare should be afforded to the paupers for Christmas Day. Hitherto it had been customary for them to be given for their dinner a glass of ale— a glass of ale. I repeat it—at public cost—a glass of ale apiece. On that occasion the Guardians unanimously agreed that the paupers should have cocoa, and not ale. Then up stood the Rector—the Rector, I repeat—and in a loud and angry voice declared: 'Gentlemen, if you will not give them their drop of ale, I will.' And he—he, a minister of the gospel or considering himself as such."—(A shudder and a groan.) "I tell you more—I tell you something infinitely worse—he sent up to the work-house a dozen of his old crusted port." (Cries of "Shame! shame!" and hisses.)

That, if you please, was the unpardonable sin.

If we are to look anywhere for local characteristics in the music of the people in any particular part of England, we may surely expect to find them in the western counties of Somerset, Devon, and Cornwall. These three counties have hitherto been out of the beaten track; they are more encompassed by the sea than others, and lead only to the Land's End.

And as a matter of fact, a large proportion of the melodies that have been collected from the peasantry in this region seem to have kept their habitation, and so to be unknown elsewhere.

I take it for granted that they are, as a rule, home productions. The origin of folk-song has been much debated, and it need not be gone into now. But it would be vain to search for local characteristics in anything that has not a local origin.

In folk-song, then, we may expect to see reflected the characteristics of the race from which it has sprung, and, as in the counties of Devon and Cornwall on one side and Somersetshire on the other, we are brought into contact with two, at least, races — the British and the Saxon — we do find two types of melody very distinct. Of course, as with their dialects, so with their melodies, the distinctions are sometimes marked, and sometimes merged in each other. The Devonshire melodies have some affinity with those of Ireland, whilst the Somersetshire tunes exhibit a stubborn individuality —a roughness, indeed, which is all their own.

Taking first the Devonshire songs, I think one cannot fail to be struck with the exceeding grace and innate refinement which distinguish them. These qualities are not always perceptible in the performance of the songs by the untutored singers; nor do the words convey, as a rule, any such impressions, but evident enough when you come to adjust to their proper form the music which you have succeeded in jotting down. It surprises you. You are not prepared for anything like original melody, or for anything gentle or tender. But the Devonshire songs are so. Their thought is idyllic. Through shady groves melodious with song, the somewhat indolent lover of Nature wanders forth without any apparent object save that of "breathing the air," and (it must be added) of keeping an open eye for nymphs, one of whom seldom fails to be seeking the same seclusion. Mutual advances ensue ; no explanations are needed ; constancy is neither vowed nor required. The casual lovers meet and part, and no sequel is appended to the artless tale.

Sentiment is the staple of Devonshire folk-song ; it is a trifle unwholesome, but it is unmistakably graceful and charming. Take such songs as " By chance it was," " The Forsaken Maiden," " The Goss-hawk," " Golden Furze ; " surely there is a gush of genuine melody and the spirit of poetry in such tunes.

In some respects the folk-song of Devonshire is rather disappointing. There is no commemoration, no appreciation, of her heroes. The salt sea-breeze does not seem to reach inland, save to whisper in a wailing tone of " The Drowned Lover," or the hapless " Cabin Boy." Sea-songs may be in her ports, but they were not born there.

Nor are the joys of the chase proclaimed with such robustness as elsewhere, any more than are the pleasures and excitements of the flowing bowl. This may be attributed to the same refinement of character of which I have spoken.

A pastoral and peace-loving community will not be expected to develop any special sense of humour. Devonshire is by no means deficient in it, but it is of a quiet sort, a sly humour something allied to what the Scotch call " pawky," of which " Widicombe

Fair " is as good an example as can be had. Of what may be called the religious element, save in Christmas and Easter carols, I have never discovered any trace.

The Rev. H. Feetwood Sheppard, who has spent ten years in collecting the melodies of Devon and Cornwall, says of them, " I have found them delightful, full of charm and melody. I never weary of them. They are essentially poetical, but they are also essentially the songs of sentiment, and their one pervading, almost unvarying theme is—The Eternal Feminine."

When we pass into Somersetshire the folk-music assumes quite a different character. The tenderness, the refinement have vanished. Judging from their songs, we might expect to find the Somersetshire folk bold, frank, noisy, independent, self-assertive; and this view would be quite in keeping with their traditional character. In Shakespeare's time bandogs and bull baiting were the special delight of the country gentry,* and Fuller describes the natives of Taunton Dean as "rude, rich, and conceited." If one turn to the music, "Richard of Taunton Dean," or "Jan's Courtship," "George Riddler's Oven," and the like, are in entire keeping with the character of the people as thus depicted. There is vigour and *go* in their songs, but no sweetness ; ruggedness, no smoothness at all ; and it is precisely this latter quality that marks the Cornish and Devonshire airs.

Take such a tune as that to which the well-known hunting song of Devon, "Arscott of Tetcott," is

* See M. DRAYTON's *Polyolbion* on this.

wedded.   The air is a couple of centuries older than
the words, for the Arscott whom the song records
died in 1788, though we can only trace the tune
back to D'Urfey at the end of the seventeenth
century.   The music is impetuous, turbulent, excited,
it might be the chasing the red deer on Exmoor;
the hunt goes by with a rush like a whirlwind to
a semi-barbarous melody, which resembles nothing
so much as that of the spectral chase in Der
Freischütz.

But Somersetshire song can be tender at times,
though not quite with the bewitching grace of
Devonia.   There is a charming air which found its
way from the West up to London some sixty years
ago, the original words of which are lost, but the
tune became immensely popular under the title of
" All round my hat," a vulgar ditty sung by all little
vulgar boys in the streets.   The tune is well worth
preserving.   It is old, and there is a kind of wail
about it which is touching.

But who were the composers of these folk-airs ?
In the old desks in west galleries of churches remain
here and there piles of MS. music : anthems, and,
above all, carols, the composition of local musicians
unknown beyond their immediate neighbourhood,
and now unknown even by name.

A few years ago I was shown such a pile from
Lifton Church.   I saw another great library, as I
may call it, that was preserved in the rack in the
ceiling of a cottage at Sheepstor, the property
of an old fiddler, now dead.   I saw a third in
Holne parish.   I have seen stray heaps elsewhere.

Mr. Heath, of Redruth, published two collections from Cornwall and one from Devon, the latter from the Lifton store in part, to which I had directed his attention. I cannot doubt that some of the popular tunes that are found circulating among our old singers—or to be more exact, were found—were the composition of these ancient village musicians. Alas! the American organ and the strident harmonium came in and routed out the venerable representatives of a musical past; and the music-hall piece is now driving away all the sound old traditional melody, and the last of the ancient conservators of folk-song makes his bow, and says :—

> " I be going, I reckon, full mellow,
> To lay in the churchyard my head,
> So say—God be wi' you, old fellow !
> The last of the zingers is dead."

NOTE.—For the history of Devon : WORTH (R. N.), *History of Devonshire*. London, 1886. For Devonshire dialect : HEWETT (S.), *The Peasant Speech of Devon*. E. Stock. London, 1892. For Devonshire folk-music : *Songs of the West*. Methuen. London, 1895. (3rd ed.) *A Garland of Country Song*. Methuen. London, 1895.

For most of what has been said above on the folk-songs of Devon I am indebted to the Rev. H. Fleetwood Sheppard, who has made it his special study.

CHAPTER II.

VILLAGES AND CHURCHES

A DEVONSHIRE village does not contrast
favourably with those in Essex, Kent, Sussex,
and other parts of England, where brick or timber
and plaster are the materials used, and where the
roofs are tiled.

But of cottages in the county there are two kinds.
The first, always charming, is of *cob*, clay, thatched.
Such cottages are found throughout North Devon,
and wherever the red sandstone prevails. They are
low, with an upper storey, the windows to which are
small, and the brown thatch is lifted above these
peepers like a heavy, sleepy brow in a very picturesque manner. But near Dartmoor stone is employed, and an old, imperishable granite house is
delightful when thatched. But thatch has given way

everywhere to slate, and when the roof is slated a great charm is gone. There is slate and slate. The soft, silvery grey slate that is used in South Devon is pleasing, and when a house is slated down its face against the driving rains, and the slates are worked into patterns and are small, they are vastly pretty. But architects are paid a percentage on the outlay, and it is to their profit to use material from a distance; they insist on Welsh or Delabole slate, and nothing can be uglier than the pink of the former and the chill grey of the other—like the tint of an overcast sky in a March wind.

I once invited an architect to design a residence on a somewhat large scale. He did so, and laid down that Delabole slate should be employed with bands of Welsh slate of the colour of beetroot. "But," said I, "we have slate on the estate. It costs me nothing but the raising and carting."

"I dislike the colour," said he. "If you employ an architect, you must take the architect's opinion."

I was silenced. The same day, in the afternoon, this architect and I were walking in a lane. I exclaimed suddenly, "Oh, what an effect of colour! Do look at those crimson dock-leaves!"

"Let me see if I can find them," said the architect. "I am colour-blind, and do not know red from green."

It was an incautious admission. He had forgotten about the slates, and so gave himself away.

The real objection, of course, was that my own slates would cost me nothing. But also of course he did not give me that reason.

Where the slate rocks are found, grauwacke and schist, there the cottages are very ugly—could not well be uglier—and new cottages and houses that are erected are, as a rule, eyesores.

However, we have in Devon some very pretty villages and clusters of cottages, and the little group of roofs of thatch and glistening whitewashed walls about the old church, the whole backed by limes and beech and elm, and set in a green combe, is all that can be desired for quiet beauty; although, individually, each cottage may not be a subject for the pencil, nor the church itself pre-eminently picturesque.

The churches of Devonshire belong mainly to the Perpendicular style; that is to say, they were nearly all rebuilt between the end of the fourteenth and the sixteenth centuries.

Of this style, this is what Mr. Parker says: "The name is derived from the arrangement of the tracery, which consists of perpendicular lines, and forms one of its most striking features. At its first appearance the general effect was usually bold and good; the mouldings, though not equal to the best of the Decorated style, were well defined; the enrichments effective and ample without exuberance, and the details delicate without extravagant minuteness. Subsequently it underwent a gradual debasement: the arches became depressed; the mouldings impoverished; the ornaments crowded, and often coarsely executed; and the subordinate features confused from the smallness and complexity of their parts. A leading characteristic of the style, and one which prevails throughout its continuance, is the square arrangement of the mouldings over the heads of doorways, creating a spandrel on each side above the arch, which is usually ornamented with tracery, foliage, or a shield. The jambs of doorways are generally moulded, frequently with one or more small shafts."

The style is one that did not allow of much variety in window tracery. The object of the adoption of upright panels of glass was to allow of stained figures in glass of angels filling the lights, as there had been a difficulty found in suitably filling the tracery of the heads of the windows with subjects when these heads were occupied by geometrical figures composed of circles and arcs intersecting.

In the west window of Exeter Cathedral may be seen a capital example of "Decorated" tracery, and in the east window one in the "Perpendicular" style.

Skill in glass staining and painting had become advanced, and the windows were made much larger than before, so as to admit of the introduction of more stained glass.

Pointed arches struck from two centres had succeeded round arches struck from a single centre, and now the arches were made four-centred.

Foliage in carving had, under Early English treatment, been represented as just bursting, the leaves uncurling with the breath of spring. In the Decorated style the foliage is in full summer expansion, generally wreathed round a capital. Superb examples of Decorated foliage may be seen in the corbels in the choir at Exeter. In Perpendicular architecture the leaves are crisped and wrinkled with frost.

In Devonshire the earlier towers had spires. When the great wave of church building came over the land, after the conclusion of the Wars of the Roses, then no more spires were erected, but towers with buttresses, and battlemented and pinnacled square heads. In the country there are no towers that come up to the splendid examples in Somersetshire; but that of Chittlehampton is the nearest approach to one of these.

In the Somerset towers the buttresses are frequently surmounted by open-work pinnacles or small lanterns of elaborate tabernacle work, and the parapets or battlements are of open tracery; but in Devon these latter are plain with bold coping, and the pinnacles are well developed and solid, and not overloaded with ornament. Bishop's Nympton, South Molton, and Chittlehampton towers are locally described as " Length," " Strength," and " Beauty."

A fine effect is produced when the turret by which the top of the tower is reached is planted in the midst of one side, usually the north; and it is carried up above the tower roof. There are many examples. I need name but Totnes and Ashburton.

A curious effect is produced among the Cornish towers, and those near the Tamar on the Devon side, of the pinnacles being cut so as to curve outwards and not to be upright. The effect is not pleasant, and the purpose is not easily discoverable; but it was possibly done as being thought by this means to offer less resistance to the wind.

The roofs are usually "waggon-headed." The open timber roof, so elaborated in Norfolk, is not common. A magnificent example is, however, to be seen in Wear Gifford Hall. But cradle roofs do exist, and in a good many cases the waggon roofs are but ceiled cradle roofs. A good plain example of a cradle roof is in the chancel of Ipplepen, and a very rich one at Beaford.

The mouldings of the timbers are often much enriched. A fine example is Pancras Week. The portion of the roof over the rood-screen is frequently very much more elaborately ornamented than the rest. An example is King's Nympton, where, however, before the restoration, it was even more gorgeous than at present. The waggon roof presents immense advantages over the open timber roof; it is warmer; it is better for sound; it is not, like the other, a make-shift. It carries the eye up without the harsh and unpleasant break from the walling to the barn-like timber structure overhead.

Wherever white Beer stone or rosy Hatherleigh stone could be had, that was easily cut, there delicate moulding and tracery work was possible; but in some parts of the county a suitable stone was lacking. In the neighbourhood of Tavistock the doorways and windows were cut out of Roborough stone, a volcanic tufa, full of pores, and so coarse that nothing refined could be attempted with it. Near Launceston, however, were the Polyphant quarries, the stone also volcanic, but close-grained and of a delicate, beautiful grey tone. This was employed for pillars and window tracery. The fine Decorated columns of Bratton Clovelly Church, of a soft grey colour, are of this stone. The run of the stone was, however, limited, and was thought to be exhausted. It was not till the Perpendicular style came in that an attempt was made to employ granite. The experiment led to curious results. The tendency of the style is to flimsiness, especially in the mouldings; but the obduracy of the material would not allow of delicate treatment, and the Perpendicular mouldings, especially noticeable in doorways, are often singularly bold and effective. A *tour de force* was effected at Launceston Church, which is elaborately carved throughout in granite, and in Probus tower, in Cornwall. For beauty in granite work Widecombe-in-the-Moor tower cannot be surpassed; there the tower is noble and the church to which it belongs is mean. In using Ham Hill stone or Beer stone, that was extracted in blocks, the pillars, the jambs of doors and windows were made of several pieces laid in courses and cut to fit one another. But when the architects of Perpendicular times had to deal with granite there was no need for this; they made their pillars and jambs in single solid blocks. A modern architect, bred to Caen stone or Bath oolite, sends down a design for a church or house to be erected near Dartmoor, or in Cornwall, and treats the granite as though it came out of the quarry in small blocks; and the result is absurd. An instance of this blundering in treatment is the new east window of Lanreath Church, Cornwall, designed by such a "master in Israel" as Mr. Bodley. The porch doorway is in six stones, one for each base, one for each jamb, and two form the arch. The old windows are treated in a similar fashion—each jamb is a single stone. But Mr. Bodley has built up his new window of little pieces of granite one foot deep. The effect is bad. Unhappily, local architects are as blind to local characteristics as London architects are ignorant of them. So also, when these gentry attempt to design hood mouldings, or indeed any mouldings, for execution in granite, they cannot do it—the result is grotesque, mean, and paltry: they think in Caen stone and Bath, and to design in granite a man's mind must be made up in granite.

In Cornwall there are some good building materials capable of ornamental treatment, more delicate than can be employed in granite. Such are the Pentewan and Catacleuse stones. The latter is gloomy in colour, but was used for the finest work, as the noble tomb of Prior Vivian, in Bodmin Church.

As stone was an intractable material, the Devonshire men who desired to decorate their churches directed their energies to oak carving, and filled them with very finely sculptured bench-ends and screens of the most elaborate and gorgeous description.

So rich and elaborate are these latter, that when a church has to be restored the incumbent trembles at the prospect of the renovation of his screen, and this has led to many of them being turned out and destroyed. South Brent screen was thus wantonly ejected and allowed to rot. Bridestowe was even worse treated: the tracery was cut in half and turned upside down, and plastered against deal boarding—to form a dwarf screen.

"What will my screen cost if it be restored?" asked a rector of Mr. Harry Hems.

"About four hundred pounds."

"Four hundred pounds! Bless me! I think I had best have it removed."

"Very well, sir, be prepared for the consequences. Your name will go down to posterity dyed in infamy and yourself steeped in obloquy."

"You don't mean to say so?"

"Fact, sir, I assure you."

That preserved the screen.

Then, again, some faddists have a prejudice against them. This has caused the destruction of those in Davidstow and West Alvington. Others, however, have known how to value what is the great treasure in their churches entrusted to their custody, and they have preserved and restored them. Such are Staverton, Dartmouth, Totnes, Harberton, Wolborough. That there must have been in the sixteenth century a school of quite first-class carvers cannot be doubted, in face of such incomparable work as is seen in the pulpit and screen of Kenton. But if there was good work by masters there was also some poor stuff, formal and without individual character—such as the screens at Kenn and Laneast.

The pulpits are also occasionally very rich and of the same date as the screens. There are noble examples of stone pulpits elaborately carved at South Molton, Bovey Tracey, Chittlehampton, and Harberton, and others even finer in wood, as Holne, Kenton, Ipplepen, Torbrian.

Among churches which have fine bench-ends may

be noted Braunton, Lapford, Colebrook, Horwood, Broadwood Widger (dated 1529), North Lew (also dated), Plymtree, Lew Trenchard, Peyhembury.

Several early fonts remain of Norman style, and even in some cases perhaps earlier. The finest Norman fonts are Stoke Canon, Alphington, S. Mary Steps (Exeter), Hartland, and Bere Ferrers. In the west, about the Tamar, one particular pattern of Norman font was reproduced repeatedly; and it is found in several churches. There are a number of village crosses remaining, a very fine one at South Zeal; also at Meavy, Mary Tavy, Staverton, Sampford Spiney, Holne, Hele, and some extremely rude on Dartmoor.

There was a churchyard cross at Manaton. The Rev. C. Carwithen, who was rector, found that the people carried a coffin thrice round it, the way of the sun, at a funeral; although he preached against the usage as superstitious, they persisted in doing so. One night he broke up the cross, and removed and concealed the fragments. It is a pity that the cross did not fall on and break his stupid head.

It is interesting to observe how late the Perpendicular style maintained itself in the West. At Plymouth is Charles Church, erected after the Restoration, of late Gothic character. So also are there aisles to churches, erected after the Reformation, of debased style, but nevertheless distinctly a degeneration of the Perpendicular.

In domestic architecture this is even more noticeable. Granite-mullioned windows and four-centred doorways under square hoods, with shields and flowers

in the spandrels, continued in use till the beginning
of the eighteenth century.

A very large number of old mansions, belonging
to the squirearchy of Elizabethan days, remain. The
Devonshire gentry were very numerous, and not extraordinarily wealthy. They built with cob, and with
oak windows, or else in stone with granite mullions,
but neither material allowed of great splendour. A
house in granite cost about three times as much as
one of a like size in brick.

The mansions are too numerous to be mentioned.
One who is desirous of seeing old houses should provide
himself with an inch to the mile Ordnance Survey
map, and visit such houses as are inserted thereon
in Old English characters. Unhappily, although this
serves as a guide in Cornwall, the county of Devon
has been treated in a slovenly manner, and in my
own immediate neighbourhood, although such a fine
example existed as Sydenham House, it remained
unnoticed ; and the only two mansions indicated in
Old English were a couple of ruins, uninhabited, that
have since disappeared. Where the one-inch fails
recourse must be had to the six-inch map.

Devonshire villages and parks cannot show such
magnificent trees as the Midlands and Eastern counties. The elm grows to a considerable size on the red
land, but the elm is much exposed to be blown over
in a gale, especially when it has attained a great size.
Oak abounds, but never such oak as may be seen in
Suffolk. The fact is that when the tap-root of an
oak tree touches rock the tree makes no progress, and
as the rock lies near the surface almost throughout

the county, an oak tree does not have the chance there that it does in the Eastern counties, where it may burrow for a mile in depth without touching stone.

Moreover, situated as the county is between two seas, it is windblown, and the trees are disposed to bend away from the prevailing south-westerly and westerly gales. But if trees do not attain the size they do elsewhere, they are very numerous, and the county is well wooded. Its rocks and its lanes are the homes of the most beautiful ferns that grow with luxuriance, and in winter the moors are tinted rainbow colours with the mosses. The flora is varied with the soil. What thrives on the red land perishes on the cold clay ; the harebell, which loves the limestone, will not live on the granite, and does not affect the schist.

The botanist may consult Miss Helen Saunders' "Botanical Notes" in the *Transactions of the Devonshire Association;* Miss Chaunters' *Ferny Combes;* and the appendix to Mr. Rowe's *Dartmoor.*

The village revel was till twenty years ago a great institution, and a happy though not harmless one. But it has died out, and it is now sometimes difficult to ascertain, and then only from old people, the days of the revel in the several villages. In some parishes, however, the clergy have endeavoured to give a better tone to the old revel, which was discredited by drunkenness and riot, and their efforts have not been unsuccessful. The clubs march to church on that day, and a service is given to them.

One of the most curious revels was that at Kingsteignton, where a ram was hunted, killed, roasted, and eaten. The parson there once asked a lad in Sunday School, "How many Commandments are there?" "Three, sir," was the prompt reply; "Easter, Whitsuntide, and the Revel."

Another, where a sheep was devoured after having been roasted whole, was at Holne. At Morchard, the standing dish at farmhouses on Revel day was a "pestle pie," which consisted of a raised paste, kept in oval shape by means of iron hoops during the process of baking, being too large to be made in a dish. It contained all kinds of meat : a ham, a tongue, whole poultry and whole game, which had been previously cooked and well seasoned.

The revel, held on the *réveil* or wake of the saint of the parish, was a relic of one of the earliest institutions of the Celts. It was anciently always held in the cemetery, and was attended by funeral rites in commemoration of the dead. This was followed by a fair, and by a deliberative assembly of the clan, or subdivision of a clan, of which the cemetery was the tribal centre. It was the dying request of an old Celtic queen that her husband would institute a fair above her grave.

CHAPTER III.

HONITON

"THIS town," said Sir William Pole in 1630, "is near three-quarters of a mile in length, lying East and West, and in the midst there is one other street towards the South." The description applies to-day, except only that the town has stretched itself during two hundred and eighty years to one mile in place of three-quarters. A quarter of a mile in about three centuries, which shows that Honiton is not a place that stands still.

It is, in fact, a collection of country cottages that have run to the roadside to see the coaches from London go by, and to offer the passengers entertainment.

The coach-road occupies mainly the line of the British highway, the Ikenild Street, a road that furnished the chief means of access to the West, as the vast marshes of the Parret made an approach to the peninsula from the North difficult and dangerous.

43

And the manner in which every prominent height has been fortified shows that the whole eastern boundary of the county has been a debated and fiercely contested land, into which invaders thrust themselves, but from which they were hurled back.

Honiton is on the Otter (*y dwr*, W. the Water) a name that we find farther west in the Attery, that flows into the Tamar. Honiton does not derive from "honey," flowing with milk and honey though the land may be, but from the Celtic *hen* (old), softened in a way general in the West into *hena* before a hard consonant.

We have the same appellative in Hennacott, Honeychurch, and Honeydykes, also in Hembury, properly Henbury, and in Hemyock. Perhaps the old West Welsh name for the place was Dunhen, or Hennadun, which the Saxons altered into Hennatun or Honeyton.

The singular configuration of the eastern confines of Devon and Dorset has been ingeniously explained. Till 1832 the two parishes of Stockland and Dalwood belonged to the county of Dorset, although surrounded entirely by Devon. In 710 a great battle was fought by Ina, King of the West Saxons, against Geraint, King of the Dumnonii, the West Welsh, on the Black Down Hills, when Geraint was defeated and fled. Then Ina built Taunton, and made it a border fortress to keep the Britons in check. Simultaneously, there can be little doubt, the men of Dorset took advantage of the situation, made an inroad and secured a large slice of territory, possibly up to the Otter.

Ina was succeeded by inert princes, or such as had their hands engaged elsewhere, and the Devonians thrust themselves forward, retook Taunton, and advanced their borders to where they had been before 710.

It has been supposed that on this occasion they were unable to dispossess the Dorset men from their well-fortified positions at Stockland and Dalwood, but swept round them and captured the two camps of Membury and Musbury. The possession of these fortresses would thrust back the Dorset frontier for some miles to the east of the Axe. So matters would remain for a considerable period, such as allowed the boundaries to become settled ; and when the final subjugation of Devon took place, this tract to the east of the Axe remained as part of the lands of the Defnas, while the Dorsaetas retained the islet which they had so long and so successfully defended. It was not till eleven hundred and twenty years had elapsed that the Devon folk could recover these points.*

Axminster was the scene of a great battle in the reign of Athelstan, in which five kings and seven earls fell. The minster, as a monastic colony, had been in existence before that, but Athelstan now endowed a college there for six priests to pray for the souls of those who fell in the battle.

Now, what battle can that have been ? In the register of Newnham Abbey is a statement made in the reign of Edward III., that the battle took place

---

* DAVIDSON, "The Saxon Conquest of Devonshire," in the *Transactions of the Devonshire Association*, 1877.

"at Munt S. Calyxt en Devansyr," and that it ended
at Colecroft under Axminster.   S. Calyxt is now
Coaxdon.

The only great battle that answers to the description was that of Brunanburgh, fought in 937.

It was fought between Athelstan and the Ethelings,
Edmund, Elwin and Ethelwin, on one side, and Anlaf
the Dane, from Ireland, united with Constantine, the
Scottish king, on the other.   It is this latter point
which has made modern historians suppose that the
conflict took place somewhere in the North.

But, on the other hand, there are grave reasons for
placing it at Axminster.

First, we know of no other battle that answers the
description.   Then, during the night before it, the
Bishop of Sherborne arrived at the head of a contingent.   The two younger Ethelings who fell were
transported to Malmesbury to be buried; clearly
because it was the nearest great monastery.   And
it seems most improbable that Athelstan should have
endowed Axminster that prayers might there be
offered for those who fell in the battle, if Brunanburgh were in Northumberland.   The difficulty about
Constantine may thus be solved.   Constantine had
been expelled his kingdom by Athelstan, and had
taken refuge in Ireland.   He had, indeed, been
restored, but when he resolved on revolt, he may
have gone to Dublin to Anlaf, and have concerted
with him an attack on the South, where the assistance of the Britons in Devon and Cornwall might
be reckoned on, whilst the North British would rise,
and the Welsh descend from their mountains.

The story of the battle is this, as given by William of Malmesbury.

The Danes from Dublin, together with Constantine and a party of Scots (Irish), came by sea, and fell upon England. Athelstan and his brother marched against them. Just before the battle Anlaf, desirous of knowing the disposition of the English forces, entered the camp in the garb of a gleeman, harp in hand. He sang and played before Athelstan and the rest, and they did not recognise him. As they were pleased with his song, they gave him a largess of gold. He took the money, but as he left the camp, he put it under the earth, as it did not behove a king to receive hire. This was observed by a soldier, who at once went to Athelstan and informed him of it. The king said angrily, "Why did you not at once arrest him and deliver him into my hands?" "My lord king," answered the man, "I was formerly with Anlaf, and I took oath of fidelity to him. Had I broken that, would you have trusted me? Take my advice, O king, and shift your quarters."

This was good advice, and Athelstan acted on it, but scarcely had he shifted his quarters than Werstan, Bishop of Sherborne, arrived, and he took up the ground vacated by the king.

During the night Anlaf made an attack and broke through the stockade, and directed his course towards the king's tent. There he fell on and killed the bishop, and massacred the Sherborne contingent. The tumult roused the king, and the fight became general, and raged till day. Great numbers fell on both sides, but in the end Anlaf was defeated, and fled to his ships. The only trace of the name Brunanburgh is in Brinnacombe, under the height whereon traditionally the fight raged; and Membury may be the place where the king was fortified. The Anglo-Saxon Chronicle calls the place Brumby: *B* and *M* are permutable letters.

Honiton has not many relics of antiquity about it. Repeated fires have destroyed the old houses; the High Street still retains its runnel, confined within a conduit, with square dipping-places at frequent intervals. The street runs straight down hill to the bridge and across the Giseage, and up again on the road towards Exeter. The town is completely surrounded by toll-gates; the tolls collected do not go to pay for the maintenance of the roads, but to defray a debt incurred by removing buildings, including the ancient shambles, from the middle of the street early in the century. This accounts for the street being particularly wide.

The Dolphin, the principal inn, is supposed to still possess some portion of the ancient building once belonging to the Courtenays, whose cognisance is the inn sign.

S. Margaret's Hospital is one of the points of interest, and is picturesquely pretty. It was intended as a leper hospital, but is now used as almshouses. It was built and endowed by Dr. Thomas Chard, the last abbot of Ford.

One thing no visitor should fail to see, and that is the superb view from Honiton Hill. It commands the valley of the Otter, with the town beneath, and the old earthworks of Hembury Fort, Buckerell Knap, and Dumpdon towering above. The flat - topped hills and the peculiar scarps are due to the formation being greensand. These scarps may be observed in process of shaping at the head of every combe. The church of S. Paul in the town is modern and uninteresting. It occupies the site of an old chapel of All Hallows. The parish church is S. Michael's on the hill, and this contains points of interest. The fifteenth-century screen is of carved oak, and stretches across nave and both aisles. The church was formerly cruciform, but north and south aisles were added to nave and chancel. Probably it formerly had a central tower. Four carved beams now support the roof where the tower should be, and bear sculptured bosses, representing an angel, a bishop, a priest, and a man in armour. Two finely carved capitals in the chancel carry the sentence, "Pray for ye souls of John Takel and Jone his wyffe." They were liberal benefactors to the church and the town.

The view from the churchyard is magnificent. On a suitable day Cosdon Beacon on Dartmoor is visible. A row of cypresses in the churchyard was transplanted from the garden of Sir James Shepperd (d. 1730).

In old times the parsons of Honiton were supposed to have been addicted to field sports, perhaps unfairly, just as one hunting abbot gave a bad name to all the abbots of Tavistock. Barclay, in his *Ship of Fools*, says :—

"For if any can flatter and beare a hawke on his fist,
He shall be made parson of Honington or of Clist."

There is much deserving of visit within reach of
Honiton, Colyton with its fine church, and the tomb
of "Little Chokebone," a good monument, long
supposed to be that of Margaret, daughter of
William, Earl of Devon, and Katherine his wife,
seventh daughter of Edward IV., who was supposed
to have been choked by a fish-bone in 1512. But
there is evidence that the lady lived long after the
date of her presumed death. What also tells fatally
against the identification is that the arms of
Courtenay are impaled with the royal arms, surrounded by the bordering componée, the well-known
token of *bastardy*. Now this belonged to the
Beauforts, and the tomb is either that of Margaret
Beaufort, wife of Thomas, first Earl of Devon, of
that name, or else of one of their daughters.

Of Colcombe House, the great Courtenay, and then
the Pole seat, but a fragment remains. At Colyton is
the Great House, a fine old building, once the residence
of the Yonges. The last of the family, Sir George
Yonge, was wont to say that he came in for £80,000
family property, received as much as his wife's
jointure, obtained a similar sum in the Government
offices he enjoyed, but that Honiton had "swallowed
it all" in election expenses. And when he stood for
the last time there, in embarrassed circumstances;
because he could not bribe as heavily as formerly,
one of the burgesses spat in his face. He died in
1812, aged eighty, a pensioner in Hampton Court,
and his body was brought down very privately to
Colyton from fear of arrest for debt. Another old
house is Sand, the seat of the Huyshe family.

Honiton has become famous for its lace, although actually the manufacture does not take place to any considerable extent in the town, but in villages, as Beer, Branscombe, Ottery, etc.

In the beginning of the sixteenth century Honiton was a centre of a flourishing trade in bone-lace, but how it was introduced is very uncertain. It has been supposed, but not proved, that Flemish refugees came to Honiton and introduced the art, but one does not quite see why they should have come so far. There is an inscription on a tombstone in Honiton church-yard to James Rodge, bone-lace seller, who died July 27th, 1617, and bequeathed to the poor of the parish the benefit of a hundred pounds. A similar bequest was made in the same year by Mrs. Minifie, a lace maker, so that both lace dealer and maker may have carried on their business for thirty years before they died.

In the latter part of James I.'s reign Honiton lace is frequently mentioned by contemporary writers. Westcote, in his *View of Devon*, 1620, says, " At Axminster you may be furnished with fine flax-thread there spunne. At Hemington and Bradnich with bone-laces now greatly in request." Acts were passed under Charles I. for the protection of the bone-lace makers, " prohibiting foreign purles, cut works, and bone-laces, or any commodities laced or edged there-with;" and these benefited especially the Devonshire workers, their goods being close imitations of the much-coveted Flemish pillow-laces.

Pillow-lace was preceded in England, as else-where, by darned netting and cut-work. A fine example of the ancient English net embroidery may be seen on the monument, in Exeter Cathedral, of Bishop Stafford, who died in 1398.

The pillow was introduced in the early part of Elizabeth's reign, and at first coarse thread-laces of geometrical design were worked on to it. Plaited and embroidered edgings, or *purles*, for the ruff, worked in silk, gold and silver wire, or thread came next, and formed the staple article during the first half of the seventeenth century. The patterns were imitated from Italian cut-work and reticella, with some marked peculiarities of workmanship and detail, such as the introduction of stars, wheels, and triangles, which are only found on English laces. The sculptor of Lady Pole's monument in Colyton Church (1623), evidently copied the bone-lace on her cape from a specimen of Devonshire make, and equally characteristic of the ancient patterns of the county is the probably plaited lace on a tucker and cuffs that adorn the effigy of Lady Doddridge in Exeter Cathedral (1614). Illustrations of these interesting examples of early Devonshire workmanship are given in Mrs. Palliser's " History of Lace." *

There is another very fine specimen in Combe Martin Church, the effigy of Judith Hancock (1637). The figure is life-size, and the dress is covered with point-lace and looped with points of ribbon.

The reason of the coarseness of early lace was that pins were rare and fetched a high price, and the humble workers in cottages employed fish-bones

* " Antique and Modern Lace," in the *Queen*, 1874. The last chapter is devoted to Honiton Lace.

about which to twist their threads, stuck into the parchment in the shape of the pattern. The bobbins were made of "sheeps' trotters." It is now very difficult to procure specimens of this fishbone-lace.

The lace produced by James Rodge and his contemporaries had large flowing guipure patterns, united by *bride* picotees, the latter worked in with the Brussels ground. *Brides* are the small stripes or connection of threads overcast with stitches which bind the sprigs together. The English lace-makers could not make this exquisite stitch with the thread that England produced, and the thread was brought from Antwerp. At the end of last century it cost from £70 to £100 per pound. Old Brussels lace was made on pillows, while the modern Brussels is worked with needles.

The visitor to Honiton, Beer, or any village around may see lace - making on pillows. The women have round or oval boards, stuffed so as to form a cushion, and placed on the knees of the worker : a piece of parchment is fixed over the pillow, with the pattern drawn on it ; into this the pins are stuck through holes marked for the purpose. Often as many as four hundred bobbins are employed at a time on a pillow. Many of the "bobbins" and "turns" to be seen in Devonshire cottages are very old : the most ancient are inlaid with silver. On some, dates are carved, such as 1678 or 1729. On some, Christian names are cut, such as John and Nicholas ; probably those of the sweethearts of the girls who used them. Jingles, or strings of glass beads, may be seen hanging to them, with a button at the end, which came from the waistcoat of the John or the Nicholas who had given the bobbin as a keepsake. What life-stories some of these old bobbins could tell ! *

Children began to make lace as early as four years old ; indeed, unless early trained to the work their hands never acquire deftness. Board schools and compulsory education are destroying the ability to work as of old, as well as too often killing the desire for work in the hearts of the children.

Boys and girls were formerly taught alike, and in some of the seaside villages fishermen took up their pillows for lace-making when ashore.

Guipure à bride and scalloped-border laces in the Louis XIV. style were followed by laces grounded with Brussels *vraie réseau*. In the working of the latter, Devonshire hands were decidedly superior to their Continental rivals. This beautiful ground, which sold at the rate of a shilling the square inch, was either worked in on the pillow after the pattern had been finished, or used as a sub-stratum for lace strips to be sewn on. The detached bouquets of the Rococo period, and the Mechlin style of design towards the end of last century, eminently suited the Devon lace-workers, as dividing the labour. Each individual hand could be entrusted with the execution of a floral design, which was repeated mechanically. The superior finish of the Honiton sprigs between 1790 and 1815 was mainly due to this, but it was fatal to all development of the artistic faculty and to general deftness. During this period Honiton produced the finest laces in Europe.

* The *Devon and Exeter Gazette*, December 31st, 1885.

What greatly conduced to the improvement of Honiton lace was the arrival of Normandy refugees at the outbreak of the French Revolution in 1793. The Normans were quicker and sharper than the Devon workers, and they stirred them up to great advance in their work. They taught them to make trolly lace, which is worked round the pillow instead of on it; and through their example the Devonshire women gave up the slovenly habit of working the ground into which they had slipped, and returned to the old double-threaded *réseau*, or ground like the old Flemish, the flowers worked into the ground with the pillow, instead of being *appliqué*.

Honiton lace made in proper fashion with sprigs was formerly paid for by covering the work with shillings.

There is a curious notice of Honiton lace in a note by Dr. James Yonge; who "was again at Honiton, April 23rd, 1702," and witnessed the rejoicings in celebration of the coronation of Queen Anne.

"Saw a very pretty procession of three hundred girls in good order, two and two march with three women drummers beating, and a guard of twenty young men on horseback. Each of the females had a white rod in her hand, on the top of which was a tossil made of white and bleu ribband (which they said was the Queen's coleurs) and bone-lace, the great manufacture. Then they had wandered about the town from ten in the morning [it was eight in the evening when he saw them] huzzaing every now and then, and then wearing their rodds. Then they returned at nine, and then break up very weary and hungary."*

* Quoted in "Some Seventeenth Century Topography," *Western Morning News*, May 9th, 1876.

Taste declined during the latter part of last century, and some of the designs of Honiton lace were truly barbarous—frying-pans, snails, drumsticks, and stiff flowers. But there were always some who did better. At the beginning of this century all taste was bad. Bald imitations of nature prevailed, without any regard to the exigencies of art. Roses and other flowers were worked in perspective ; it was thought sufficient to servilely copy nature and leave grouping to chance.

Queen Adelaide had a dress made of Honiton lace. By her desire all the flowers were copied from nature, and the first letter of each spelt her name.

> Amaranth.
> Daphne.
> Eglantine.
> Lilac.
> Auricula.
> Ivy.
> Dahlia.
> Eglantine.

The present Queen also had her wedding-dress of Honiton lace, and it cost a thousand pounds.

Unhappily, design sank very low. Perhaps the lowest stage of degradation in design was reached in 1867, when a Honiton lace shawl sent to the Paris Exhibition from Exeter received a prize and commendation. Nothing can be conceived worse. That it should have been rewarded with a medal shows that either the judges pardoned the ineptitude in design for the sake of the excellence of the work, or else that they themselves stood on the same level of artistic incompetence which then prevailed. Since then, happily, design has been more studied. There is still a good deal of very sorry stuff produced—as far as artistic design is concerned—but at the same time there is much faithful copying of good antique work. All old work is not good; there were bad artists in the past, but the general taste was better than it is now. I was once in the shop of one of our foremost furniture dealers and decorators in town, when a young married couple came in to choose curtains and carpets for their new home. I had been talking with the head of the establishment about artistic furniture, and he had shown me carpets, curtains, and wall-papers, such as no designer in the fifteenth, sixteenth, or seventeenth centuries would have blushed to produce. The young couple passed all these samples by—blind to their merits, and pounced on and chose some atrocious stuff, bad in colour and bad in art. When they were gone, the proprietor turned to me: "You see," he said, "the public is still uncultivated; we are forced to keep rubbish in our trade to satisfy those whose taste does not rise above rubbish." Now it is the same with regard to lace. There is badly designed lace as well as that which is as good as anything drawn by a great master in the past. Let the public eye be discerning to choose the good and reject the evil, and then the poor lace-workers will not be set to produce stuff that never ought to have time, labour, eyesight devoted to it.

There are some trades that are hurtful to those employed in them. The lace-making by machinery at Nottingham is said to induce decline.

The following letter I have received on the subject of the Honiton lace-workers :—

"They are most certainly not a short-lived lot—until within the last eight or nine years Mrs. Colley was the youngest worker I knew, and she is fifty-one ; Mrs. Raymond is sixty-four. There are a good many over sixty, and several still at work over seventy. I have never had cases of decline come under my notice, and if there was any I must have known it. Until the fresh impetus was given to the trade by exhibitions, the younger workers stopped learning, and there was no school, so that the trade depended on the old ones, and all have to commence the work from five to seven years of age. I think it may fairly be assumed to be at any rate not injurious to health, and judging from the age to which they continue to work, not to the sight either."

Thus the buyers of lace can do it with a safe conscience.

There is a woman's name associated with Devon, who was a great landed proprietress and an heiress, and this was Isabella de Fortibus. She was sister of Baldwin, Earl of Devon, a De Redvers, and on his death, without issue, she inherited the splendid estates of the earls of Devon, and became Countess of Devon in her own right. She, however, also died without issue in 1292.

On Farway Common, near Honiton, three parishes meet, and there were incessant disputes as to the boundary. Isabella decided it thus. She flung her ring into the air, and where it fell that was to be the point of junction for Gittisham, Farway, and Honiton. The spot is still called "Ring-in-the-Mere." Such at least is the local legend accounting for the name.

In the neighbourhood of Honiton are the ruins of Dunkeswell Abbey, but they are reduced to a gateway only. It belongs to Mrs. Simcoe, of Walford Lodge, Dunkeswell, a handsome house built about the end of last century by General Simcoe, famous in the American Revolution as the commander of Simcoe's Rangers. He was Governor of San Domingo at the time of the insurrection, and afterwards Governor-General of Canada. Mrs. Simcoe possesses interesting relics connected with him, as well as Napoleonic relics that belonged to her father, Lieut.-General Jackson, *aide-de-camp* to Sir Hudson Lowe at St. Helena.

Mohuns-Ottery, once a great seat of the Carews, was burnt down in the beginning of this century, and all that remains of the mansion are three arches. The Grange, Broadhembury, has been more fortunate; it has a magnificent oak-panelled room, with ghost stories attached, and there are those alive who declare that they have seen the ghost. The church possesses, among other points of interest, a curious window with projecting corbels that represent the spirits of the good in happiness within, and the spirits of the bad without in discomfort—not to put too fine a point on it, as Mr. Snagsby would say.

There are several fine fortifications, as already said: Dumpden, accessible only on foot, and Hembury are the most important.

Books to be consulted :—

ROGERS (W. H. H.), *Memorials of the West.* Exeter, 1888.

FARQUHARSON (A.), *The History of Honiton.* Exeter, *n.d.*, but 1868 (*scarce.*)

For the Axe Valley : PULMAN (G. P. R.), *The Book of the Axe.* London, 1875.

CHAPTER IV.

A LANDSLIP

THERE are a good many more curious things to
be seen in England than is generally supposed,
if we will but go out of the highways to look for
them. Certainly one of the most extraordinary and
impressive is the great landslip between the mouth
of the Axe and Lyme Regis; one which even
extended further west beyond the estuary. On this
bit of coast, where Devonshire passes into Dorset,
the cliff scenery is very fine. The White Cliff is a
magnificent headland that possesses the peculiarity
of appearing to lean over preparing to slide into the
waves, owing to the inclination of the varicoloured
strata of which it is composed. To understand the
phenomenon which occasioned the subsidence of a
whole tract of coast with the alteration of the coast-
line, something must be said of the cause of the
catastrophe. The chalk bed striped with lines of
glistening black flints is superposed upon a bed of
what is locally termed fox earth, a bed of gravel or
sand that intervenes between it and the clay beneath.

Now the rain that falls on the chalk downs infiltrates and, reaching the sand and unable to sink through the clay, breaks out in land springs.

But where the chalk cliffs start sheer out of the sea, there the springs ooze into the sea itself, and, dissolving the texture of the sandy bed, resolve it into a quicksand, liable at the time of great floods to be washed out from under the superincumbent chalk. Should this take place, there is no help for it, but down the chalk bed must go. If you were lying on a bed, and the mattress under your feather bed were pulled away, you would descend, sinking to a depth equivalent to the thickness of the sub-tracted mattress. That is plain enough.

Now all along the coast to the east of Lyme Regis there is an undercliff—evident tokens of a subsidence of this description which has taken place at some time. When this undercliff has been eaten up by the sea, and a fresh face of crag exposed, then again there will occur a displacement, a pulling out of the mattress, and down will go the chalk above with all the houses and fields upon it. But the sea has not as yet done more than nibble at this undercliff.

It was not quite so to the west of Lyme. There sheer cliffs of glistening white rose above the pebbly shore, so abruptly and with such slight undulations, that several miles ensued before it was possible for those on the height to descend to the beach. Naturally, where the rain-water percolated through the chalk it formed no valleys with streams.

Thus the cliffs stood—for no one knows how long —till the end of December, 1839.

Previous symptoms of the approaching convulsion were not altogether wanting. Cracks had been observed for more than a week opening along the brow of the Downs, but they were not sufficiently remarkable to attract much attention, as such fissures are by no means uncommon on this bit of coast. However, about midnight of December 24th, the labourers of Mr. Chappel, the farmer who occupied Dowlands (about a quarter of a mile inland from the brow of the cliff, and over half a mile from the nearest points of the approaching convulsion) were returning from a supper given them by their employer, whereat the ashen faggot had been burnt according to custom, and were making their way to their cottages, situated near the cliff. Then they noticed that a crack which crossed their path, and which they had observed on their way to the Christmas Eve supper, had widened, and that the land beyond had sunk slightly. Nevertheless they did not consider the matter of great importance, and they went to their homes and to bed. About four o'clock in the morning they were roused by their houses reeling, by the concrete floors bursting and gaping, and the walls being rent. They started from their beds in great alarm, and about six o'clock arrived at the farm to rouse their master; they had found their escape nearly cut off, as the crack had widened and the land on the sea side had sunk considerably, so that they had, with their wives and children, to scramble up—and that with difficulty, and, in the darkness, with no little danger.

Happily all escaped in time.

During Christmas Day there was no great change;

parties of the coastguard were stationed on the Downs throughout the ensuing night to watch what would happen.

About midnight a great fissure began to form which ran in almost a direct line for three-quarters of a mile. This fissure rapidly widened to 300 feet, descending, as it seemed at first, into the very bowels of the earth, but as the sides fell in it finally was choked at a depth of 150 feet.

One James Robertson and a companion were at that hour crossing the fields which then extended over this tract, and stumbled across a slight ridge of gravel, which at first they thought must have been made by some boys, but one of them stepping on to it, down sank his leg, and his companion had to pull him out of a yawning chasm. Next moment they saw that the whole surface of turf was starred and splitting in all directions, and they fled for their lives. The sound of the rending of the rocks they described as being much like that of the tearing of cloth or flannel. Two other members of the coastguard, who were stationed on the beach, now saw something begin to rise out of the sea like the back of a gigantic whale; at the same time the shore of shingles on which they stood lifted and fell, like the heaving of a breast in sleep. The water was thrown into violent agitation, foaming and spouting, and great volumes of mud rushed up from below. The great back rose higher and ever higher, and extended further till at last it formed a huge reef at a little distance from the beach. This ridge was composed of the more solid matter, chert and other pebbles, that had been in the sand under the chalk, and which by the sinking of the chalk was squeezed out like so much dough. It remained as a reef for some years, but has now totally disappeared, having been carried away by the waves.

As the great chasm was formed, the masses from the sides falling in were, as it were, mumbled and chewed up in the depths, and to the eyes of the frightened spectators sent forth flashes of light; they also supposed that an intolerable stench was emitted from the abyss. But this was no more than the odours given out by the violent attrition of the cherty sandstone and chalk grinding against each other as they descended.

Throughout the 26th the subsided masses of the great chasm continued sinking, and the elevated reef gradually rising; but by the evening of that day everything had settled very nearly into the position in which it remains at present, although edges have since lost their sharpness and minor rents have been choked.

A writer whose reminiscences have been recently published describes briefly the aspect of the place after the sinkage.

" I rode over to see this huge landslip. The greater part of a farm had subsided a hundred feet or more. Hedges and fields, with their crops of turnips, etc., were undisturbed by the fall, and broken off sharply from the ground a hundred feet above. There was a rather dislocated ridge on the shore, which formed a sort of moraine to the slip. On this part were some cottages twisted about, but still holding together, and having their gardens and even their wells attached; yet the shock of the falling mass had been so great as to cause the upheaval of an island off shore."

The aspect of the landslip on the farms of Bindon, Dowlands, Rousdon, and Pinhay at present is full of interest and of picturesque beauty. Ivy has grown luxuriantly and mantles the crags, elder bushes have found the sunk masses of rock suitable to their requirements, and in early summer the air is strong with the scent of their trusses of flowers, and in autumn the whole subsidence is hung with thousands on ten thousands of shining black clusters of berries. Above a sea of foliage the white cliffs shoot out in the boldest fashion, and out of the gorge start horns, pinnacles of chalk of the most fantastic description. The whole is a labyrinth of chasms, not to be ventured into with good clothing, as the brambles grow in the wildest luxuriance and are clawed like the paws of a panther. But, oh! what blackberries may be gathered there—large, sweet, luscious as mulberries. Moreover, the whole sunk region is a paradise for birds of every description, and not a step can be taken that does not disturb jackdaws, magpies, warblers of every kind. One of the cottages that went down has been rebuilt with the old material. As already said, it descended at least a hundred feet with its well. The well still flows with water; that, however, is not now marvellous— how it was that it held water previously is the extraordinary fact.

At the extremity of the landslip the visitor will see that there is still movement going on, but on a small scale—cracks are still forming and extending through the turf. It may be safely said that the landslip between the mouth of the Axe and Lyme

Regis is one of the most interesting and picturesque scenes to be found in England.

There is a good deal more in the neighbourhood to be seen than the landslip at Rousdon and Pinhay. If the cliffs be explored to the west of the mouth of the Axe, they will be found to well repay the visit. The splendid crag of the White Cliff towers above the sea, showing the slanting beds of the cherty matter below the dazzling white of the chalk, and from their inclination giving to the whole cliff an appearance of lurching into the waves. Beyond this is Beer, a narrow cleft in the hills, in which are fishermen's cottages, many of them very picturesque, and above them rises a really excellently designed modern church.

A walk up the valley leads to the famous Beer quarries that have been worked for centuries. This splendid building-stone lies below the chalk with flints. There are eight beds, forming a thickness of twelve feet four inches, resting on a hard, white, calcareous rock five or six feet thick, which reposes in turn on sandstones. There is very little waste from these quarries, which are carried on underground; and all that is seen of them are the yawning portals in a face of white cliff. But a shout at the entrance will summon a workman, who will conduct the visitor through the labyrinth underground. The roof is sustained by large square pillars formed by portions of the workable beds left standing.

The stone is nearly white, and chiefly composed of carbonate of lime, with the addition of some argillaceous and silicious matter, and a few scattered particles of green silicate of iron. When first quarried this stone is somewhat soft, and is easily worked, but it rapidly hardens on exposure.

Opposite the new quarry are the mounds that mark the site of the old quarry, from which the stone was extracted for Exeter Cathedral. The subterranean passages there are now blocked, but during the time of the European war they were much used by smugglers, who abounded in Beer. The *Memoirs of Jack Rattenbury*, the most notorious of these, were published at Sidmouth in 1837, but are not of conspicuous interest. Beer Head has suffered from landslips, and is broken into spires of rock in consequence.

Books on the Landslip, and on Seaton :—

CONYBEARE and DAWSON, *Memoir and Views of Landslips on the Coast of East Devon*, 1840. A very scarce work.

HUTCHINSON (P. O.), *Guide to the Landslip near Axmouth*. Sidmouth, 1840.

DAVIDSON (J. B.), "Seaton before the Conquest," in *Transactions of Devonshire Association*, 1885.

MUMFORD (G. F.), *Seaton, Beer, and Neighbourhood*. Yeovil, *n.d.*

CHAPTER V.

EXETER

EXETER, the Isca Dumnoniorum of the Romans,
was the Celtic Caer Wisc; that is to say, the
caer or fortress on the Usk. The river-name has
become Exe; it derives from the Celtic word which
signifies water, and which we have in whiskey and
Usquebaugh, *i.e.* fire-water.

The same word has become also Ock. Thus the
Ockment River at Okehampton, a few miles down,
becomes the Exe, at Exbourne; and a tributary of
the Exe is the Oke, that flows into it near Bampton.

There have been but few Roman remains found in
Exeter, and it can never have been an important
settlement. Several Roman roads converge on it
and radiate from it.

The great Fosseway, that ran from Lincoln through
Leicester, reached it. It struck from Honiton,
by Rockbeare and Clyst Honiton, and shows its

antiquity by being the bounds of Broadclyst and Rockbeare, Sowton and Pinhoe parishes. It entered Exeter by Heavitree. Another Roman road from Lyme Regis enters Exeter by Wonford, where it joins the Fosseway. This road also proclaims its high antiquity by being a parish boundary. From Exeter an ancient road ran direct for Launceston: it is called in places the Old Street. It branched at Okehampton, and a road ran thence to Stratton, in Cornwall.

The Fosseway continued to Moreton Hampstead, and crossed Dartmoor, where it has served as the equator of that desolate region; all above it is esteemed the northern half, all below the southern half of Dartmoor. Further it has not been traced.

Another road, the Ridgeway, ran from Exeter to Totnes, and thence has been followed to Plympton Castle.

Whether these roads proceeded far in Cornwall cannot now be determined.

That these ways were possibly pre-Roman, but improved by the conquerors of the world, is probable. Hard by the roadside at Okehampton, in 1898, was found a hoard of the smallest Roman coins, all of the reign of Constantine the Great. It had probably formed the store of a beggar who "sat by the wayside begging." He hid it under a rock, and probably died without having removed it. About 200 coins were found, all dating from between A.D. 320 and 330.

The Saxons must have crept in without violent invasion, across the Axe, rather than through the gaps in the Black Down and Exmoor—for to the

north, as already said, the vast morasses were a
hindrance—and have established themselves without
violent opposition by the riversides. Their manner
of life was unlike that of the Britons. The latter
clung to the open highlands, their *Gwents* as they
called them, clear of trees, breezy downs; whereas
the Saxons, accustomed to forests, made their stock-
ades in the flat *hams* and *ings* by the rivers, in
worths and on *hangers*.

Very probably the Dumnonii suffered their in-
trusion with reluctance, but they did not venture
on forcible resistance, lest they should bring down
on themselves the vengeance of Wessex.

When, however, the Saxons had established themselves in sufficient numbers, they had their headquarters in Exeter; but there they did not amalgamate
with the natives. The Saxon town was quite apart
from that occupied by the Britons, or West Welsh, as
they called our Dumnonians. That part of Exeter
which contains dedications to Celtic saints was the
British town, as was also Heavitree,* with its daughter churches of S. Sidwell and S. David; but the
Saxons occupied where now stands the Cathedral;
and each settlement was governed by its own laws.
It was not till 823 that Egbert, by a decisive battle
at Gavulford (*Gafl* a holdfast, and *ffordd* a road),
established Saxon supremacy. He apparently drove
the Devonshire Celts back along the Old Street, or
Roman road, past Okehampton, till they made a

---

* Names of places, as Heavitree, Langtree, Plymtree, take the
"tree" from the Welsh "tref," a farm or habitation. Heavitree is
Tre-hafod, the summer farm.

stand at Coombow (*Cwm-bod* = the habitation in a combe). There the hills close in on the road on both sides, and the way branched to Lydford. Commanding both roads is Galford Down ; there the Britons threw up formidable entrenchments, or, what is more probable, occupied an earlier camp that remains intact to the present day. Here they made a desperate stand, and were defeated ; after which the king, Egbert, cast up a *burgh* beyond the old *dun*, which gives its second name to the place, Burleigh, or Burgh-legh. The last relics of the independence of the Dumnonian kingdom disappeared after Athelstan's visit in 926 and 928. A relic of this visit may be seen in Rougemont Castle, Exeter, where the Anglo-Saxon work—notably some herring-bone masonry, and windows rudely fashioned without arches—remains.

A Saxon school had been established in Exeter before A.D. 700, to which S. Boniface, or Wynfrith as he was then called, had been sent. He was a native of Crediton, then a Saxon stockaded settlement, and over the palisades, as a boy, he had looked with scorn and hatred at the native Britons occupying the country. When he was in Exeter he, in like manner, regarded the native Christians with loathing as heretics, because they did not observe Easter on the same day as himself, and perhaps with accentuated hate, because he knew that they had possessed Christian teachers and Christian privileges three centuries before his own people had received the Gospel. Perhaps also his German mind was offended at the freshness, vivacity, and maybe as well the

fickleness of purpose of the native Celt. This early
acquired aversion lasted through life, and when he
went into Germany and settled at Mainz, to posture
as an apostle, he was vexed to discover that Celtic
missionaries had preceded him and had worked
successfully among his Teutonic forefathers in their
old homes. Thenceforth he attacked, insulted, and
denounced them with implacable animosity, and did
his utmost to upset their missions and supplannt
them with his own. Virgilius, an Irishman, with a
fellow Paddy, Sidonius, was at Salzburg, and Virgilius
was bishop there. Boniface beat about for an excuse
to get rid of them both. He found that the bishop,
having discovered that one of his priests had been
accustomed to baptise using a bad Latin formula,
had acknowledged this man's baptisms as valid, for
the will was present: the fault was due to ignorance
of the Latin tongue. Boniface, hearing of this, laid
hold of it with enthusiasm, and denounced Virgilius
at Rome. Pope Boniface, however, took the side of
the Irishman against his over-zealous henchman.

Mortified at this rebuff, Boniface lay in wait to
find another excuse for ruining Virgilius. He ascertained presently that the Irishman taught that the
earth was round, and that there was an antipodes
to those living in Germany. Now the Irish schools
were the most learned in Europe, and Irish saints
had sailed far into the west over the Atlantic: they
had formed their own opinions concerning the shape
of the world. Boniface wrote to the Pope to denounce
the doctrine of Virgilius as "perverse and unjust,
uttered against God and his own soul."

This doctrine Pope Zacharias hastened to condemn as heretical.* Virgilius had to go to Rome to justify his opinion before ignorant Latin ecclesiastics—with what results we do not know.

Athelstan came to Exeter in 926, and drove out the British inhabitants. He built towers and repaired the old Roman walls; he it was who founded the monastery of SS. Mary and Peter, afterwards to become the Cathedral; and, we are told, he gave to it relics of S. Sidwell. This was a local saint, of whom very little is known, save that she was the sister of Paul, who became abbot and bishop of Léon, in Brittany. She had two sisters, Wulvella and Jutwara, called also Jutwell and Eadware. Though the names seem Saxon, they are corruptions of Celtic originals. Wulvella became an abbess at Gulval, near Penzance, where she entertained her brother as he was on his way to Armorica. Sidwell is supposed to have been a martyr, possibly to Saxon brutality, but this is very uncertain, as her story has not been preserved. She has as her symbols a scythe and a well—"canting" symbols framed from her name. Her brother Paul founded a church that still retains his name, in the British portion of Exeter.

The bishop's seat had been at Crediton: the Saxon

* In my *Lives of the Saints*, written in 1874, I accepted M. Barthélemy's view, that Virgilius held that there were underground folk, gnomes; but I do not hold this now, knowing more than I then did of the learning of the great Irish scholars, and of the voyages made by the Irish. The earliest gloss on the *Senchus Mor* says, "God formed the firmament around the earth; and the earth, in the form of a perfectly round ball, was fixed in the midst of the firmament."—I. p. 27.

bishops did not like it. There were no walls there, and the Danes made piratical excursions. So Bishop Leofric induced Edward the Confessor to move the seat to Exeter, and this was done by Edward in person, in 1050.

In Fore Street is an odd misshapen little church, S. Olave's. This was endowed by Gytha, sister of Sweyn, the Danish king, and wife of Earl Godwin. She was the mother of Harold. She is said to have endowed it (1053) that prayer might be offered for the soul of her husband, and in honour of Olaf, King of Norway, who had fallen in battle in 1030. As S. Olaf fought against the Danes, and it was through the machinations of Canute that he came to his end, it is hard to see how a Danish lady should have felt any enthusiasm about Olaf, who was regarded as a saint and martyr by the national Norwegian party, which was bitterly opposed to the Danish. I suspect that the church already existed, and was dedicated to S. Gwynllyw of Gwent, who at Newport was also converted into Olave, by the English-speaking colonists. Both Gwynllyw and Olaf were kings, and it is noticeable that S. Olave's Church is in the British portion of Exeter. When William the Conqueror arrived before the city, Gytha, who was within the walls, escaped and took refuge in Flanders. William gave the church, with her endowments, to Battle Abbey. But I am not writing a history of Exeter. For those who desire to learn its story in full, I must refer them to the work of Mr. Freeman.

The Cathedral is disappointing, and that because it is built, not of the warm, red sandstone that abounds in the neighbourhood, and is very good building material, but of Beer stone, which is cold and grey. It has another defect: it is too low; but this was determined by the towers. When it was resolved to rebuild the Cathedral, it was decided to preserve the Norman towers, employing them as transepts. This settled the business. The church could not be made lofty; and on entering the western doors the visitor is at once disappointed. He feels a lack of breathing-space; the vaulting depresses him. The architectural details are not to be surpassed, but the whole effect is marred by the one mistake made at the outstart. One cannot wish that the towers had been removed, but one does regret that they were allowed to determine the height of nave and choir. The choir was begun by Bishop Quivil, in 1284, when also the great and incomparably beautiful windows were inserted in the towers. The nave was finished by Bishop Grandisson, in 1369, the year of his death.

Grandisson was a friend of the detestable John XXII., one of the Avignon Popes; and John appointed his intimate to Exeter in total disregard to the rights of the chapter to elect. He was consecrated at Avignon. Hitherto almost all the bishops had been local men.

Grandisson was a man very Romanly inclined, and appointed to a see that was redolent with Celtic reminiscences. He did not relish these. Whenever he had the chance of rededicating a church he endeavoured to substitute a patron from the Roman calendar in place of the British founder. He drew up a **Legendarium, a book of Lessons on Saints'**

Feasts to be used in the Cathedral Church, and ignored nearly every saint whose name was not approved by admission into the Latin martyrology.

"The Church of Exeter is a remarkable case of one general design being carried out through more than a hundred years. It was fixed once for all what the new Saint Peter's should be like, and it grew up after one general pattern, but with a certain advance in detail as the work went westward. Bishop Grandison, when the church was about half built, said that when it was finished it would surpass in beauty all churches of its own kind in England and France. Whatever he meant by '*genus suum*,' the prediction was safely risked. As far as outline and general effect goes, the Church of Exeter forms a class by itself."—FREEMAN.

A more remarkable church than the Cathedral of Exeter is that of Ottery S. Mary, also built by Grandisson. It is, of course, not by any means so large. It gave, perhaps, the original type to Exeter, for there also the towers have been employed as transepts, and was begun in the Early English style. But there a stateliness and an originality of effect are reached that Exeter cannot approach.

There the side aisles have but lancet windows, and a flood of light pours down through the very original clerestory lights. There is no east window. What the general effect must have been before the levels were wantonly altered at the "restoration" one can now hardly surmise. But the church, in spite of this and some odiously vulgar woodwork, is one of the most striking in England, and perhaps the boldest in originality of conception.

The Guildhall, in High Street, is a good example of Elizabethan architecture, in bad stone.

A beautiful excursion may be made from Exeter to Fingle Bridge,* on the Teign, where the river winds between the hills densely wooded with coppice, that close in on each other like the fangs of a rat-trap. With this may be combined Shilstone cromlech, the sole perfect specimen of the kind remaining in the county, and once but a single member in a series of very remarkable monuments.

The Teign is frowned down on by several strongly fortified camps. Fingle should be seen when the hills are clothed in flowering heather, as though raspberry cream had been spilt over them. White heather may be picked there.

Fulford House is a quadrangle in a sad state of dilapidation ; originally of Tudor architecture, but disfigured by bad alterations in the Prince Regent's days, when cockney Gothic was in vogue. In the house is a bad portrait of the " Royal Martyr," presented by Charles II., and one of " Red Ruin," a spendthrift Fulford. In the hall is some superb carved panelling, early Tudor.

Exeter may be made a centre for ecclesiological excursions of no ordinary interest. Dunchideock Church has a well-restored screen ; but by far the richest carved oak rood-screen in the county is that of Kenton, where also the pulpit is of incomparable beauty. The carver employed thereon was a man of no common talent, and the work is one of brilliant

* *Ffin*—limit, *gal*—the level land, *i.e.* in comparison with the Dartmoor highlands.

execution. There is much difference in the carving in the county—some is common, mechanical; that in the Kenton screen and pulpit is of the very finest quality.

In the little church of S. Mary Steps, in Exeter, may be seen a portion of the screen removed from S. Mary Major when that monstrosity was erected. At Plymtree the screen bears on it contemporary portraits of Prince Arthur (son of Henry VII.) and Cardinal Morton. That of Bradninch has on it paintings of the Sibyls, the Doctors of the Church, and the Legend of S. Francis.

Pinhoe was the scene of a great battle with the Danes in 1001. They had come up the Exe, and burned Pinhoe, Broadclyst, and some of the neighbouring villages. Levies in Devon and Somerset met them, but were defeated with great slaughter. The church contains a fine coloured screen with the vaulting-ribs and gallery. The alms-box is curious: it represents a serving-man supporting himself with a stick in one hand, the other extended soliciting alms.

East Budleigh should be visited for its fine bench-ends, some very curious; one represents a cook roasting a goose; another a ship in full sail. Their date is 1534. There is a screen, but not of first quality.

Littleham, near Exmouth, has a good screen. Screens are the features of Devonshire churches: a church was built to contain one. Without it the proportions are faulty.

Books on Exeter :—
    FREEMAN (E. A.), *Historic Towns: Exeter*. 1895.
    NORTHY (T. J.), *Popular History of Exeter*. 1886.
    JENKINS (A.), *History of Exeter*. 1841.

CHAPTER VI.

CREDITON

A CURIOUS, sleepy place, the houses like the great church built of red sandstone, where not of the red clay or cob. But in the latter case the cob is whitewashed. No house can be conceived more warm and cosy than that built of cob, especially when thatched. It is warm in winter and cool in summer, and I have known labourers bitterly bewail their fate in being transferred from an old fifteenth or sixteenth century cob cottage into a newly-built stone edifice of the most approved style. As they said, it was like going out of warm life into a cold grave.

The art of building with cob is nearly extinct. Clay is kneaded up with straw by the feet, and then put on the rising walls that are enclosed in a frame-

work of boards, but this latter is not always necessary
as the clay is consistent enough to hold together,
and all that is required is to shave it down as the wall
rises in height.   Such cob walls for garden fruit are
incomparable.   They retain the warmth of the sun
and give it out through the night, and when pro-
tected on top by slates or thatch will last for centuries.   But let their top be exposed, and they
dissolve in the rain and flake away with the frost.
They have, however, their compensating disadvan-
tage—they harbour vermin.

Crediton takes its name from the Creedy river
that flows near the town.   The river is designated
(*Crwydr*) from its straggling character, crumbling
its banks away at every flood and changing its
course.   At a very early period the Saxons had
succeeded in establishing a settlement here, a *tun*,
and here Wynfrith, better known as S. Boniface,
was born in 680.   Willibald, a priest of Mainz who
wrote his life, tells us that his father was a great
householder, and of "eorl-kind," or noble birth.   He
loved his son Wynfrith above all his other children,
and for a long time withheld his consent to his
embracing the monastic life.   During a serious ill-
ness, however, when death seemed near at hand, he
relented, and Wynfrith was sent to school at Exeter.
Thence he moved to Nutschelle, where he assumed
the name of Boniface.   At the age of thirty he was
ordained.   King Ina, of the West Saxons, honoured
him with his confidence, and he might have risen to
a high office in his native land, but other aspirations
had taken possession of his soul.   No stories were

listened to at his time in the Anglo-Saxon monasteries with greater avidity than those connected with the adventurous mission of Archbishop Willibrord among the heathen Frisians, and Boniface longed to join the noble band beyond the sea. The abbot opposed his design, but Boniface was obstinate, and with three brethren left Nutschelle for London; there they took ship and landed in Frisia in 716. But the time was unpropitious, and he was forced to return to Nutschelle.

Next year he went to Rome, and then the Pope urged him to establish papal authority in Germany, which had been converted by Celtic missionaries, who had their own independent ways, that were not at all relished at Rome. Boniface, who hated the Celts and all their usages, eagerly undertook the task, and he went into Thuringia. He did a double work. He converted, or attempted to convert, the heathen, and he ripped up and undid what had been done independently by the Irish missionaries. In his old age he resumed his attempt to carry the Gospel into Frisia, and was there killed, A.D. 755.

A Saxon see was established at Crediton about 909, and was given three estates in Cornwall—Poulton, Lawhitton, and Callington. The Bishop was charged to visit the Cornish people year by year " to drive away their errors," for up to that time "they had resisted the truth with all their might, and had disobeyed the Apostolic decrees," that is to say, they clung to their ecclesiastical independence and some of their peculiar customs.

Crediton remained the seat of the Romano-Saxon bishops till 1046, when Leofric got the see moved to Exeter, where his skin would be safer behind walls than in exposed Crediton.

The church, dedicated to the Holy Cross, is a very stately building; the tower is transition Norman at the base. The rest is Perpendicular, and a fine effect is produced by the belt of shadow under the tower, with the illumined choir behind, which has large windows. The east window was mutilated at the "restoration." It was very original and delightful; it has been reduced to the same commonplace pattern as the west window.

Crediton was a great seat of the cloth trade, and many of those whose sumptuous monuments decorate the church owed their wealth to "Kirton serge." Westcote says that the "aptness and diligent industry of the inhabitants" (in this branch of manufacture) "did purchase it a pre-eminent name above all other towns, whereby grew this common proverb, 'as fine as Kirton spinning' (for we call it briefly Kirton), which spinning was very fine indeed, which to express the better to gain your belief, it is very true that 140 threads for woollen yarn spun in that town were drawn together through the eye of a taylor's needle, which needle and threads were for many years together to be seen in Watling Street, in London, in the shop of one Mr. Dunscombe, at 'The Sign of the Golden Bottle.'"

Crediton is now a great centre of apple culture and cider-making. The rich red soil lends itself admirably to the production of delicious apples.

It is quite a mistake to suppose that any fruit serves for cider. There are certain kinds that are vastly superior to others for this purpose, as the Bitter-sweet, the Fox-whelp, the Kingston Black and Cherry Pearmain; but the best all round is the Kingston Black.

When there is going up a general cry for legislation to ameliorate in some way the condition of agriculture, it is a satisfaction to think that one act of Government has had a beneficial effect on the English farmer, if not throughout the land, at all events in the West of England and in other cider-making counties, and that act was the laying of heavy duty on foreign sparkling wines. Quite as much champagne is drunk now as was before the duty was increased, but unless we are very much mistaken some of that champagne comes from the apple and not from the grape.

·A story is told that a gentleman the other day applied to a large apple-orchard farmer in the West of England for a hogshead or two of his sparkling cider. The farmer replied that he was very sorry not to be able to accommodate him as in previous years, but a certain London firm had taken his whole year's "pounding." He gave the name of the firm and assured his customer that he could get the cider from that house. The gentleman applied, and received the answer :—

"SIR,—We are not cider merchants. You have made some mistake. We are a firm of champagne-importing merchants from the celebrated vineyards of MM. So-and-so, at So-and-so."

Well, the money goes into English pockets, into those of the hardly-pressed and pinched English farmers. And cider is the most wholesome and sound of beverages. So all is well.

There are, as may have been noticed, three cold nights in May—not always, but often. At Crediton, and throughout the apple-growing districts in North Devon, these are called "Francémass" or "S. Frankin's days;" they are the 19th, 20th, and 21st May. When a frost comes then it injures the apple blossom. The story relative to this frost varies slightly. According to one version there was an Exeter brewer, of the name of Frankin, who found that cider ran his ale so hard that he vowed his soul to the devil on the condition that he would send three frosty nights in May to annually cut off the apple blossom. The other version of the story is that the brewers in North Devon entered into a compact with the Evil One, and promised to put deleterious matter into their ale on condition that the devil should help them by killing the blossom of the apple trees. Accordingly, whenever these May frosts come we know that his majesty is fulfilling *his* part of the contract, because the brewers have fulfilled *theirs* by adulterating their beer. S. Frankin, according to this version, is an euphemism for Satan.

Our dear old friend, the apple, not only serves as a kindly assistant to help out the supply of wine, but also forms the basis of a good many jams. With some assistance it is converted into raspberry and plum, but no inducement will persuade it to become strawberry. It is certainly instructive to pass a jam factory in October and thence inhale the fragrance of raspberries.

For some twenty or thirty years the orchards were sadly neglected. The old trees were not replaced, there was no pruning, no cleaning of the trunks, the cattle were turned into the orchard to gnaw and injure the bark and break down the branches, no dressing was given to the roots, and the pounding of apples was generally abandoned. But thanks to the increased demand for cider—largely, no doubt, to be drunk as cider, also, it is more than suspected, to be drunk under another name—the farmers in Somersetshire, Devonshire, Hereford, and Worcestershire have begun to cultivate apple trees, and care for them, as a means of revenue.

In former days there were many more orchards than at present; every gentleman's house, every farmhouse had its well - stocked, carefully pruned orchard. Beer ran cider hard, and nearly beat it out of the field, and overthrew the apple trees, but the trees are having their good times again.

There is a curious song of "The Apple Trees" that was formerly sung in every West of England farmhouse. It was a sort of Georgic, giving complete instructions how apples are to be grown and cider to be made. It is now remembered only by very old men, and as it has, to the best of my knowledge, never appeared in print, I will quote it in full :—

> "An orchard fair, to please,
>   And pleasure for your mind, sir,
> You'd have—then plant of trees
>   The goodliest you can find, sir ;

In bark they must be clean,
   And finely grown in root, sir,
Well trimmed in head, I ween,
   And sturdy in the shoot, sir.

O the jovial days when the apple trees do bear,
We'll drink and be merry all the gladsome year.

  " The pretty trees you plant,
     Attention now will need, sir,
  That nothing they may want,
     Which to mention I proceed, sir.
  You must not grudge a fence
     'Gainst cattle, tho't be trouble ;
  They will repay the expense
     In measure over double.

          O the jovial days, &c.

  " To give a man great joy,
     And see his orchard thrive, sir,
  A skilful hand employ
     To use the pruning knife, sir.
  To lop each wayward limb,
     That seemeth to offend, sir ;
  Nor fail at Fall, to trim
     Until the tree's life end, sir.

          O the jovial days, &c.

  " All in the month of May,
     The trees are clothed in bloom, sir,
  As posies bright and gay,
     Both morning, night and noon, sir.
  'Tis pleasant to the sight,
     'Tis sweet unto the smell, sir,
  And if there be no blight,
     The fruit will set and swell, sir.

          O the jovial days, &c.

  " The summer oversped,
     October drawing on, sir ;
  The apples gold and red
     Are glowing in the sun, sir.

As the season doth advance,
    Your apples for to gather,
I bid you catch the chance
    To pick them in fine weather.
          O the jovial days, &c.

" When to a pummy ground,
    You squeeze out all the juice, sir,
Then fill a cask well bound,
    And set it by for use, sir.
O bid the cider flow
    In ploughing and in sowing,
The healthiest drink I know
    In reaping and in mowing.
          O the jovial days, &c."

This fresh and quaint old song was taken down from an ancient sexton of over eighty near Tiverton.

The young apple trees have a deadly enemy in the rabbit, which loves their sweet bark, and in a night will ruin half a nursery, peeling it off and devouring it all round. Young cattle will break over a hedge and do terrible mischief to an orchard of hopeful trees that promise to bear in another year or two. The bark cannot endure bruising and breaking—injury to it produces that terrible scourge the canker. Canker is also caused by the tap-root running down into cold and sour soil; and it is very customary, where this is likely, to place a slate or a tile immediately under the tree, so as to force the roots to spread laterally. Apple trees hate standing water, and like to be on a slope, whence the moisture rapidly drains away. As the song says, the orchard apples when ripe glow "gold and red," and the yellow and red apples make the best cider.

The green apple is not approved by the old-fashioned cider-apple growers. The maxim laid down in the song, that the apples should be "the goodliest you can find," was not much attended to some thirty years ago when orchards were let down; farmers thought that any trees were good enough, and that there was a positive advantage in selecting sour apples, for that then the boys would not steal them. It is now otherwise; they are well aware that the quality of the cider depends largely on the goodness of the sort of apple grown. The picking of apples takes place on a fine windy or sunny day. The apples to be pounded are knocked down with a pole, but those for "hoarding" are carefully picked, as a bruise is fatal. After that the fallen apples have been gathered by women and children they are heaped up under the trees and left to completely ripen and be touched with frost. It is thought that they make better cider when they have begun to turn brown. Whether this be actually the case, or the relic of a mistaken custom of the past, the writer cannot say.

All apples are not usually struck down—the small ones, "griggles," are left for schoolboys. It is their privilege to glean in the orchard, and such gleaning is termed "griggling."

What the vintage is in France, and the hop-picking is in Kent and Bavaria, that the apple-picking and collecting is in the cider counties of England. The autumn sun is shining, there is a crispness in the air, the leaves are turned crimson and yellow, of the same hues as the fruit. The grass of the orchard is bright with crimson and gold as though it were studded with jewels, but the jewels are the windfalls from the apple trees. Men, women, and children are happy talking, laughing, singing snatches of songs— except when eating. Eat they must—eat they will —and the farmer does not object, for there is a limit to apple-eating. The apple is the most filling of all fruit. And yet how unlimited seems the appetite of the boy, especially when he gets into an orchard! The grandfather of the writer of this book planted an orchard specially for the boys of the parish, in the hope that they would glut themselves therein and leave his cider orchard alone. It did not answer; they devoured all the apples in their special orchard and carried their ravages into his also.

The farmer knows that the apple is tempting, and the apple-pickers and collectors are allowed to eat— within limits. But he can afford to be generous. In a good year how abundant is the supply on every tree! How every tree resembles those that Aladdin saw in the enchanted world underground laden with topaz and ruby!

There was a curious custom in Devon, now completely gone out, which consisted, on Old Christmas Day, in going at night into an orchard and firing blank charges from fowling-pieces at the apple trees. It was supposed that this ensured there being a good harvest of apples the ensuing year. In Somersetshire the wassailing of the trees continued till within the memory of old folk. Sir Thomas Acland related to Mr. Brand, in 1790, that in his neighbourhood on Christmas Eve it was customary for the country people to sing a wassail or drinking song, and drink the toast from the wassail-bowl to the apple trees in order to have a fruitful year. And Herrick alludes to this when he enjoins :—

> "Wassaile the trees, that they may bear
> You many a plum, and many a peare ;
> For more or lesse fruits they will bring,
> As you do give them wassailing."

The wassail song was as follows :—

"Old Apple tree, we are come to wassail thee,
All for to bloom, and to bear thy flowers and fruit so free.
Wassail ! wassail ! all round our town ;
Our cups are white and our ale is brown.
Our bowl is made of a good ashen tree,
And here's kind fellows as will drink to thee.

> Hats full, caps full, five-bushel bags full,
> Barns full, floors full, stables full, tallats full,
> And the little hole under the stairs, three times three !
> Hip, hip, hurrah ! shout we."

When the apples are considered fit to pound, which is usually in November, they are taken to the crusher. This consists of a large circular stone trough with a rim about it, and in this rolls a great stone wheel, set in motion formerly by a horse attached to a "roundabout." The great wheel revolved and crushed the apples to a pulp. The crushing was, however, also done by the hand, in small quantities. There is, however, a method of cutting them small between rollers. The machine is now commonly set in motion by water.

The pounded apple pulp is called pomage, or

apple-mock (mash). The apples are ground to one consistence, with kernels and skins. The kernels give flavour, and the skins colour; or are supposed so to do.

The pulp is next conveyed to the cider-press, where it is placed in layers, with clean straw or haircloths between the layers. Below is the vat; in Devonshire and Cornwall commonly called the "vate." Above are planks with a lever beam weighted, so as to produce great pressure, or else they are pressed by means of a screw. The pressing-planks are locally termed the "sow." The cider now begins to flow. The first flow is by no means the best.

The pulp thus squeezed is termed the "cheese." This is pared down, and the parings added to the block and again subjected to pressure.

The cider as it flows away is received in "kieves." No water whatever is added to the apples. What comes away is the pure unadulterated juice. When, however, the cider has been wholly pressed out, then it is customary to make a hole in the "cheese" and pour in some water, which is left to be absorbed by the spongy matter. This is afterwards pressed out, and goes by the name of "beverage." It is not regarded as cider. It is sharper in taste, and is appreciated by workmen.

Outside old farms is often to be seen a huge block of stone, with a ring at the top. This was the weight formerly attached to the beam. The pressing of the "cheese" was anciently performed by men pulling the wooden beam, weighted with the great mass of granite or other heavy substance that

pressed down the "sow." A later contrivance was
a wheel with a screw, by means of which far more
pressure could be brought on the "cheese." The
cider that oozed out under pressure ran out of the
trough by a lip into a flat tub called a "trin;" or
into the "kieve." The great scooped-out stones in
which the apples were crushed were often of great
size, as much as ten or even twelve feet in diameter.
The stone that rolled in them was termed the
"runner." Where much pains was taken with the
cider, there the several kinds of apples were crushed
separately, and also pressed separately. But the
usual custom was to throw in all together into the
"chase" or crushing basin. In a good many places
small discarded "chases" may be seen. These were
employed not for making cider, but cider spirit,
which was distilled. This is indeed still manufactured in some places on the sly. In Germany it is
largely distilled and sold as "schnaps," and very
fiery, nasty stuff it is. The manufacturers of British
spirits know the use of cider spirit as a base for
some of their concoctions.

Formerly a duty of ten shillings a barrel was
imposed on the making of cider, but this was repealed in 1830.

The "cheese" of the apples is of little value. It
is given to pigs. Keepers are glad of it for the
pheasants they rear; and made into cakes it serves
as fuel, smouldering and giving forth a not very
aromatic smoke.

The juice of the apples is left in the "kieves" for
a period that varies according to the weather and

the temperature, but generally is from three to four days.

During this period fermentation commences, and all the dirt and impure matter come as a scum to the surface. This head is skimmed off as it forms. If this be not done, after a time it sinks, and spoils the quality of the cider. The liquid, by fermentation, not only develops alcohol, but also cleanses itself. The fresh, sweet cider is of a thick and muddy consistency. By fermentation it purifies itself, and becomes perfectly clear.

The cider is now put into casks. In order to make *sweet* cider the cask is " matched." A bucketful of the new cider is put in, then brimstone is lighted in an old iron pot, and a match of paper or canvas is dipped in the melted brimstone and thrust into the cask through the bung-hole, which is closed. The fumes of sulphur fill the vessel, and when the barrel is afterwards filled with cider all fermentation is arrested. Sweet cider, if new, is often rather unpleasant from the taste of the sulphurous acid.

This may be avoided by " racking," that is to say, the cider when made may be turned from one hogshead to another at intervals, whenever it shows signs of fermenting. This continuous " racking " will arrest the progress of fermentation as effectually as " matching."

The sweet cider is in far greater demand by the general public than that which is " rough," but a West Country labourer will hardly thank you for the cider that will be drunk with delight by the cockney. He prefers it "rough," that is to say acid,

the rougher the better, till it almost cuts the throat
as it passes down.

Unless bottled, cider is difficult to preserve owing
to the development of lactic acid.　Moreover, in
wood it turns dark in colour, and if allowed to stand
becomes of an inky black, which is not inviting.　This
is due to having been in contact with iron.

It is bottled from Christmas on till Easter, and
so is sold as champagne cider; sometimes as champagne without the addition, we strongly suspect.

The amount of alcohol produced by fermentation
varies from five and a half to nine per cent.　In the
sweet sparkling cider the amount is very small, and
it would take a great deal of it to make a man
inebriate.

Much difference of opinion exists as to the good
of cider for rheumatic subjects.　The sweet cider
is of course bad, but it is certain that in the West
of England a good many persons are able to drink
cider who dare not touch beer—not only so, but
believe that it is beneficial.　Others, however, protest
that they feel rheumatic pains if they touch it.

The manufacturers of champagne cider very commonly add mustard to the liquid for the purpose
of stinging the tongue; but apart from that, cider
is the purest and least adulterated of all drinks.

In conclusion I will venture to quote another West
of England song concerning cider, only premising
that by "sparkling" cider is not meant that which
goes by the name in commerce, but the homely
cask cider; and next, that the old man who sang
it to the writer of this article—a Cornish tanner—

claimed (but the claim may be questioned) to have composed both words and melody, so that the song, though of country origin, is not very ancient :—

> " In a nice little village not far from the sea,
> Still lives my old uncle aged eighty and three,
> Of orchards and meadows he owns a good lot,
> Such cider as his—not another has got.
>
> > Then fill up the jug, boys, and let it go round,
> > Of drinks not the equal in England is found.
> > So pass round the jug, boys, and pull at it free,
> > There's nothing like cider, sparkling cider, for me.
>
> " My uncle is lusty, is nimble and spry (lively),
> As ribstons his cheeks, clear as crystal his eye,
> His head snowy white, as the flowering may,
> And he drinks only cider by night and by day.
>
> > Then fill up the jug, &c.
>
> " O'er the wall of the churchyard the apple trees lean
> And ripen their burdens, red, golden, and green.
> In autumn the apples among the graves lie;
> 'There I'll sleep well,' says uncle, 'when fated to die.
>
> > Then fill up the jug, &c.
>
> " ' My heart as an apple, sound, juicy, has been,
> My limbs and my trunk have been sturdy and clean;
> Uncankered I've thriven, in heart and in head,
> So under the apple trees lay me when dead.'
>
> > Then fill up the jug, &c."

Near Crediton, at Creedy Bridge, was born John Davy, the composer of the popular song " The Bay of Biscay." He was baptised on Christmas Day, 1763, at Upton Hellions, and was an illegitimate child ; but he was tenderly brought up by his uncle, a village blacksmith, who played the violoncello in Upton Hellions Church choir.

When in Crediton one day as a child with his uncle, he saw some soldiers at the roll-call, and was vastly delighted at the music of the fifes; so much so that he borrowed one and very soon learned to play it. After that he made fifes with his penknife of the hollow-stalked weeds growing on the banks of the Creedy, locally called "bitters," and sold them to his playfellows.

A year later the chimes of Crediton made such an impression on this precocious child, that he purloined twenty or thirty horseshoes from his uncle's smithy, and the old fellow was sadly perplexed as to what had become of them, till he heard a mysterious chiming from the garret, and on ascending to it, found that John had suspended eight of the horseshoes from the rafters so as to form an octave, and with a rod was striking them in imitation of the Crediton chimes.

This story getting to the ears of the rector of the parish, Chancellor Carrington, he felt interested in the child and showed him a harpsichord, on which he soon learned to play. Davy also at this time applied himself to learn the violin.

When Davy was eleven years old the rector introduced him to another parson, named Eastcott, who possessed a pianoforte, an instrument of recent introduction. With this the boy soon became familiar. An effort was now made by these two kindly clergymen, and they placed him with Jackson, the organist of Exeter Cathedral, with whom he remained some years and completed his musical education.

He then went to London, where he was employed

to supply music for the songs of the operas of that day, and was retained as a composer by the managers of the Theatre Royal until infirmities, rather than age, rendered him incapable of exertion, and he died, before he was sixty-two, in penury. It was due only to a couple of London tradesmen, one of whom was a native of Crediton, that he was not consigned to a pauper's grave. He wrote some dramatic pieces for the theatre at Sadler's Wells, and composed the music for Holman's opera of *What a Blunder*, which was performed at the little theatre in the Haymarket in 1800. In the following year he was engaged with Moorhead in the music of *Perouse*, and with Mountain in that of *The Brazen Mask*. His last opera was *Woman's Will*. Some of his songs have obtained a firm hold, as "Just Like Love," "May we ne'er want a Friend," "The Death of Will Watch the Smuggler," which I have heard a village blacksmith sing, and "The Bay of Biscay."

He was buried in St. Martin's churchyard, February 28th, 1824.

There are some fine seats and parks near Crediton: Creedy Park, that of Sir H. Fergusson Davie, Bart.; that of Shobrooke, the seat of Sir I. Shelly, Bart.; and Downes, the property of Sir Redvers Buller. This latter place takes its name from the *dun* which occupied the hill-top between the Yeo and Creedy, which unite below it. All traces of the old ramparts have, however, disappeared under cultivation. There is a somewhat pathetic story connected with Shobrooke and Downes. The latter belonged to William

Gould, and James Buller, of Morval, obtained it by marrying his eldest daughter and heiress Elizabeth, born in 1718. The younger and only other sister, Frances, married John Tuckfield, of Shobrooke Park, then known as Little Fulford. This was in 1740, when she was only eighteen. The respective husbands quarrelled about money and politics, and forbade their wives to meet and speak to each other. John Tuckfield was member for Exeter 1747, 1754, 1760, when he died. The sisters were wont to walk every day to a certain point in the respective grounds and wave their handkerchiefs to each other, and they never met in this world again, for Elizabeth died in 1742.

There is not much of great interest in the neighbourhood of Crediton. Perhaps the church that most deserves a visit is Colebrook, with its curious wood carving and a fine original and late piece of screen - work. There is also Coplestone Cross, a very remarkable piece of early Celtic interlaced work, such as is not to be found elsewhere in England except in Northumbria. It is mentioned in a charter in 974, but it is far older than that. It stands at the junction of three parishes, and has given a name to a once noted family in the county, that comes into an old local rhyme, which runs :—

> " Crocker, Cruwys, and Coplestone,
>   When the Conqueror came were found at home."

But who the ancestors of these families were at the time of the Conquest we have no means of knowing. Of the few English thegns who retained their lands in Devonshire after the Conquest, not one is recorded as holding any of the estates that later belonged to these families. The cross is of granite, and stands 10 feet 6 inches high. It is, unhappily, mutilated at the top.

At Nymet Rowland, near Crediton, the savages lived, to whom Mr. Greenwood drew attention. They were dispersed by becoming a prey to typhoid, when their hovel was torn down. The last of them, an old man, lived the rest of his life and died in the parish of Whitstone in a cask littered with straw, the cask chained to a post in an outhouse. I have given an account of them in my *Old English Home*.

At Lapford is a fine screen, and the carved benches are deserving of attention. Lapford was for long, too long, the place over which " Pass'n Radford " brooded as an evil genius. I have told several stories of him in my *Old Country Life*, under the name of Hannaford. He has been sketched in Mr. Blackmore's *Maid of Sker* beside Parson Froude, of Knowstone. The latter has been drawn without excessive exaggeration.

At Down S. Mary the screen has been admirably completed from a fragment by the village carpenter. There is a good screen at Bow.

A good walk through pretty scenery to Dowrish, an ancient mansion, and once dating from King John's reign, but modernised in suburban villa style. Though there is nothing remaining of interest in the house, the view thence, stretching across the richly wooded land of the new red sandstone to the heights of Dartmoor, will repay the walk. For

many years Crediton was the residence of the
Rev. Samuel Rowe, the Columbus of Dartmoor.
He laboriously explored that region, till then almost
unvisited, and chronicled its prehistoric relics.
Although he was hopelessly involved in the pseudo-
antiquarianism of his period, and put everything
prehistoric down to the Druids and Phœnicians, yet
his researches were most valuable, and he has
recorded the existence of many relics that have
since disappeared. His *Perambulation of Dartmoor*
was published in 1848. He had indeed been preceded in 1832 by the Rev. Edward A. Bray, vicar
of Tavistock, but the visits of the latter to Dartmoor
had been confined to the immediate neighbourhood
of the town of which he was parson.

CHAPTER VII.

TIVERTON

Two-fords Town—The Seven Crosses—Numerous chapels—Tiverton
Church—Blundell's School—Parson Russell—Washfield—Sampford
Peverell Ghost—"Old Snow"—White Witches—Instance of evil
done by them—The Four Quarters—Machine lace—John Heath-
coat—Cullompton—Bampfylde Moore Carew—Bampton Pony Fair
—The Exmoor ponies.

TIVERTON, or, as it was originally called,
Twyford, takes its name from being planted
between the Exe and the Loman (Gael. *liomh*,
smooth or sluggish *), which are here fordable. It
rises picturesquely above the Exe, and the height
when crowned with castle as well as church must
have presented a remarkably fine group of towers.
The main castle tower was, however, pulled down
and left as a stump about thirty-five years ago.

The castle was a great Courtenay stronghold, and
occupied a site that had doubtless been previously
fortified. There is, however, a large and strong
earthwork, Cranmore, that occupies the height above
Collipriest and looks down upon the town.

At Hensleigh, a hamlet to the west of the town,
is a spot called "The Seven Crosses." The origin

---

* The same in Loch Lomond and in Lake Leman, in the Lyme
in Dorsetshire, and the Leam by Leamington.

of this name is, according to a generally accepted tradition, as follows :—

One day the Countess of Devon was taking her walk abroad in the direction of Hensleigh, when she met a tailor descending the hill, laden with a large covered maund, or basket. As he passed, she heard a cry from the hamper. She stayed her steps and inquired what he was carrying.

"Only seven puppies that I be going to drown in the Exe," was his reply.

"I want a dog," said the Countess. "Open the hamper."

The tailor tried to excuse himself, but in vain. The Countess insisted, and, on the lid being raised, seven little babes were revealed.

"Alas, my lady!" said the tailor. "My wife gave birth to all seven at once, and I am poor, poor as a church mouse. What other could I do than rid myself of them?—they are all boys."

The Countess saw that they were lovely and vigorous babes, and she made the tailor take them back to his wife, and charged herself with the cost of their bringing up and education. When they were sufficiently old she had them all sent to Buckfast Abbey, to be reared for the priesthood, and in due time they were ordained and became —that is, four of them—rectors of Tiverton (for Tiverton had four together), and the three others their curates. As they were all of a birth, they loved each other, and never disagreed; and that was—so it is averred—the only instance within a historic period that the rectors of the four portions

of Tiverton have agreed, and have got on smoothly
with each other and with their curates. As the seven
hung together in life, in death they were not parted.
All died in one day, and were buried on the spot
where the Countess of Devon saved their lives,
and there above their heads seven crosses were
reared, but not one of these remains to the present
day.

Formerly there were in Tiverton parish eighteen
chapels, of which the only remains are found in a
cottage at Mere, and a restored chapel at Cove.
Tidcombe Rectory was built by a former rector,
named Newte, on the graveyard of one of these
chapels, and it is pretended that none of the eldest
sons of the Newte family have ever since come of
age, as a punishment for this act of profanation.

Tiverton Church, dedicated to S. Peter, represents
three periods of architecture. In the north aisle is
a Norman doorway, with zigzag moulding. The
tower, a hundred feet high, is the most beautiful
feature — Perpendicular. The nave, chancel, and
north aisle are of early Perpendicular work ; the
south aisle, with its Greenway chapel, dates from
early in the sixteenth century. It was built by John
Greenway, a rich merchant of Tiverton, and running
round it, represented in relief, are twenty scenes from
the life of our Lord, beginning with the Flight into
Egypt, and ending with the Ascension. The roof of
the south porch is also Greenway's work, and is very
fine. He and his wife Joan are represented over the
door kneeling in adoration. He died in 1529, but the
chapel was built in 1517. The exterior is covered

with lavish enrichments—representations of ships, wool-packs, men, and horses. Formerly this chapel was separated from the south aisle by a richly-carved, gilt and coloured screen of stone, containing paintings in panels. This was wantonly destroyed in 1830, but the fragments were happily rescued by the Earl of Devon and removed to Powderham. At the "restoration" in 1854 the rood-screen was also removed, but was secured by the Rev. W. Rayer, rector of Tidcombe Portion, who had just purchased the whole of the Holcombe estate from the Blewett family, and his son had it restored and erected in Holcombe Rogus Church.

The screen was in a very worm-eaten condition, and its restoration was a very expensive matter.

Blundell's Grammar School was founded in 1604, and was for many years the leading school of Devonshire. Under Dr. Richards it contained the largest number of pupils, 200, ever within the walls, until the new buildings were erected on a suitable spot to the east of Tiverton, where there are now 250 boys.

Dr. Richards was a good teacher, but a very severe disciplinarian. Perhaps the most famous of his pupils, both as a clergyman and sportsman, was the late John Russell, "Parson Jack" as he was called. He was a great favourite as a school-boy, and always showed a considerable amount of shrewdness. With another boy, named Bovey, he kept a scratch pack of hounds. Having received a hint that this had reached the ears of Dr. Richards, he collected his share of the pack, and sent them off to his father. The next day he was summoned to the master's desk.

"Russell," said the Doctor, "I hear that you have some hounds. Is it true?"

"No, sir," answered Russell; "I have not a dog in the neighbourhood."

"You never told me a lie, so I believe you. Bovey, come here. You have some hounds, I understand?"

"Well, sir, a few—but they are little ones."

"Oh! you have, have you? Then I shall expel you."

And expelled he was, Russell coming off scatheless. I tell the following tale because it was told in Blundell's School of Russell, during his lifetime, as one of his pranks, but I mistrust it. I believe the story to be as old as the twelfth century; and if I remember aright, it occurs in one of the French Fabliaux of that period.

Dr. Richards had some very fine grapes growing against his garden wall, under the boys' bedroom windows. "Jack was as good as his master," and the young scamp was wont to be let down in a clothes-basket by night, by his mates, to the region of the grapes, and to return with a supply when hauled up.

The Doctor noticed how rapidly his grapes disappeared, and learning from his man John the cause, took his place under the vine along with his gardener, who was ordered to lay hold of the boy in the basket and muffle his mouth, lest he should cry out. This he did when Russell descended; and Dr. Richards took his place in the clothes-basket. The boys hauled away, wondering at the accession of weight, but when they saw the Doctor's head level with the window, panic-stricken they let go their hold of the rope, and away went Doctor and basket to the bottom.

No bones were broken, and nothing came of it, the Doctor being rather ashamed of the part he had played in the matter.

It was said of Russell, as Napoleon said of Ashton Smith, that he was "le premier chasseur d'Angleterre." His love for sport made him always a poor man. On one occasion he invited a young curate to breakfast with him, and preach for him. After breakfast two likely-looking hunters, perhaps a little screwy, were brought round and steadily mounted.

"No time for going round by the road," said Parson Jack ; "we will ride to my church across country, and so save a couple of miles."

Off they rode. The curate presently remarked, "How bare of trees your estate is," as they crossed lands belonging to Russell. "Ah !" responded the sportsman "the hounds eat 'em." Coming to a stiff gate, Russell, with his hand in his pocket, cleared it like a bird, but looking round, he saw the curate on the other side crawling over the gate, and crying out in piteous tones, "It won't open."

"Not it," was the reply, "and if you can't jump a gate like that, I'm sure you can't preach a sermon. Good-bye."

But he was not only a mighty hunter, he was also an excellent parish priest and a fine preacher, though not always depending on his own sermons. He was ordered to preach at one of Bishop Phillpotts' visitations. His sermon was good, and at the consequent dinner the Bishop complimented him in almost exaggerated terms for "his splendid sermon." Russell knew that the Bishop when most oily was most dangerous, and suspected that he had recognised the sermon, so, as always, ready, he said in returning thanks, "As to the sermon, my lord, I quite agree with you. I have ever considered it as one of Barrow's best." Needless to say, the Bishop collapsed.

I can cap that with another anecdote.

The late Dr. Cornish, of Ottery S. Mary, was pompous and patronising. A curate under him, recently ordained, preached his first sermon. In the vestry the vicar, swelling out, said, "For a beginner it was not wholly bad." "Ah, Doctor, I must not take any credit to myself. It is one of Bishop Andrews' finest discourses." Needless to say that Doctor Cornish's stomach went in.

There have not been many conspicuous lights from Blundell's. Perhaps the most famous of them is the present Archbishop of Canterbury.

The school has passed through many vicissitudes. By a Chancery decision in 1846 all boarders were swept away and the school reduced to seventeen boys. £10,000 were put into the lawyers' pockets in defending the suit, whereby the school was reduced well-nigh to bankruptcy. By another decision of the courts and at the cost of another £10,000, boarders were restored, and new buildings were erected. The old school has been altered into private dwellings.

Near Tiverton is Washfield, where there is a very

fine Jacobean screen with the arms of James I. upon it, and in the north aisle those of Charles as Prince of Wales. It deserves a study. In this church the old parish orchestra still performs on Sunday, or did so till recently. There is here a curious church-house with an oriel window.

Outside the churchyard was buried a squire of the parish, so wicked that he was denied a place in consecrated ground. Three times were Acts of Parliament passed to enable either sale of property or the management to be taken from successive squires as one after another was mad. Worth House has now passed away from the family of that name, which has died out in the male line.

In 1810 much public interest was excited by a report of spiritual manifestations at Sampford Peverell, five miles from Tiverton, and the Rev. C. Colton published an account of them. They consisted of the usual rappings, dealing of heavy blows, and the throwing about the room of heavy articles. That these were produced by some cunning servant-maid cannot be doubted. Mr. Colton, who vouched for the truth of the phenomena, did not bear a good character; he ended his days by suicide, after having been "unfrocked," and his last years spent in gambling-houses.

That these tricks were at one time not unfrequently resorted to is probable. The Germans give them as the work of a Poltergeist. In my own neighbourhood, in or about 1852, a precisely similar exhibition took place. Stones, cups, pans flew about a room, and strange knockings were heard. Many people went to witness them, and came away convinced that they were the work of spirits; especially was it so with one yeoman, whose hat was knocked off his head by the spirit. My father investigated the matter, and came to the conclusion that the whole was contrived by a girl of low intelligence but of much cunning. It is now, with the advance of education, persons of a superior grade who are the dupes of spirit-mediums. Education will not give brains, but it will varnish emptiness.

At Tiverton lived, till a few years ago, "Old Snow," a rather famous "white witch," to whom many persons had recourse, among others a farmer who was a churchwarden and a well-to-do man. I knew him well, and in 1889 believed him to be a doomed man, with a hacking cough, worn to a shred, and bent by weakness. Having consulted all the prominent doctors in the south of the county, he went in desperation to "Old Snow." What the white witch did to him I cannot say, but I can testify he was a changed man from that day, and is at present a robust, hale man, looking good for another twenty or thirty years.

In an article I wrote on "White Witches" for the *Daily Graphic* I mentioned this case. Some days after I met the farmer. "Why," said he, "you have put me in the papers." "So I have," I answered, "but what I told was literally true." "True—aye," he said, "every bit. Old Snow cured me when the faculty gave me up. *How* he did it, neither you nor I know."

The white witch is an institution that has not been

killed by board schools in the West, nor, as far as can be judged from the favour in which he is still regarded, is he likely to die. A witch is generally supposed to be the feminine of wizard, but in the West of England " witch " is of common gender, and those in highest repute are men. Their trade consists in prescribing for the sick, in informing those who have been " overlooked " whose evil eye has influenced them for ill, where lost articles are to be found, and how spells cast on their cattle are to be broken.

A white witch is one who repudiates utterly having any traffic with the Evil One. His or her knowledge is derived from other sources—what, not specified. I had for many years as a tenant in one of my cottages a woman who was much consulted as a white witch. She is now dead, and her decease is a matter of outspoken regret.

The village inn frequently had guests staying there to undergo a course of "blessing" from this woman. She was an ill-favoured person, with a wall-eye, and one eye higher in her head than the other. She was bent, heavy-featured, and stoutly built. A worthy woman, scrupulously neat in her person, and who kept her cottage in beautiful order. She certainly believed in her own powers, and as certainly performed very remarkable cures, which it was not possible to deny, though they might be explained. For instance, in the hayfield in a parish four miles distant as the crow flies, eight by road, a young man cut his leg with the scythe, and the blood spurted out. At once the farmer dipped the man's handkerchief in the blood, mounted one of his men on a horse, and sent him galloping to the white witch, who took the kerchief, blessed it, and simultaneously four miles off as the crow flies, the blood was stanched. The son of the largest farmer in the place, a man who is worth his thousands, was suffering from glandular ulcerations in the neck. The village doctor attended him and did him no good. He consulted the principal medical man in the nearest market town, also to no advantage. Time passed and he was no better; he gave up consulting doctors, who sent him in bills and left him rather worse than when they began on him. At last he went to the white witch. Whether she "struck" his glands or prescribed some herbs I cannot say, but what I do know is that within a month the young man was perfectly well.

The woman, who was my tenant, was no conscious impostor, of that I am convinced. What her secret was she would not communicate, but most earnestly did she deprecate any communication with evil spirits. Not only did the village innkeeper derive a certain revenue from patients lodging in his house to be under treatment by her, but the postmen of the neighbourhood also earned their crumbs by carrying kerchiefs blessed by her to sufferers within their districts. It was no uncommon sight to see a walking postman careering along with arms extended holding a kerchief in each hand, fluttering as he walked. It is held that the blessing is drawn out of the material if it be folded, put in a pocket, and handled other than most gingerly between finger and thumb.

When among the educated, the cultivated classes, we find belief in faith-healing, and so-called "Christian Science," is it to be wondered at that in classes lower down in the scale there should be credulous persons who not only believe in white witches, but believe in their own powers as white witches?

It is the same as in the Lourdes miracles; the imagination acts on the nervous system, and that stimulates the body to throw off disease. That is the true secret.

I cannot doubt but that in many cases herbs are employed that have been sadly neglected ever since our doctors have gone in for mineral medicines. The latter act violently, but the herbs slowly, and, in many instances, more surely.

However, in the majority of cases the white witches are mere impostors, and may do much harm, as in that I will now record, which took place three years ago only. I shall, for obvious reasons, not give the true names, nor indicate the locality.

A cattle dealer in 1896 had a daughter, who two years previously had been a victim to influenza. This had affected her head and produced profound melancholy. As doctors proved unavailing, the man went to Exeter and consulted a white witch there. According to his statement the witch showed him the face of a neighbour, Mrs. Thomas, in a glass of water, and told him that his daughter was "overlooked" by the person he saw. The white witch further informed him that the individual who had "ill wished" his daughter passed his door every day, but had hitherto never entered it, but that on the following Saturday she would do so. The cattle dealer returned home, and, sure enough, next ensuing Saturday Mrs. Thomas entered his house and asked if he would take of her a little meat she had to spare, as she had been killing a pig.

Next night the Thomases' house was set on fire. It was thatched, and six persons slept under the thatch. By the merest chance Mr. Thomas woke in the night, and hearing a strange sound went outside his house to see what was the matter, and found his roof in flames. He had barely time to rouse and bring forth his wife and family before the roof fell in.

It was ascertained by the police that the thatch had been deliberately fired. The incendiary had struck two matches, which had failed, and in drawing the matches from his pocket had dropped two halfpenny stamps. He had climbed on to a hedge to effect his object, and the third match had ignited the thatch. But it was never ascertained *who* had done the deed.

A few years ago I wrote the little account of "Devonshire White Witches" for the *Daily Graphic* already referred to. This brought down on me a copious shower of letters from all parts of England, entreating me to furnish the addresses of some of our white witches, as the correspondents had found it profitless and expensive to apply to medical practitioners, and they were anxious to try the cures of these conscious or unconscious impostors.

Tiverton parish was ecclesiastically divided into

four quarters, each under an independent rector, and all co-equally regnant in the parish church. The arrangement was not happy—and led to constant ruffles and conflict of opinion. The condition was so unsatisfactory that the late Bishop of Exeter and present Archbishop carried an Act to alter it.

Tiverton is a seat of machine-lace manufacture, introduced by Mr. John Heathcoat in 1816.

Lace is said to have been brought into France by Mary de Medici from Venice; and the making of this beautiful work of art rapidly spread and took root in the Low Countries. Refugees from Flanders brought it into England, when they settled at Cranfield, in Bedfordshire. The lace made was Brussels point; the network was formed by bone bobbins on a pillow, which held the threads, and the sprigs were worked with a needle.

The introduction of machinery told heavily on the commoner and coarser lace-making.

In the reign of George II., or about a hundred and fifty years after the introduction of the first knitting machines, many additions and improvements were made in them, and the so-called "tickler," guided by mere accident, was now applied for the first time to the manufacture of lace. This attempt was succeeded by a "point-net" machine, an invention that was nearly, but not entirely, successful.

In 1768 a watchmaker, named Hammond, applied the stocking-frame to the manufacture of lace, but it worked slowly and without accuracy. Attempts were made in various parts of the kingdom to make fishing-nets by machinery, and a workman discovered, by observing a child at play, the secret of the "bobbin and carriage," which was first applied to the manufacture of fishing-nets. It was not, however, till 1809 that Mr. Heathcoat patented his machine, which combined the discoveries of the past with immense improvements of his own.

The point-net frame had been invented in the early years of the century. Attempts were made to produce a twist mesh. Heathcoat divided the warp threads and put them on a beam, apart from the transverse threads, which latter he wound upon thin bobbins, and arranged them so that they could pass around and amongst the former.

This machine was, however, complex, having twenty-four motions to the series for twisting the mesh, and four for the pins to secure the twist when unravelling, but after the expiration of the patent it was simplified so as to require only six, with two motions to prevent the unravelment.

The introduction of mechanism threatening the manufacture at home provoked grave riots in the counties of Nottingham, Derby, and Leicester, headed by a weaver named Ludd, who gave his name to the riots. The man himself was really insane. Troops of men went about breaking machines and intimidating workers in the factories. William Horsfall, a Marsden manufacturer, they murdered. This was in 1813. Although peremptory punishment fell on the rioters, still insecurity to life and property continued for some years, and induced Mr. Heathcoat to transfer his frames to and start as a manufacturer in Tiverton in 1816, and abandon his factory at Loughborough. He brought with him as a foreman Mr. Asher, who had been shot at and wounded in the back of his head by the rioters. This transfer was so much loss to Loughborough and gain to Tiverton, and that not temporary, but lasting, for what was begun in 1816 is continued to this day in full vigour, finding employment for 1400 hands and 130 children. John Heathcoat's only child and daughter married a solicitor named Amory, and their son was made a baronet by Mr. Gladstone in 1874, a well-deserved honour, as, but for the introduction of the lace manufacture, Tiverton would have sunk to the position of a stagnant county town.

The Exe valley below Tiverton presents pleasant scenery, but nothing fine. An excursion should be made to Cullompton in the Culm (Welsh *cûll*, Gael. *caol*, narrow, slender) valley to see the interesting church with its fine restored screen in all the splendour of colour. Cullompton had the wit to preserve and cherish what Tiverton cast away. Uffculme has also a screen; near this is Bradfield House, a rare treasury of old oak carving. Culmstock has a stone screen, which has stupidly been converted into a reredos.

Holcombe Rogus is a very fine specimen of an Elizabethan house and hall. In the church is some beautiful cinque-cento carved screenwork to the manorial pew.

At Bickleigh was born Bampfylde Moore Carew in 1693. His father was the rector, and the son was educated at Blundell's School at Tiverton, where he showed considerable ability. He and other boys kept a pack of hounds, and as these, with Carew and others behind them, once gave chase to a deer strayed from Exmoor over standing corn, so much damage was done that the farmers complained.

Bampfylde Moore Carew was too great a coward to wait and take his whipping. He ran away from school, and sheltered among some gipsies. He contracted such a love for their vagrant life, and such satisfaction in getting their applause for thefts that manifested low cunning, that nothing would induce him to abandon their mode of life and return to civilisation. At one time he postured as a non-juring parson who had been forced to leave his rectory, and preyed on the sympathy of the Jacobite gentry. Then learning from a newspaper that a cargo of Quakers bound for Philadelphia had been wrecked on the Irish coast, he disguised himself as a Friend, and traded on the charity of the Quakers by representing himself as one of those who had been rescued from the sea.

He was elected King of the Beggars on the death of Clause Patch, who had reigned previously over the mendicants. At last he was arrested, tried at the quarter sessions at Exeter, and transported to Maryland, where he was sold to a planter, and as he tried to escape an iron collar was riveted about his neck. He again escaped; this time succeeded in getting among the Indians, who relieved him of his collar. He stole a canoe from his benefactors, and got on board a vessel sailing for England. What became of him is not known, but he is thought to have died in obscurity in 1770, aged 77, but where buried is unknown. The fellow was a worthless rogue, without a redeeming quality in him.

The Bampton Fair is an institution that should not be passed by unsought by the visitor to North Devon, if he be a lover of horseflesh or a student of mankind. He will see there choice specimens alike of Exmoor ponies and of North Devon farmers, and will catch many a waft of the broadest dialect of the borders of Somerset and Devon.

A writer in *S. Paul's Magazine*, December 12th, 1896, says :—

"As a dead-alive, archæologically interesting place, the Devon Bampton on the Exe is a more or less desirable centre for the angler and the hunting man, but ordinarily, in the eyes of the unsporting, sane person, it is a useful hole to strive to avoid.

"Bampton Fair, however, is a celebration once to be seen by every woman or man who has eyes, ears, and nose for novelty. Such lowing of oxen, bleating of sheep, and assemblage of agrestics and congregation of ponies! The side shows are naught. Who cares for gingerbread, pasties, cockles, fairings, tipsy yokels, trolloping hussies, and other attributes of Bœotia let loose? The play's the thing—that is, the pony exhibition. Nijni Novgorod is all very well—quite unique in its way; Rugby, Barnet, and Brampton Brian fairs are things apart. But Bampton Fair is absolutely *sui generis*. Exmoor ponies throng the streets, flood the pavements, overflow the houses, pervade the place. Wild as hawks, active and lissom as goats, cajoled from the moors and tactfully manœuvred when penned, these indigenous quadrupeds will leap or escalade lofty barriers in a standing jump, or a cat-like scramble, whilst the very 'suckers' have to be cajoled with all the Dædalian adroitness with which the Irish pig has to be induced to go whither it would not."

The great sale of ponies formerly took place at Simonsbath, but it was moved to Bampton in 1850, and is held on the last Thursday in October.

"Seventy years ago," said a bailiff, "there were only five men and a woman and a little girl on Exmoor, and that little girl was my mother. She drew beer at Simonsbath public-house. There were a rough lot of customers then, I promise you."

The moor was the property of the Crown, and it was leased in part to Sir Thomas Dyke Acland since 1818, and was used for the rearing of ponies and the summering of sheep.

There was a good deal of horse stealing in the early days of this century. In spite of the severe laws on this sort of theft, and of the Acland brand of the anchor, a good many ponies were spirited away by the shepherds and disposed of in Wiltshire. The Acland breed is pure, and can only be obtained from the Baronet. All the rest are the result of crossing. Sir Thomas moved his stock away from Exmoor to the Winsford Hills, and left only a dozen mare ponies to preserve the line, when the father of the late Sir Frederick Knight rented 10,000 acres of the moor and added 6000 subsequently.

"An after-dinner conversation led Mr. Knight to consider the great pony question in all its bearings. The party met at Sir Joseph Banks's, the eminent naturalist. They discussed the merits of the Dongola horse, which had been

described as an Arab of sixteen hands and peculiar to the
regions round Nubia. Sir Joseph proposed to the party to
get some of the breed, and accordingly Lords Headly,
Morton, and Dundas, and Mr. Knight then and there gave
him a joint £1000 cheque as a deposit for the expenses.
The English consul in Egypt was applied to, and in due
course the horses and mares which he sent bore out Bruce's
description to the letter. In addition to their height, they
were rather Roman-nosed, with a very fine texture of skin,
well chiselled under the jowl, and as clean-winded as all
their race. About ten or twelve arrived, and Mr. Knight
was so pleased with them that he bought Lord Headly's
share. His two sires and three mares were then brought to
Simonsbath, where he had established a stud of seven or
eight thoroughbred mares and thirty half-breeds of the
coaching Cleveland sort.

"The first cross knocked out the Roman nose as completely as the Leicester destroys the Exmoor horn, but the
buffy stood true to its colour, and thus the type was never
quite lost. The half Dongolas did wonderfully well with
the West Somerset, which often came to Exmoor to draw
for a fox, and they managed to get down the difficult hills
so well, and crossed the brooks so close up with the
hounds, that the vocation of the white-clad guides on
chase days gradually fell into disuse."*

The average height is 12½ hands, and bays and
buffy bays with mealy noses prevail; in fact, are
in a majority of at least three to one.

The older ponies live all through the winter on the
hills, and seek out sheltered spots for themselves
during the continuance of wind and rain. These
favourite nooks are well known to the herdsmen,

* Condensed from "The Exmoor Ponies," by "DRUID," in *The
Sporting Magazine*, October, 1860.

who build up stacks of hay and straw, which are doled out to them in times of snow. "Still, like honest, hard - working labourers, the ponies never assemble at the wicket till they have exhausted every means of self-support by scratching with their fore-feet in the snow for the remnants of the summer tufts, and drag wearily behind them an ever lengthening chain of snowballs."

A writer in *All The Year Round* for May, 1866, says :—

"Throughout North Devon and Somersetshire and wherever ponies are famed, the Exmoor breed have a great reputation, not without reason, for they are not only hardy and sure-footed, but from their earliest years the foals follow their dams at a gallop down the *crees* of loose stones on the steep moorland sides; they are extraordinarily active and courageous. The writer once saw an Exmoor, only 44 inches high, jump out of a pound 5 feet 6 inches in height, just touching the top bar with his hind feet."

Well, let a visitor go to Bampton Fair, and see the pranks of these wild, beautiful creatures, and note as well the skill with which they are managed by the men experienced in dealing with them. Such a sight will remain in his memory, and when he gets back to town he will have something to talk about at dinner, and if he has a bit of descriptive power in him he will hold the ears of those who are near him at table.

NOTE.—HARDING (Lt.-Col.), *The History of Tiverton.* Tiverton, 1845.

CHAPTER VIII.

BARNSTAPLE

The *stapol* of Branock's district—The Irish settlers—Branock badly received in South Wales—Situation of Barnstaple—Huguenot refugees—Samuel Pepys's wife—Jacques Fontaine—French names altered—Barnstaple the starting-point for Ilfracombe and Lynton—The coast road—Exmoor—Combe Martin—The Valley of Rocks —The Wichehalses of Lee—Brendon—S. Brendan's voyages—Churches near Barnstaple.

THIS town was the *stapol*, port or mart, of the district of Barum, Braun, or Brannock, an Irish saint, confessor, and son-in-law to Brychan, King of Brecknock, who settled at Braunton, formerly Llan-Brynach, then Brannock-stow. The northern cheek of Barnstaple Bay is formed by a peninsula, the centre of which is this same Braunton, where Branock had his monastic establishment. As intimately associated with this district, a few words on him may be allowed.

In the fifth century the whole of North Devon and North-east Cornwall was invaded and occupied by Irish and half-Irish hordes. Irish accounts relate that these invasions began about 378, and continued till the reign of Dathi, 428.

The Irish had made themselves masters of Breck-nock, where their prince, Aulac or Amalghaid, claimed the throne in virtue of his wife Marchell, daughter and heiress of the native Welsh king. Brychan, the son, succeeded him ; he had as tutor to his children an Irishman named Brynach or Branock, who was his confessor, and to whom he gave one of his daughters in marriage. Branock did not have a pleasant time of it in South Wales, and he migrated to North Devon, where, by some means, he obtained a grant of a considerable tract of country.

His legend was extant at the time of the Reformation, and Leland, Henry VIII.'s antiquary, who travelled in Devon and Cornwall, saw it, and says it was full of fables about Branock's cow, his staff, his well, and his serving-man, Abell.

Unhappily, this has been lost, and all we know concerning him is from a Latin life, composed in Wales, that passes hurriedly over his life elsewhere and relates mainly what took place when he returned to South Wales. There he was very ill received, owing to the hatred entertained towards the Irish. A woman— the author of the life does not say as much, but we may suspect it, his wife—instigated a man to assassinate him. Brynach was wounded, but not killed, and he had to shift his quarters. He probably returned to Devon and died there.

Braunton Church contains some fine oak carving, and deserves a visit.

Barnstaple lies stretched along the bank of the Taw, and from the river has a prepossessing appearance. There are, however, few objects of interest in the town. The church of S. Peter, with a lead spire that leans, is interesting internally from the many monuments it contains of wealthy Barnstaple merchants.

A tall, good tower to Holy Trinity helps greatly to give dignity to an otherwise unattractive town, made pre-eminently so by the unsightliness of the ranges of suburban residences that line the roads out of it.

But Barnstaple is important as having given shelter to a number of refugees at the revocation of the Edict of Nantes, and their descendants still live in the town, though under names that have become much altered. Among these refugees was the family of St. Michel, and Samuel Pepys married one of the daughters. The St. Michels were of good family, of Anjou, but a son having taken up with Huguenot religious notions, was disinherited, and came to England. There he married the daughter of Sir Francis Kingsmill, and had a son and daughter. He returned to France, but was in very indigent circumstances, and during an absence from home his children were removed to an Ursuline convent. St. Michel, however, recovered them and fled with them and his wife to England, and arrived at Barnstaple, but settled near Bideford. How Samuel Pepys met Elizabeth St. Michel we do not know. He was married to her before the justice of peace on December 1st, 1655, but as he always observed October 10th as his wedding day it is probable that he, like many another, had been secretly married by a priest of the Church of England, and merely conformed to the law afterwards on December 1st. She was fifteen only when Pepys married her, and the young couple found an asylum in the family of Pepys's cousin, Sir Edward Montagu, afterwards Earl of Sandwich. She was a pretty, but a silly woman, and much inclined to jealousy, but indeed Sam gave her good cause for that.

"1668–9, Jan. 12. This evening I observed my wife mighty dull, and I myself was not mighty fond, because of some hard words she did give me at noon, out of a jealousy at my being abroad this morning, which, God knows, it was upon the business of the Office unexpectedly; but I to bed, not thinking but she would come after me. But waking by and by, out of a slumber, which I usually fall into presently after my coming into the bed, I found she did not prepare to come to bed, but got fresh candles, and more wood for her fire; it being mighty cold, too. At this being troubled, I after awhile prayed her to come to bed; so, after an hour or two, she silent, and I now and then praying her to come to bed, she fell out into a fury, that I was a rogue, and false to her. I did, as I might truly, deny it, and mighty troubled, but all would not serve. At last, about one o'clock, she came to my side of the bed, and drew the curtains open, and with the tongs red hot at the ends, made as if she did design to pinch me with them, at which, in dismay, I rose up, and with a few words she laid them down; and did by little and little, very sillily, let all discourse fall; and about two, but with much seeming difficulty, came to bed, and there lay well all night, and lay in bed talking together, with much pleasure, it being, I knew, nothing but her doubt at my going out yesterday, without telling her of my going, which did vex her, poor wretch! last night, and I cannot blame her jealousy, though it do vex me to the heart."

One of the Huguenot refugees was a pastor, Jacques Fontaine, who came over with Mlle. de Boursaquotte, to whom he was affianced.

They were taken in and hospitably received. He kept a diary, which has been published. At first he joined the communion of the Church, but later on, when the Corporation placed S. Anne's Chapel at the disposal of the French refugees, he became their minister. The diary narrates his difficulties.

"God had not conducted us to a haven there [at Barnstaple] to perish with hunger. The good people of Barnstaple were full of compassion, they took us into their houses, and treated us with the greatest kindness; thus God raised up for us fathers and mothers in a strange land. I was taken into the house of a most kind and charitable gentleman—a Mr. Downe. He was a bachelor, of some forty years of age, and had an unmarried sister living with him; they were kindness itself, and I was completely domesticated with them. My intended wife had been received into the house of a Mr. and Mrs. Fraine."

Unfortunately, Miss Downe, a short, thin, sallow old maid, marked with small-pox, fell in love with the French refugee, and made advances to him which were unmistakable. She plainly told him that she thought that he and the Boursaquotte were a pair of fools to think of being married, when they had not a penny between them to bless themselves with; and finally, as M. Fontaine would take no hints, she fairly threw herself at his head with an offer of her person and fortune. The minister retired in dismay, and sought his host.

"What is to be done?" said he. "Your sister has shown me the honour of offering herself to me, but—but I am engaged to Mlle. de Boursaquotte."

"Make yourself easy on that score," said Mr.

Downe. "I am enamoured of that lady, and I will relieve you of her."

The result was a hasty marriage between M. Fontaine and Mlle. Boursaquotte; they were united by the vicar, in the parish church, on February 8th, 1686, and in the register are entered as "James Fountain and Elizabeth Buzzacott." This latter name is still common in the town.

Other Huguenot names continue equally altered. L'Oiseau has been translated into Bird, and Roches into Roach. I came across elsewhere in the parish registers another Huguenot family, Blanchepied, which has degenerated into Blampy.

Barnstaple is the starting-point for the grand and almost unsurpassed coast line from Ilfracombe to Porlock. Other coasts may have bolder cliffs, but none such a combination of boldness and luxuriance of vegetation. It has, moreover, a great advantage— that a good road runs along it from Ilfracombe to Combe Martin. But from this point the coast is deserted, and the road climbs a thousand feet to the Trentishoe Down, then dives into the Heddon valley to the sweet and peaceful "Hunter's Inn," climbs again over moor, and makes for Lynton. The road, however, should be deserted, the Heddon stream followed to the mouth, when a good path will be found skirting the cliffs to Wooda Bay, a lovely spot; and thence through the grounds of Lee Abbey to the Valley of Rocks, and Lynton.

Lynton, and the same may be said of Wooda Bay, has the advantage which Ilfracombe has not, of having had an architect to design mansions and hotels for it that are no disfigurement to the place, and are not a blot on the scenery.

From Lynton the road follows the coast to Countisbury, after which it deserts it.

For Exmoor Mr. Blackmore's *Lorna Doone* is a good preparation, but the visitor who expects to find the Doone valley and the slide of the waters at all equal to the description given in that book must expect disappointment.

To return on our traces. Combe Martin is one long street of not interesting or ancient houses, save "The Pack of Cards," but it has a fine church, beautifully situated, with a good tower and a well preserved screen. Saints are painted on the panels. There are fine canopied niches for SS. Peter and Paul. The vaulting of the screen was removed in 1727. The parvise over the porch is good, and there are eight old carved bench-ends.

There is a curious double lock to the vestry; a small key has to be turned before the lock can be made to act under the large key. An Early English triplet is in the south aisle. Behind the brass in the wall of William Hancock, Gent., 1587, is his skull in a recess.

Watermouth Castle, that was passed on the way to Combe Martin, is modern and unsuccessful. A gateway into the gardens is made up of carved armorial coats removed from Berrynarbor, and dating from 1525. The Berrynarbor Church tower is finer than that of Combe Martin. There is a good deal to interest in the church. In the Valley of Rocks are hut circles, but so mutilated and over-

grown with fern as not to be easily distinguishable.
Lynton Church has been well enlarged and is very
pleasing. It is fabled that a band of marauding
Danes succeeded in landing at Lynmouth, ascended
the cliffs, and were surrounded and massacred in the
Valley of Rocks, which bears the name of "The
Danes" or "Danes' Combe." But this is one of
those many legends invented to explain a name;
the original signification has been lost. It was
called originally *Dinas*, the castle or camp. Lee
Abbey never was an abbey. It was the seat of the
De Wichehalse family, refugees, it is pretended, from
the Low Countries in or about 1570. But, as a
matter of fact, the Wichehalse family first turns up
at Chudleigh nearly half a century before their
reputed flight from Flanders. They were cloth merchants apparently, and one of the family, Nicholas
Wychalse, the third son of Nicholas of Chudleigh,
having married a wife from Pilton, settled at Barnstaple and died there in 1570. As merchants in the
wool trade the Barnstaple branch did well, and married
into some of the best county families. All the rigma-
role about their being *De* Wichehalse, and being of
noble Flemish ancestry, and of their having fled from
Alva's persecution, may be dismissed as pure fable.

The story goes that in the reign of Charles II.
Sir Edward de Wichehalse was the head of the house
and lived in splendour at Lee Abbey. He had an
only child, a daughter, who was wooed and proved
over-fond towards a nobleman high in the favour
of James II. The lover proved faithless, and the
deserted damsel threw herself from the cliffs at

Duty Point. The father in vain sought redress by petitioning the king, and when the Duke of Monmouth landed at Lyme, De Wichehalse raised levies and hasted to his support. After the battle of Sedgemoor Sir Edward returned to Lee, but emissaries of the king were sent to apprehend him, and when De Wichehalse learned that they were approaching, he and his family embarked in Lee Bay on board a small smack, intending to fly to Dutch William and the land whence the ancestral noble had come. The night, however, proved stormy, and the boat was lost with all on board.

Lee "Abbey" came into the possession of the "De" Wichalse family in 1620; there is a monument in Lynton Church to Hugh Wichalse, gent., in 1653. From the Wichalses it passed by *sale* to the family of Short. I can find no Sir Edward in the pedigree, as given by Colonel Vivian, so it may be hoped that the story is altogether baseless, as the fable of the noble origin of the wool merchant family.

At Lynton is the fine mansion of Sir George Newnes, the publisher of *Tit-Bits* and many kindred papers, who was created a baronet by Mr. Gladstone for political services.

Exmoor in some respects is finer than Dartmoor, in others less fine. It is finer in that it soars up out of the sea to its full height, whereas the land rises some eight hundred feet to the roots of Dartmoor. But Exmoor is rounded and lumpy, and has no tors.

It served as the great barrier to the Dumnonii, broken only by the portal at Dulverton. The Black Down is its continuation. Indeed the county has

a natural frontier. The height of Exmoor never
attains the altitude of Dartmoor, and is not loftier
than the Bodmin moors.

The long stretches of down without rocks and
without bad bogs render Exmoor a choice place
for stag-hunting.

The valleys to the south of Exmoor that are
watered by the Yeo, the Bray, the Mole, contain
scenery that is pleasing, but never rises to boldness.

Exmoor is interesting as harbouring a strong body
of the earlier dusky population that occupied the
country before the invasion of the Celts. But the
river names savour of the Irish settlers rather than
of the Britons. Such are the Bray (Ir. *brag*, running
water: there is a Bray in Wicklow); the Mole
(Ir. *malda*, gentle, slow); Barle (Ir. *fuarlach*, *barlach*,
chilly).

But the finest Exmoor scenery is on the Somersetshire side, where the hills rise boldly above the sea,
and where rich vegetation clothes the shores of the
Bristol Channel. From Exmoor, moreover, a grand
view is obtained of the Welsh mountains across the
Severn sea. One can quite understand S. Branock
escaping from a population that looked on him with
an evil eye, to the blue hills that rose above the sea
not so far to the south, and easily reached in a
summer sail—and where, moreover, the land was
occupied by his countrymen — the Irish, as conquerors.

The road to Countisbury passes remarkable earthworks, the Oldburrough, of uncertain, but probably
prehistoric, date.

On the immediate outskirts of Exmoor is Brendon. The church itself is of no particular interest, beyond its dedication to S. Brendan, the Irish navigator, who spent seven years exploring the western seas for the Isles of the Blessed, and who may perhaps have reached America in the sixth century. The narrative of his voyage is, however, full of fable; but the fact of his having made two exploring expeditions is fairly well authenticated. The cause of his undertaking the voyage was this. One day he and a couple of pupils, brothers, went together in a boat to an islet off the west coast of Ireland. Brendan left the younger lad with the boat, and ascended into the island with the elder. Presently, as the wind rose, the young man said to his master, "I do not think my brother can manage the boat alone, with this wind and the rising tide."

"Be silent," said Brendan. "Do you not suppose I care for the boy as much as you do yourself?"

And they went further. But the young man became more uneasy, and he again remonstrated. Then Brendan lost his temper and swore at him. "Begone—and be drowned to you!"

So the young man returned to the beach and found the boy struggling with the boat. He rushed into the water—and was himself swept away by a wave and perished.

Now when Brendan returned and found what had happened, he was full of self-reproach, and hurried off to S. Itha, his nurse, to ask her what was to be done.

"You will be in trouble," she said. "All his relatives will take this up, and it will occasion a blood feud. Make yourself scarce. Besides, you deserve punishment for your inconsiderate and passionate conduct. Go to sea."

And to sea he went in three wicker-work vessels, each covered with three coats of tanned hides, and each with a leather. sail, and thirty men in each boat.

In the immediate neighbourhood of Barnstaple is Pilton Church, that should be seen for its fine screen and curious hour-glass; Tawstock for its Bourcher tombs; Chittlehampton for its beautiful tower; and Atherington for its screen, a fragment, but that fragment complete in every member, a superb specimen. Hall, on the Taw, is the fine mansion of the Chichester family.

Swymbridge Church should on no account be omitted. It possesses a magnificent screen, and an ancient pulpit with figures in niches. The modern reredos is bad.

The Chichester monuments are curious, notably one of a youthful Chichester, whose portrait is given, and whom the bird of Jove is represented as carrying off to serve as Ganymede in heaven.

Littleham possesses an ancient fresco of S. Swithun, and a rich screen and benches, that have been carefully and judiciously restored.

NOTE.—Books on Barnstaple are:—

CHANTER (J. R.), *Sketches of some Striking Incidents in the History of Barnstaple.* 1865.

CHANTER (J. R.), *Memorials of the Church of S. Peter, Barnstaple.* 1887.

CHANTER (R.), *Sketches of the Literary History of Barnstaple, with the Diary of Philip Wyott. n.d.*

CHAPTER IX.

BIDEFORD

Ugly modern buildings—"Westward Ho!"—Roman roads—The Torridge—The story of King Edmund—The ravages of the sons of Lodbrog—Hingvar and Hubba defeated at Appledore—Brictric the Golden-haired—Bideford Bridge—The herriot—Sir William Coffin —The Newfoundland Fisheries—Sir Richard Grenville—Colonisation of Wokohen—Captain White—The story of the life of Sir Richard Grenville—The *Revenge*—The north coast to Wellcombe— The Hobby Drive—Hartland—S. Nectan—The Promontory of Hercules—Wellcombe—Mutilation of the Church—Wear Gifford.

BARNSTAPLE and Bideford are towns that the jerry-builders have done their utmost to make hideous with white brick villas banded with red. It is a curious fact, but fact it is, that a builder without a grain of taste, if ambitious to make one of his domestic monstrosities attractive, will look into the pattern-book of a maker of terra-cotta, and select the most obtrusive ridge-tiles and, above all, hip-knobs he can find, frizzle the spine of his roof with the former, clap the latter on his gable, and think that the product is stylish. The foliations of the ridge-tiles get broken after a frost, and the roof acquires a mangy look, but not till after the villa has been let as a handsome suburban residence.

When one encounters this sort of thing, repeated

again and again, the heart turns sick, and the visitor is impatient to fly from towns thus vulgarised.

To Bideford he comes full of thoughts of "Westward Ho!" and expects to find an Elizabethan flavour about the place, only to be woefully disappointed. Even the church is new; only the bridge remains, and that has been menaced with destruction.

Bideford has memories, but modern Bideford has made herself æsthetically unworthy of them.

To begin with, the old Roman, or pre-Roman, road from North Cornwall passing through Stratton, that takes its name from the street or road, ran to the ford on the Torridge and passed on to Barnstaple.

At the beginning of the ninth century the estuary of the Taw and Torridge (*Dur*, water, and *Dur-rhyd*, the water ford*) invited the entry into the land of the Northmen.

A memorable incident in one of these incursions is connected with a romantic story that shall be told in full.

Roger of Wendover gives the tale, founding it on old ballads.

"There was, not long ago, in the kingdom of the Danes, a certain man named Lodbrog (Hairy-breeches), who was sprung from the royal race of that nation, and had by his wife two sons, Hingvar and Hubba. One day he took his hawk and went unattended in a little boat to catch small birds and wild-fowl on the seacoast and in the islands. While thus engaged he was surprised by a sudden storm, and carried out to sea, and after having been tossed about

---

* The ford gave its distinctive appellation to the river above it.

for several days and nights, was at last carried in sore distress to the English coast, and landed at Redham, in the province of Norfolk. The people of that country by chance found him with his hawk, and presented him as a sort of 'prodigy to Edmund, king of the East Angles, who, for the sake of his comely person, gave him an honourable reception. Lodbrog abode some time in the court of the monarch, and as the Danish tongue is very like English, he began to relate to the king by what chance he had been driven to the coast of England. The accomplished manners of King Edmund pleased Lodbrog, as well as his military discipline and the courtly manners of his attendants. Emulous of the like attainments, Lodbrog asked permission of the king to remain in his court, and having obtained his request, he attached himself to the king's huntsman, whose name was Bjorn, that he might with him exercise the hunter's art. But such was the skill of Lodbrog, that he was always successful in hunting or hawking, and being deservedly a favourite with the king, Bjorn became jealous of him, and giving way to deadly hatred, one day, when they were hunting together, he attacked him and slew him, and left his body in a thicket. This done, the wicked huntsman called off his dogs with his horn, and returned home. Now Lodbrog had reared a certain greyhound in King Edmund's court, which was very fond of him, and, as is natural, when the huntsman returned with his own dogs, remained watchful by his master's body.

"Next day, as King Edmund sat at table, he missed Lodbrog from the company, and anxiously asked his attendants what had befallen him, on which Bjorn, the huntsman, answered that he had tarried behind in a wood, and he had seen no more of him. But as he was speaking, Lodbrog's dog came into the hall and began to wag his tail and fawn on all, and especially on the king, who, on seeing him, said to his attendants, ' Here comes Lodbrog's dog ; his master is not far behind.' He then began to feed the dog, hoping soon to see his master. But he was disappointed, for when the greyhound had satisfied his appetite, he returned to keep his accustomed watch over his master's body. After three days he was compelled by hunger to return to the king's table, and Edmund, greatly wondering, gave orders to follow the dog when he left the hall, and watch whither he went. The king's servants fulfilled his commands, and followed the dog till it led them to Lodbrog's lifeless body. On being informed of this the king was greatly disturbed, and directed that the body should be committed to a more honourable sepulchre. King Edmund then caused diligent inquisition to be made touching the death of Lodbrog; and Bjorn, the huntsman, was convicted of the crime, and by order of the king, the captains and wise men of his court passed sentence on him. The judges unanimously agreed that the huntsman should be put into the boat in which Lodbrog had come to England, and should be exposed on the sea without sail or oar, that it might be proved whether God would deliver him."

Roger of Wendover goes on to tell how Bjorn was wafted across to Denmark, and there was examined by torture by Hubba and Hingvar, sons of Lodbrog, who recognised their father's boat. Bjorn, under torture, declared that Lodbrog had been put to death by Edmund, king of the East Angles. The Danes accordingly assembled an army and invaded East Anglia to avenge on Edmund the murder of their father.

The Norse story does not agree with this at all. According to the Sagas, Ragnar Lodbrog was seized by Ælla, king of the Northumbrians, and was thrown

into a dungeon full of serpents, in which he sang his
dying song, the famous Krakumal. His sons, they
say, were called Eirekr, Agnarr, Ivar, Bjorn Ironside,
Hvitserkr, and Sigurd Worm-in-the-eye.

Edmund encamped at the royal vill of Haeles-
dune (Hoxne), when Hingvar and Hubba landed
at Berwick-on-Tweed, and ravaged the country
on their march through Northumbria. In 870
Hingvar entered East Anglia, and was attacked
by Edmund whilst his force was divided from that
of Hubba. Both sides suffered severely. Hubba
joined Hingvar at Thetford, and the united army
fought Edmund again. His force was far out-
numbered. He was routed, and he and Humbert,
bishop of Elmham, were taken in a church; Humbert
was despatched with the sword. Edmund was tied
to a tree, and the Danes shot at him with their
arrows, till they were tired of the sport, when he was
decapitated, and his head flung into a thicket of the
forest of Hoxne.

So far we have had nothing about Bideford. But
now we come to this parish.

Hingvar and Hubba (Agnarr and Ivar of the Norse
version) were provided by their sisters with an ensign
before starting, on which, with their needles, they
had wrought the figure of a raven, in symbol of the
carnage that their brothers were to cause in revenge
for the death of their father. Hingvar and Hubba
in 866 ravaged East Anglia and Mercia; they
wintered in Essex, and in 867 crossed the Humber
and took York. In 868 they devastated as far as
Nottingham. In 870 Edmund fell. Every successive

year was marked by fire and slaughter. In 876 the Danes were in Exeter, and again in 877. In the winter of 878 Hubba came with twenty-three ships into the estuary of the Taw and Torridge with the raven standard, and landed at Appledore (*Aweddwr*, W. running water). Here the men of Devon were encamped at Kenwith,* now Henny Castle, north-west of Bideford, where earthworks remain to this day in the wood. The Danes attacked the camp, and were repulsed, with the loss of twelve hundred men and their raven banner. Hubba was also slain. He was buried on the shore near his ships, and a pile of stones was thrown up over him. The place bears the name of Whiblestone, or Hubbastone, but all traces of the cairn have disappeared, swept away by the encroachment of the sea. So the men of Devon avenged the blood of S. Edmund and of the men of Mercia and East Anglia.

In the time of Edward the Confessor the manor of Bideford belonged to Brictric the Golden-haired. He was sent by the king to the court of Baldwin V., Count of Flanders, where Matilda, the Count's daughter, cast on him an eye of affection. But Brictric did not reciprocate, and Matilda felt all the rage and resentment entertained by a flouted fair. Her chance came at last. She was married to William the Bastard, who conquered England. For fourteen years she had waited, nursing her wrath. Now, at last, the opportunity had arrived for revenge. At her instigation Brictric was made to surrender

* Observe the Goidelic for *Cen* for the Brythonic *Pen*. Kenwith is " The Head of the Wood."

all his honours and lands, and was conveyed to Winchester, where he died in prison, and was hurriedly buried.

William the Conqueror gave Bideford to the son of Hamo the Toothy, Richard de Grenville, and the place has never since lost its association with the Granville family.

Sir Theobald Granville in the fourteenth century was a large benefactor to the town in assisting in the building of the bridge, rendered advisable by the great loss of life at the ford or in the ferry. It was, however, said to have been set on foot at the prompting of Richard Gurney, the parish priest, who dreamed two nights running that there was a rock below the ooze on which a pier might rest. But one pier did not suffice, and how to sustain others on mud was a puzzle. It was—so tradition says—solved by sinking bags of wool and laying the bases of the piers on these, a story not so improbable as appears on the face.

For a long time the vicars of Bideford had a herriot, that is, a right to the second best horse or cow of any parishioner who died. In 1529 this led to a scene. Sir William Coffin was passing one day by the churchyard, when, seeing a crowd collected, he asked the occasion, and learned that a corpse had been brought there to be interred, but that the vicar refused to read the burial service unless the dead man's cow were surrendered. But as the deceased had left no other property whatever, the heirs demurred. On hearing this Sir William sent for the priest, and reasoned with him on the impropriety of his conduct; however, the vicar was obstinate and would not give way.

"Very well, then," said the knight, "stick me in the grave, and cover me up instead of the corpse, and you shall have my second best cow."

He was proceeding to get into the grave, when the vicar thought prudent to yield. I suppose that the matter became notorious by the complaint of the parson, for Sir William was actually summoned before Parliament on a charge of violating the rights and privileges of the Church. But partly through his favour at court, and partly by his being able to represent the mischievous consequences of the arbitrary demand for "mortuaries," Parliament passed an act which put a stop to them, or, at all events, in favour of the poor, limited the extent of these claims.

Bideford was not a place of much importance till the reign of Queen Elizabeth; it started into significance through the Newfoundland cod-fisheries, which were almost entirely in the hands of the Barnstaple, Bideford, and Bristol men as far as England was concerned.

As early as 1504 the Portuguese had begun to catch fish on those coasts. In 1578 England had fifty vessels, Portugal as many, and France and Spain together, a hundred and fifty, occupied in reaping the harvest of the sea in the North Atlantic. From 1698 to 1700 Bideford had twenty-eight vessels engaged in the fishery, whilst Barnstaple had only seven or eight; London sent out seventy-one, and Topsham thirty-four.

But the raising of Bideford into a port of importance was due mainly to the enterprise of the famous
Elizabethan admiral, Sir Richard Grenville.

"Sir Richard was born most probably at Stowe, the
Cornish seat of the family, in the parish of Kilkhampton,
in the year 1546. His father, Roger, was a captain in the
navy, and met with a watery grave at Portsmouth, in a ship
called the *Mary Rose*, a vessel of 600 tons, and one of the
finest in the navy, commanded by Sir George Carew. She
sank with all on board, July 19th, 1545, from a similar
accident to that which happened to the *Royal George* near
the same place, June 28th, 1782. Being at anchor in calm
weather with all ports open, a sudden breeze caused the
ship to heel over, when the water entered through the lower
ports and sank her. Some guns recovered many years after
are preserved in Woolwich Arsenal. Richard Granville was
early distinguished among his companions for his enthusi-
astic love of active exercises, and at the age of sixteen he,
in company with several other chivalrous scions of our
nobility, obtained a licence from Queen Elizabeth to enter
into the service of the Emperor of Hungary against the
Turks."*

He was engaged in the battle of Lepanto, in
which Don Juan of Austria, with the combined
fleets of Christendom, destroyed the Turkish galleys.
One can but wish that a combined fleet would once
more try conclusions with the Turk.

Then Richard Granville in 1569 was made Sheriff
of Cork, but he remained in Ireland two years only.
By his interest with Queen Elizabeth he obtained for
Bideford a charter of incorporation, 1574. He was
High Sheriff of Cornwall in 1578, and was then

* GRANVILLE (R.), *History of Bideford.* n.d.

knighted. But the bias of his mind was towards
adventure at sea, and he united with his relative, Sir
Walter Raleigh, in the exploration which led to the
discovery of Virginia and Carolina in 1584.

"Two ships belonging to Sir Walter's company, and in
the command of Captain Philip Amadas and Arthur
Barlow, brought home that important news. The mag-
nitude and eligibility of the territory acquired by the
Crown were on everyone's lips; for the accounts of those
who had been eye-witnesses of the country, its productions
and inhabitants, hastened onwards Raleigh's preparations
for taking possession of his newly-found dominions. As
soon as the good news spread among the country people in
the west, hundreds of hardy adventurers offered themselves
as the pioneers of colonisation in that quarter. A fleet of
seven ships, of which Sir Richard took the command, was
got ready with all possible despatch, and when the anchor
was weighed at Plymouth on the 9th of April, 1585, there
were none amongst the thousands there assembled but
shared the belief that their relatives and friends were
departing for a land flowing with milk and honey. The
voyage was a pleasant one, being favoured with a prosperous wind, but the inveterate hostility of Sir Richard
towards our national enemies, the Spaniards, led him to
prolong its duration. He accordingly pursued his course
by the roundabout way of the West India islands, and was
rewarded by the capture of several valuable prizes during
his cruise there. They did not reach the island of
Wokohen, on the coast of Carolina, until the 26th of
June, thus consuming valuable time on their passage. We
are told they were in about 34 degrees North latitude,
when, just as they were on the point of entering the roads,
the admiral's ship, from some mischance or other, drove on
a reef of rocks and went to pieces. It was fortunate that

no loss of life heightened the gloom of this inauspicious
opening. After great exertions the men rescued the crew
of the doomed vessel, and proceeded for the island of
Roanoke, a little farther to the northwards. The admiral
went at once from that island to the continent, and, on his
landing, proceeded to see what sort of country the promised
land was. Whilst engaged in this survey, the natives, who
were unaccustomed to the sight of beings so different
from themselves in colour, costume, and bearing, crowded
around, plying them with questions by signs and gestures.
Sir Richard appeased their inquisitiveness with the few
trifling articles he had designed for them as presents; but
their appetites being rather sharpened than appeased by
these acquisitions, one of the natives, instigated by the rest,
entered Sir Richard's tent, and, attracted by a massive silver
goblet belonging to that knight, without more ado walked
off with it. The despoiled owner happened at the time to
be employed in 'prospecting' the country, but on his return
instantly missed the favourite piece of plate. Enraged
at this mark of ingratitude when from his conciliatory
kindness he had expected good faith, he adopted severe
measures on the natives around. He soon after set sail to
Roanoke, which all accounts concur in representing as an
incommodious station, deficient in all the requisites for a
good harbour, and all but uninhabited. Here, having
founded a settlement, he left in it a company of 180 men.
Mr. Ralph Lane, a man of experienced judgment, was elected
governor of the infant colony, which ranked among its
members several names not unknown to fame. Men well
skilled in the different sciences were there, to instruct and
improve the growing intelligence of the colony. Of these,
Hariot, a mathematician of first-rate eminence in his day,
is especially mentioned. Sir Richard made for home with
the avowed intention of procuring a reinforcement sufficiently powerful to subdue and colonise the continent of

Virginia and Carolina. His good fortune led him in his homeward voyage to fall in with a Spanish register ship, almost as richly laden as the treasure ship the *Cacafuego*, which had enriched, by its capture, his relative Sir Francis Drake and his crew. In this vessel, which Sir Richard engaged and boarded, was stowed away a cargo worth more than £50,000 sterling."*

When Sir Richard Granville had retired, the colonists wasted their time in searching for gold in place of cultivating the soil. Consequently they were in a condition of starvation when Sir Francis Drake, touching there on his way to England, rescued them from their impending fate.

"Not long after, Sir Richard Granville with three ships hove in sight. Ignorant of what had happened he landed with the confident hope of adding vigour and strength to the infant colony for whose welfare he had toiled and sacrificed; but after making the most laborious searches for the absentees, without obtaining any indications of their fate, he set sail, leaving fifteen of his crew ashore for the purpose of retaining possession. This handful of men soon became involved in hostilities with the natives, and were by them destroyed to the last man. However disheartening this unlooked-for succession of disasters might have proved to men of ordinary stamp, they only incited the elastic dispositions of Raleigh and Granville to more vigorous operations. Early, therefore, in the following year (1587), they fitted out three more ships, which were entrusted to the command of Captain John White, a native of Devonshire, a man well versed in all the difficulties and trials attending enterprises of this nature. He brought

* *Grenvilles of Stowe,* by "A BIDEFORDIAN."

together a more numerous and determined body of adventurers than had composed the former expedition under Lane; but upon their arrival the same disadvantages which had daunted their predecessors in the colony appeared so forcibly before their senses that, deeming the continuous mass of forest and the endless savannahs of the country only fit for the abode of savages, they with one accord solicited their leader, White, to return to England and bring a fresh supply of articles, that their uncomfortable position might at least be made tolerable. He accordingly retraced his footsteps, arriving in this country at a time when the eyes of the entire nation were intent upon warfare, and, receiving no encouragement from their patrons, the unfortunate colony in Roanoke obtained no assistance; and the painful fact must be repeated, that our first settlers in Virginia were suffered to perish miserably by a famine or to fall ignominiously from the savage hatred of the tribes who surrounded them."

Kingsley is wrong in stating that Sir Richard was at sea, and assisted in the destruction of the Armada; at the time he was acting under orders to remain in Cornwall.

Three years after, in 1591, he was in command of the *Revenge*, as Vice-Admiral of England, in which he achieved the glorious action off the Azores in which he met his death. His object was to intercept the richly-laden fleet of the Spaniards, on its return from the West Indies; a service of the utmost importance, as thereby England stopped the sources of Philip's power.

Towards the end of August, the Admiral, Lord Thomas Howard, with six of Her Majesty's ships and as many small vessels, was at anchor at Flores, when news arrived of the near approach of the great Spanish fleet. Many of the Englishmen were ill on shore, and others were filling the ships with ballast. Imperfectly manned and ballasted as they were, there was nothing for it but to make an attempt to escape out of the trap in which they were caught, and the ships slipped their cables. Sir Richard, as Vice-Admiral, was the last to start, delaying to do so till the final moment, in order to collect those of his sick crew who were on shore; and this delay was fatal.

The two great Spanish squadrons hove in sight and intercepted him. However, he resolved to force his way through. The Spanish fleet consisted of fifty-three vessels. Eleven out of the twelve English ships had escaped. Sir Richard weighed, uncertain at first what to do. The Spanish fleet were on his weather bow, and he was advised to cut his mainsail, cast about, and run before the wind, trusting to the fleetness of his ship. But Sir Richard utterly refused to turn his back on the enemy, alleging that he would die rather than show that to a Spaniard.

The wind was light. The *San Philip*, a huge high-cargoed ship of 1500 tons, hove to windward, took the wind out of the sails of the *Revenge*, and attempted to board her. The Spanish vessels were filled with soldiers: in some two hundred, in some five hundred, in others eight hundred.

The *San Philip* had three tiers of ordnance, with eleven pieces on every tier.

Then, as Tennyson tells the tale :—

" Sir Richard spoke and he laughed, and we roared a hurrah,
  and so
 The little *Revenge* ran on sheer into the heart of the foe,
 With her hundred fighters on deck, and her ninety sick below,
 For half of their fleet to the right, and half to the left were
  seen,
 And the little *Revenge* ran on thro' the long sea-lane between."

The fight began at three o'clock in the afternoon and continued all that evening. The *San Philip*, having received the lower tier of the *Revenge*, charged with cross-bar shot, was to some extent disabled, and shifted her quarters. Repeated attempts made to board the English vessel were repulsed. All that August night the fight continued, the stars shining overhead, but eclipsed by the clouds of smoke from the cannon. Ship after ship came in upon the *Revenge*, so that she was continuously engaged with two mighty galleons, one on each side, and with the enemy boarding her on both. Before morning fifteen men-of-war had been engaged with her, but all in vain ; some had been sunk, the rest repulsed.

" And the rest, they came aboard us, and they fought us hand
  to hand,
 For a dozen times they came with their pikes and musqeteers,
 And a dozen times we shook 'em off, as a dog that shakes
  his ears,
 When he leaps from the water to land."

All the powder at length in the *Revenge* was spent, all her pikes were broken, forty out of her hundred men were killed, and a great number of the rest wounded.

Sir Richard, though badly hurt early in the battle, never forsook the deck till an hour before midnight, and was then shot through the body while his wounds were being dressed, and again in the head, and his surgeon was killed while attending on him. The masts were lying over the side, the rigging cut or broken, the upper work all shot in pieces, and the ship herself, unable to move, was settling slowly in the sea, the vast fleet of the Spaniards lying round her in a ring, like dogs round a dying lion and wary of approaching him in his last dying agony. Sir Richard, seeing it was past hope, having fought for fifteen hours, ordered the master-gunner to sink the ship; but this was a heroic sacrifice that the common seamen opposed. Two Spanish ships had gone down, above fifteen hundred men had been killed, and the Spanish admiral could not induce any of the rest of the fleet to board the *Revenge* again, as they feared lest Sir Richard should blow himself and them up.

Sir Richard was lying disabled below, and too weak and wounded to contest with those who opposed the sinking of the vessel. The captain now entered into parley with the Spanish admiral, and succeeded in obtaining for conditions that all their lives should be saved, the crew sent to England, and the officers ransomed. Sir Richard was now removed to the ship of Don Alfonso Barsano, the Spanish admiral, and there died, saying in Spanish :—

" Here die I, Richard Granville, with a joyful and quiet mind, for that I have ended my life as a true soldier ought to do that hath fought for his country, queen, religion, and honour : whereby my soul most joyfully departeth out of this body, and shall always leave behind it an everlasting fame of a valiant and true soldier that hath done his duty as he was bound to do."

Froude well says :—*

" Such was the fight at Flores in that August, 1591, without its equal in such of the annals of mankind as the thing which we call history has preserved to us. At the time England and all the world rang with it. It struck a deeper terror, though it was but the action of a single ship, into the hearts of the Spanish people, it dealt a more deadly blow upon their fame and naval strength, than the destruction of the Armada itself, and in the direct results which arose from it it was scarcely less disastrous to them. Hardly, as it seems to us, if the most glorious actions which are set like jewels in the history of mankind are weighed one against the other in the balance, hardly will those three hundred Spartans, who in the summer morning sat combing their long hair for death in the passes of Thermopylæ, have earned a more lofty estimate for themselves than this one crew of modern Englishmen. After the action there ensued a tempest so terrible as was never seen or heard the like before. A fleet of merchantmen joined the armada immediately after the battle, forming in all one hundred and forty sail ; and of these one hundred and forty, only thirty-two ever saw Spanish harbour ; the rest all foundered or were lost on the Azores. The men-of-war had been so shattered by shot as to be unable to carry sail ; and the *Revenge* herself, disdaining to survive her commander, or as if to complete his own last baffled purpose, like Samson, buried herself and her two hundred prize crew under the rocks of St. Michael's."

* *Forgotten Worthies.*

Bideford is the starting-point for the north coast of Devon, from the mouth of the Torridge to the Cornish border, and thence to Bude.

The beauty of this coast is almost unrivalled, equalled only by that from Ilfracombe to Minehead.

Clovelly, with the Hobby Drive, is something to be seen, and one's education is incomplete without it.

And one can combine archæology with the quest of beauty, if a visit to Clovelly be combined with one to the "Dykes," sadly mutilated by roads cut through the embankments. Nevertheless, sufficient remains of Clovelly Dykes to make it a fair representative of a British king's *Dun*. Beyond Clovelly, somewhat spoiled by being a place of resort, but always maintaining much picturesqueness, is Hartland, the settlement of S. Nectan, reputed son, but probably grandson, of King Brychan of Brecknock. He is represented in a niche on the tower. His name is Irish; Nectans were not uncommon in the Green Isle.

Very little is known of S. Nectan. He is said to have been killed, his head cut off—not improbably by the chief at Clovelly Dykes, who cannot have relished having the country overrun and appropriated by a horde of half Irish half Welsh adventurers. And this took place precisely at the time when the Irish grip on Britain was relaxing.

A stone was marked with his blood where he was killed. He got up and carried his head to where now stands the church. But "they all did it." These Celtic saints had a remarkable faculty for not only losing their heads, but finding them again.

There is a grand screen painted and gilt in the church.

At Hartland Point, the promontory of Hercules of the ancients, is a lighthouse. When the wind is from the west the Atlantic thunders and foams on one side of the headland, whilst on the other in the bay the sea lies glassy, and reflects the purple-red slaty cliffs. The point rises 300 feet out of the sea, and was probably at one time occupied by a cliff-castle. A visit to Hartland Quay reveals the most extraordinary contortions in the slate rock. The cliffs are sombre, the strata thrust up at right angles to the sea, and over them foam streamlets that discharge themselves into the ocean.

Hartland Abbey was founded by Gytha, the wife of Earl Godwin, and mother of Harold, in honour of S. Nectan, who, she believed, had come to the assistance of her husband in a storm and saved him from shipwreck—as if a true Celtic saint would put out his little finger to help a Saxon! But there was unquestionably a monastery here long before—from the sixth century, when S. Nectan settled on this wild headland.

The large parish was at one time studded with chapels, but these have all disappeared, or been converted into barns. The church is two miles from the village of Hartland.

A walk along the cliffs may be carried to Well-combe, another foundation of S. Nectan, where is his holy well, recently repaired. The church contains a screen earlier in character than is usually found. There were interesting bench-ends with very curious heads. At the "restoration" a few of the ends were plastered against the screen, and their unique heads sawn away so as to make them fit the place into which they were thrust, but never designed to occupy. Their places were taken by mean deal benches. I suppose as the patron, S. Nectan, lost his head, these chief ornaments of the church were doomed to the same fate.

Wellcombe Mouth is worth a visit; a narrow glen descending to the sea, which here rages against precipitous cliffs.

Another excursion from Bideford should be made to Wear Gifford, where is one of the finest oak-roofed halls in England.

The mansion stands on a slope, rising gently from the meadows near the Torridge, yet rears itself into the semblance of a stronghold by a scarped terrace, which extends along the south front.

Half concealed in luxuriant vegetation, on the right is the embattled gateway tower, still one of the entrances. In approaching the house we see two projecting gables, and between them is the entrance and the hall, the latter with its massive chimney.

From the entrance the broad oak staircase, having a handsome balustrade, is ascended. The walls are hung with tapestry. On reaching the minstrels' gallery an excellent view is obtained of the superb roof, "one of the most ornate and tasteful specimens of Perpendicular woodwork to be met with in England. Every portion is carved with the spirit and stroke of the true artist; and the multiplied enrichments seen in detail from our elevated position quite surprise the spectator."*

Elaborately carved wainscot panelling surrounds the walls, covering about ten feet in height. It is adorned with heraldic shields, and opposite the fireplace are the arms of Henry VII.

This small, perfect, and beautiful specimen of an old English mansion was the cradle of one of the best of Devonshire families, the Giffards, a branch of which was at Brightley. The last of the Wear Gifford stock conveyed the estate and mansion with his daughter and heiress to the Fortescues. But the Giffard race is by no means extinct, it is now well represented by the Earl of Halsbury.

* Ashworth : " The Ancient Manor House of Wear Gifford," in *Trans. of the Exeter Diocesan Architect. Soc.*, vol. vi., 1852.

Note.—Book on Bideford :—
Granville (R.), *History of Bideford*. Bideford, 1883.

CHAPTER X.

DARTMOOR AND ITS ANTIQUITIES

Geological structure of Dartmoor — Granite — " Clitters " — Building with granite—The bogs—The rivers—Rock basins—Logan stones — Kaoline deposits — Hut circles — Cooking‧stones — Pottery — Pounds—Grimspound—Position of women in early times—Approximate period to which the relics belong—The cromlech—The kistvaen—The stone circle—The stone row—The menhir—Cairns —Modes of interment among the pagan Irish—Stone crosses— Tinners' burrows and stream works—Blowing-houses.

THE great irregular tableland of Dartmoor, an upheaval of granite over a thousand feet above the sea, and in places attaining to above two thousand, occupies two hundred and twenty-five square miles of country. Of that, however, less than one half is the " Forest " and belongs to the Duchy of Cornwall. Around the forest are the commons belonging to the parishes contiguous to the moor.

The moor is almost throughout of granite. At the outskirts, indeed, gabbro and trap exist, that have been forced up at the points where the granite has burst through the slate, and these later uprushes of molten matter have greatly altered the granite in contact with them, and have produced an elvan.

The most extraordinary difference in kinds and composition exists throughout the granitic area.

Some granite is very coarse, full of what are locally called " horse - teeth," crystals of felspar, other is finely grained. Some is black with schorl, some, as that of Mill Tor, white as statuary marble. Granite was not well stirred before it was protruded to the surface. The constituents of granite are quartz, felspar, and mica ; the latter sometimes white, at others usually black and glistering. The felspar may be recognised as being a dead white. The black shining matter found near where are veins of tin, is schorl.

It is the opinion of modern geologists that the granite never saw daylight till cold and consolidated, and that granite when in fusion and erupted to the surface resolves itself into trap. The pressure of superincumbent beds prevented perfect fusion. In its altered condition when perfectly fused it may be seen in Whit Tor, near Mary Tavy.

But, it may be asked, what has become of the beds that overlay the granite? They have been washed away. In Exmoor we do not meet with the granite. It had heaved the slates, but not sufficiently to so dislocate them as to enable the rains and floods to carry them away and reveal the granite below. If Dartmoor granite could but have retained its covering matter, the region would have been indeed mountainous. In Shavercombe, a lateral valley of the upper Plym, may be seen traces of the original coverlet of slate, much altered by heat.

The granite looks as though stratified, but this is deceptive. It is so unequally mixed that some flakes or layers are harder and more resistant to atmospheric forces than are others, and where the granite is soft it gives way, presenting a laminated appearance. Moreover, the granite is full of joints. Where these joints are vertical and numerous, there the rocky masses break into fragments. Bellever Tor is a good instance. This imposing mass looks as though, when rising out of the Flood, it had shaken itself, like a poodle, to dry itself, and in so doing had shaken itself to bits. Lustleigh Cleave is another instance. Every tor is surrounded by a " clitter " (Welsh *clechir*), and these clitters are due to the disintegration of the granite in horizontal beds, and then on account of their joints horizontal and diagonal, falling into confused heaps. Where the joints are not numerous and not close together, there the rocks cohere and form tors. In many, as Vixen Tor and Mis Tor, the pseudo-bedding lines are very distinct. Where the soft beds are infrequent, there the granite forms great cake-like blocks as in Hey Tor. The tors are, in fact, the more solid cores as yet not overthrown by natural agencies. Such a core is Bowerman's Nose, and around it is the " clitter " of rock that once encased it.

Granite is very pervious to water, as everyone knows who lives in a house built of it by modern architect and masons.

The ancients were not such fools as we take them to have been. They did condescend to consider the capabilities and the disadvantages of their building material before employing it. The " old men," when they constructed a wall of granite, always gave it two faces, and filled in with rubble between. By this means the rain did not drive through, although they did not employ mortar ; and the ancient tenement houses on the moor are dry as snuff. But the modern architect insists on having the walls built throughout with lime, in courses, and the rain enters by these as by aqueducts. Then, to remedy the evil, the whole face of the house is tarred over or cemented, with what result to the prospect may well be conceived. The granite, though pervious, is so to a very limited extent when compared with limestone, and through a granite country there are no springs that issue from subterranean reservoirs. All the rain that falls on the surface runs off superficially, but not all at once, for on the granite lie enormous beds of peat, the growth and decomposition of moor plants through vast ages. These beds of peat are like sponges ; they absorb the rain, retain it, and slowly give it up during the summer. In limestone districts the making of a river goes on within the bowels of the mountain, but in a granite district it takes place on its outside. Remove the beds of turf and peat, and there will be torrents after a shower, and then dry torrent beds.

To north and south of the equator of the moor lie vast tracts of bog in which the rivers are nursed, and without which they could not be. No visitor can realise what Dartmoor really is in the economy of nature as the mother of the Devonshire rivers till he has visited either Cranmere Pool, or the ridge on the south, where are the meres from which spring the Avon, the Erme, the Yealm, and the Plym.

The granite being of unequal hardness, its constituent crystals become separated by the action of the weather into an incoherent gravel, which in Cornwall is called growan. The process may be seen in full activity on any tor. Sometimes water lodges on a slab, and finding a soft spot begins to decompose it; then, when this is the case, the wind swirls the water about, and with it the grit is spun round and round, and this continues the work of disintegration, and finally a rock basin is produced.

Of these rock basins some fine samples exist: that on Caistor Rock has had to be railed round, to prevent sheep from falling in and being drowned. Mis Tor has another, the Devil's Frying-pan. There are plenty of them to be seen in all conditions, from the rude beginning to the complete bowl.

At one time it was supposed that they were Druidical vessels employed for lustration, and archæologists talked long and learnedly concerning them. But what is quite certain is that they were produced by Nature unassisted.

When a hard bed of granite lies on one that is very soft, the latter becomes disintegrated and eaten completely away. The hard bed is left either balanced on one point or more, or else has its centre of gravity so placed as to precipitate it from its position. Plenty of rocks may be seen in all these conditions. If it should chance that a rock remains poised on one point, then possibly a little pressure at one end of the slab will set it in motion. This, then, is known as a logan, or rocking stone, which antiquaries of old pronounced to have been employed by the Druids as oracles, or for purpose of divination. All this was bred out of the phantasy of the antiquaries. There is absolutely not a particle of evidence to show that they were supposed to be mysterious, or were employed in any rites, and it is also absolutely certain that they were formed by the hand of Nature alone.

There are many logan rocks on Dartmoor. One is on Black Tor, near Princetown. It is instructive, as it not only shows the process of weathering which made it what it is, but it has on top of it a rock basin that decants by a lip over the edge of the stone when the latter is made to vibrate.

The "Nutcracker" stone near Amicombe Hill above the West Ockment rolls in a high wind like a boat that is anchored. There were two very fine logans on Staple Tor above Merivale Bridge, but quarrymen wantonly destroyed the whole of one of the steeples, together with the finest logan on Dartmoor that was on it. The other remains. On Rippon Tor is one, another in Lustleigh Cleave.

The felspar dissolved by the rain was carried away, and has been deposited in many places, filling up an ancient lake-bed and forming Bovey Heathfield, coating plains and hills with a deposit white as snow; this is kaolin, and is worked as china clay at Lee Moor and in Shaugh. The water flowing from the works is like milk, and, curiously enough, cows relish it.

Having got rid of the rock basins and logan stones as pseudo-antiques, we will now address ourselves to those which are genuine.

Such are the menhir, the kistvaen, the so-called
"sacred" circle, the stone rows, the hut circles,
barrows, and cairns. All these abound on Dartmoor.
Nowhere else in England can be seen such an extent
of land undisturbed by cultivation, and carrying on
its surface so many hoary monuments of a prehistoric population. It may be premised that all
kinds of theories have been floated as to their purport and as to the period to which these relics belong,
and the loudest and most positive have always been
those who had no experience with spade and pick,
which can alone solve the problem of their object and
age. Systematic and persistent investigation into
these monumental remains has been carried on for
six years by a committee acting under the authority
of the Devonshire Association for the Advancement
of Science, Literature, and Art, and five reports of
their proceedings have been already published in the
Transactions of the Association.

It may be said that, at all events with regard to
the hut circles, their position in the order of civilisation has been made out almost to a certainty, for
something like a hundred and fifty of these have
been carefully examined. With these accordingly
we will begin.

They are strewn in thousands over the surface of
the moor, and such as remain are but the merest
fraction of those that must have existed formerly, for
incalculable numbers have been destroyed by those
who have made enclosures.

The hut circle is all that remains of the primitive
dwelling of a people that were pastoral, and were
clothed mainly, though not exclusively, in skins.

The foundations of the circular dwellings are formed of blocks of granite, sometimes set vertically and sometimes placed in horizontal layers, enclosing a space from eight to thirty feet in diameter. The roof rested on the circular wall, which was never over four feet high, and was doubtless of wood covered with rushes, heather, or skins; a low doorway facing south or south-west gave access to the interior; and a hole in the apex of the roof served as chimney. The thorough exploration of the floors of these huts has resulted in the discovery of fireplaces, cooking-holes, and raised platforms of stones forming seats by day and beds at night, not so uncomfortable as it sounds, when covered with rushes and dry fragrant heather.

That the inmates played games is probable, from the number of small rounded quartz pebbles found that may have served for a game. Cooking-pots rudely made by hand of coarse earthenware, imperfectly baked, have been found, standing in the cooking-holes made in the floor, with the "cooking-stones" in and around them. These are river pebbles of dense, hard granite, which were placed in a fire and heated to such a pitch that dropped into the pot containing water they brought it to the boiling-point, and maintained it, by fresh additions, until the cooking operation was complete. These pots were fragile, and like modern crockery ware got broken; in one prehistoric cooking-vessel it took the form of a fracture in the bottom—perhaps due to the careless dropping in of the cooking-stones by some inexperienced or impatient cook—but somebody was equal to the occasion, for the bottom was neatly mended with china clay. These vessels, or as much as stood in view above the floor of the hut, were usually ornamented with patterns of the herring-bone type, or merely with dots and lines conveying no idea of consecutive pattern. Their interiors are much blackened with cooking, and imprisoned in the shreds there may yet be found, by the expert analyst, oily globules, remains of prehistoric fat from beef and mutton. Cooking was performed in holes in the ground as well as in pots, just as modern savages cook at the present time. Hot stones in a pit, green grass, meat, more hot stones, and the whole turfed in, and you have a result which an epicure would relish. Some patience is necessary, perhaps twenty hours for a whole pig.

There is a curious passage in the life of S. Lugid, of Clonfert, who died at the beginning of the seventh century. When a youth he served in the monastery, and as his biographer says, at that time it was customary to warm water by dropping into the vessel a ball of iron that had previously been heated in the fire. Lugid had to put such a ball into the drinking-vessel of the abbot, S. Coemgall, and he took it out of the fire with a pair of tongs, but Coemgall for some reason drew his hand back, and the ball fell on the table instead of into his cup, and it was so hot that it burnt a hole through the board.

Most of the cooking-pots found in the Dartmoor hut circles have rounded bottoms, and are of too poor a paste to resist the direct action of the fire.

An example of one such, removed from the hole in which it was, is preserved in the Plymouth Municipal Museum.

One cooking-pot was found with a cross at the bottom of thicker clay, the object being to strengthen it, as experience showed that these pots always yielded first at the bottom. Some of the largest hut circles, those presumedly used in summer, had their kitchens separate from them, smaller huts, where the floors have been found thick with charcoal and fragments of this wretched fragile pottery.

The larger huts had their roofs supported by a central pole, and the socket-hole in which it stood has been found in some of them. In many huts also a flat, smooth stone bedded in the floor has been noticed, presumedly employed as a block on which to chop wood or fashion bone implements.

It is remarkable that one specimen only of a spindle-whorl has been discovered. No metal objects have so far been found in the Dartmoor hut circles. Implements of flint, sandstone, and granite abound; they are mostly scrapers, borers, knives, and rubbing or smoothing tools; a few arrow-heads have turned up, but these are mostly outside the huts, probably shot away in hunting.

The examination of the graves discloses the same kind of pottery, but with better finish and more elaborate ornamentation. Implements of stone and some bronze objects were yielded by the graves, and the evidence of the exploration of the Dartmoor remains has thus far connected them with the period of culture known as the late Neolithic and Early

Bronze Age, which means that the folk were still using stone for their tools and weapons, but were just beginning to employ bronze, an alloy of copper and tin. It is not surprising that bronze has not hitherto been found in the dwellings; it was far too valuable to be left about in such a manner as to be lost, and no surprise need be expressed that it has been discovered in sepulchral monuments appertaining to the same people, for nothing was too good as an offering for the use of the dead in the happy hunting-grounds above.

That at least some of these huts belonged to "medicine men" is probable, from the finding in them of large, clear quartz crystals, such as are employed by several savage races as mediums for conjuring spirits.

Some of the hut circles are enclosed within "pounds." Many examples exist. The most noteworthy is Grimspound. The circumference of the wall measures 1500 feet, and it includes within it twenty-four hut circles. The wall is double, with small openings as doors into the space between, two of which are perfect; but for what purpose the interspace between the walls was left is most uncertain. It can hardly have been filled in with earth or rubble, as no traces of such filling remain. The entrance to the pound is in a very perfect condition. There is a hut circle outside the enclosing wall, just as in the prehistoric forts of Ireland.

A curious passage may be quoted from the gloss to the Law of Adamnan, which shows how women were treated among the early races.

In the hovels, very similar to our hut circles, a hole was dug in the floor from the door to the hearth about three feet deep. In this, in a condition of stark nudity, the women spent the day, and the object of the hole was partly decency and partly to keep the women in their places, so that—without joking—they were not on the same level as man. They did all the cooking, turning the spits. They made candles of fat, four hands'-breadth long. These they were required to hold aloft whilst the men ate and drank. At night the women were put to sleep in bothies like dog-kennels, *outside* the enclosure, so as to keep guard over their lords and masters, like watch-dogs.

In Wales, Iltyd the knight sent his wife out stark naked in a bitter wind to collect the horses and drive them into pound, whilst he lay cuddled up in the blankets.

Verily men had the upper hand then. *Nous avons changé tout cela.*

Near Post Bridge were numerous pounds containing hut circles; most have been destroyed—one only remains intact, at Broadun. Adjoining it was another, much larger; there the enclosing wall has been destroyed, but not all the hut circles. At Archerton a plantation of firs has been made within one of these enclosures, of course to the destruction of the monuments it contained.

What we learn from the hut circles on Dartmoor is that they were built and occupied by a people who, though they knew bronze, held it in high value, as we do gold.

II. Of the characteristic dolmen, which we in England call cromlech, we have but a single good example, that at Drewsteignton. Cornwall possesses numerous and fine specimens; they abound in Wales and in Ireland. But although we have one only remaining, it can hardly be doubted that formerly there were others, wherever the name of Shillstone (Shelfstone) remains, as near Modbury, and in Bridestowe.

The dolmen belonged to the period before bodies were burnt; it was the family or tribal ossuary. As it became crowded with skeletons, the earliest were unceremoniously thrust back to the rear, to make room for the last comers. The *allée couverte* in France, and the chambered barrows of Denmark, North Germany, Scotland, Ireland, and England, are but extensions of the dolmen to hold a larger number of the dead. The dolmens usually have a hole at one end, or a footstone that is removable at will, to allow for food to be passed in to the dead, and for the introduction of fresh applicants for house-room in the mansion of the departed.

Some of these holed dolmens have the stone plugs for closing the holes still extant. On Dartmoor in the kistvaens a small stone at foot or side was placed, to be removed at pleasure.

III. The kistvaen, or stone chest, is a modification of the dolmen, and is usually of a later date; when incineration was become customary, the need for such enormous mortuary chapels, or tombs, as the dolmens and *allées couvertes* ceased. The dead could be packed into a much smaller space when reduced to a handful of ash. Nevertheless, it is probable that some kistvaens belong to the period of carnal interment, and were erected for the reception of single bodies, which for some reason or other could not be conveyed to the family mausoleum. In Derbyshire carnal interment is found in cists, which are miniature dolmens, or kistvaens, sometimes standing alone, sometimes congregated together like cells of a honeycomb, each containing its crouched skeleton. On Dartmoor we have hundreds of kistvaens. Most have been rifled, but such as have been explored show that they belonged to the same people and period as those who occupied the hut circles.

In the fine kistvaen at Merivale Bridge, plundered and mutilated though it had been, a flint knife and a polishing stone were found ; and flint flakes have been picked out of the ploughed soil round the Drewsteignton cromlech. At King's Oven is a ruined circle surrounding a demolished kistvaen, of which, however, some of the stones remain. A flint scraper was found wedged between two of the encircling stones. Some fine specimens are to be seen near Post Bridge.

IV. The stone circle is called by the French a cromlech. The purport of this is conjectural. Undoubtedly interments have been found within them, but none, so far, in those on Dartmoor. In the great circle on Penmaen-mawr there were interments at the foot of several of the monoliths, and, indeed, one of these served as the backstone of a kistvaen. Stone uprights surround many cairns, in the midst of which is a kistvaen ; but such circles as the Grey

Wethers, Scaur Hill, and that on Langstone Moor, never enclosed cairns or kistvaens, and must have had some other purpose. Among semi-barbarous tribes it is customary that the tribe and the clan shall have their places of assembly and consultation, and these are marked round by either stones or posts set up in the ground. Among some of these tribes, if one of the constituent clans fails to send its representative, the stone set up where he should sit is thrown down. It is possible that the circles of upright stones on Dartmoor, not connected with cairns, may have served such a purpose. They are usually placed on the neck of land between two rivers. There are on Dartmoor about a dozen.

V. The stone row is almost invariably associated with cairns and kistvaens, and clearly had some relation to funeral rites. The stone settings are often single, sometimes double, or are as many as eight. They do not always run parallel ; they start from a cairn and end with a blocking-stone set across the line. In Scotland they are confined to Caithness. The finest known are at Carnac in Brittany. It is probable that just as a Bedouin now erects a stone near a fakir's tomb as a token of respect, so each of these rude blocks was set up by a member of a tribe, or a household, in honour of the chief buried in the cairn at the head of the row. It is remarkable how greatly the set stones vary in size ; some are quite insignificant, and could be planted by a boy, while others require the united efforts of three or four men, with modern appliances of three legs and block to lift and place them. Usually the largest

stones are planted near the cairn, and they dwindle
to the blocking-stone, which is of respectable size.
There is no known district so rich as Dartmoor in
stone rows. The number of these still remaining
in a more or less dilapidated condition is surprising. Some five-and-twenty have been counted, and
quantities must have been destroyed, and these the
very finest examples, as the big upright stones lent
themselves readily to be converted into gate-posts.
Indeed of those that have been allowed to remain
many have lost their largest stones.

The most important stone row is that on Stall
Moor, a single range, that can be discerned even from
Cornwood Station, and looks like a number of
cricketers in flannels stalking over the brow of the
hill. A fine one is on Down Tor ; here the largest
stones had been thrown down for the sake of removing them for gate-posts, and the marks of the
levers were visible. Happily the Dartmoor Preservation Society interfered and re-erected the stones
which had been cast down. At Drizzlecombe are
three sets of stone rows leading from tall menhirs.
The stone avenue that led from the Longstone, near
Caistor Rock for over a mile, was wantonly destroyed
by a farmer a few years ago, when building a new-
take wall hard by. A good example is on the brow
of the hill opposite Grimspound, but the stones are
not large. The Merivale Bridge remains consist of
two sets of double rows, the stones very small, but
the rows fairly intact. But the most remarkable row
of all is that near the Erme Valley, which, starting
from a great circle of upright stones, extends for two

miles and a quarter, descending a dip and crossing a stream to mount the opposite hill.

VI. The menhir, or tall stone, is a rude, unwrought obelisk. In some cases it is nothing other than the blocking-stone of a row which has been destroyed. But such is not always the case. There were no rows in connection with the menhir at Devil's Tor and the Whitmoor Stone.

That the upright stone is a memorial to the dead can hardly be doubted ; it was continued to be erected, with an inscription, in Brito-Roman days, and its modern representative is in every churchyard. The menhirs, locally termed longstones, or langstones, must at one time have been numerous. Those round the moor have been carried away to serve as window-sills, door-jambs, even church pillars. Several places and moors, by their names, assure us that at one time these monuments were there.

Menhirs are still erected by the dolmen builders on the Brama-pootra, the Khassias, and always in commemoration of the dead. The Chinese hold that the spirits of the deceased inhabit the memorials set up in their honour ; and the carved monoliths in Abyssinia, erected by the same race when it passed from Arabia to Africa, have carved in their faces little doors for the ingress and egress of the spirits. Holed menhirs are found in many places.

There are several menhirs on Dartmoor, as the Beardown Man (*Maen*, stone), near Devil Tor, in a wild and desolate spot far from the haunts of man; the highest is at Drizzlecombe, height eighteen feet, and weighing six tons.

It may well be doubted whether in any part of England such a complete series of remains of a vanished population exists as on Dartmoor, where we have their houses and their tombs. But the monuments are not of great size.

VII. Cairns on Dartmoor are numerous, but all the large ones have been opened and robbed at some unknown period. They would not have been dug into at the cost of time and labour unless they had rendered results of value. One ruined cairn with a kistvaen in it is still called "The Crock of Gold," but probably bronze was the metal chiefly found. A cairn opened on Hameldon yielded a bronze knife with an amber handle with pins of gold. A cairn at Fernworthy gave up an urn with a button of Kimmeridge coal, and a small bronze knife, together with another of flint. But the cairns were not always raised over the bodies of the dead. Sometimes, perhaps, only over the head, which has long since disappeared; sometimes over the place where the body was burnt, and sometimes as mere memorials.

What makes ancient Irish usage so valuable is that there we have traditional pagan customs recorded, and after Christianity was adopted the ancient usages were but slightly modified. I will quote a passage from Professor Sulivan that explains the various methods of interment. And it must be borne in mind that in Ireland the Celt was superposed on the Ivernian just as in Devon and Cornwall, and that in both the dominant race largely adopted the religious views and customs of the subjugated people.

"From the ancient laws and other sources we have direct evidence that the ritual of the dead varied with the rank, sex, and occupation of the deceased, and that it was more splendid and elaborate in the case of great men." *

The various kinds of monument were the *Derc*, the *Fert*, the *Leacht*, the *Duma*, the *Cnoc*, and the *Carn*.

The *Derc* was a hollow, a pit, or hole, dug in the ground; in fact, a simple grave.

The *Fert* was a rectangular chamber, composed of stones set upright, and covered horizontally with flags; in a word, a kistvaen.

The *Leacht* seems to have been a larger-sized kistvaen, a cromlech or dolmen, but a single upright stone was also called a leacht. When a number of persons were buried in a single mound, then a stone was set up in commemoration of each round the tumulus or cairn. A good specimen may be seen beside the road to Widecombe from Post Bridge. The cairn has been almost levelled, but the ring of stones remains.

The *Cnoc* was a rounded, sugar-loaf mound of earth, and the *Duma* was a similar mound raised over a kistvaen.

The *Cairn* or *Carn* was a mere pile of stones, generally made over a grave, but sometimes having no immediate connection with one. Here is a curious

* Introduction to O'CURRY, *Manners and Customs of the Ancient Irish*, 1873, i., p. cccxxix.

passage which will explain why some cairns contain
no interments :—

"The plunderers started from the coast, and each man
took with him a stone to make a carn, for such was the
custom of the Fians when going to plunder or war.   It
was a pillar-stone they planted when going to give a general
battle ; and it was a cairn they made this time, because it
was a plundering expedition. . . . Every man who survived
used to remove his stone from the cairn, and the stones
of those who were slain remained in place, and thus they
were able to ascertain their losses."—*The Book of the
Dun Cow.*

Sometimes, after a battle, when it was not possible
to carry away a body, the head of the man who
had fallen was buried by his friends under a cairn,
because the ancient Irish were wont to carry off
heads as trophies ; but to violate a cairn, even when
raised by a foe, was regarded as sacrilege.

On Dartmoor, in addition to prehistoric antiquities,
numerous rude stone crosses remain ; some of these,
if not all, indicate ways, and were employed as
landmarks.   Only one bears an inscription, "Crux
Siwardi."

The whole of the moor, in the stream bottoms,
is seamed with streamers' "burrows" and deep work-
ings.   It is not possible to fix their date.   Throughout the Middle Ages stream tin was extracted from
Dartmoor.   Fresh activity was shown in the reign of
Elizabeth.   Beside the mounds may be seen the
ruins of the old "blow-house," where the tin was
smelted, and very probably among the ruins will be
found the moulds into which the tin was run.   I post-

pone what I have to say on the tin-working to a chapter on that topic in the ensuing portion of my book, on Cornwall.

Books on Dartmoor :—

ROWE (S.), *Perambulation of Dartmoor* (new ed.). Exeter, 1896. A caution must be given that the original work was written in 1848, when archæology was a matter of theorising, and when Druids and Phœnicians cut great figures. In reading Rowe's book the reader must pass over all this.

CROSSING (W.), *Amid Devonia's Alps*. London and Plymouth, 1888. A pleasantly written little book, and free from the arrant nonsense of pseudo-antiquarians of fifty years ago, cooked up afresh.

PAGE (J. L. W.), *An Exploration of Dartmoor*. London, 1889. All the archæologic lore in this book must be rejected. Otherwise it is good.

CRESSWELL (B. F.), *Dartmoor and its Surroundings*. London, 1898. A handy 6d. guide, very useful, and commendably free from false theorising on antiquarian topics.

SPENCER (E.), *Dartmoor*. Plymouth, 1894. A fresh and pleasant book, trustworthy as to the geology, but wildly erroneous as to the antiquities.

For the Archæology :—

Reports of the Dartmoor Exploration Committee of the Devonshire Association, 1894-9.

For the History of the moor :—

Reports and publications of the Dartmoor Preservation Society.

For the Crosses :—

CROSSING (W.), *The Ancient Crosses of Dartmoor*. Exeter, 1887.

CROSSING (W.), *The Old Stone Crosses of the Dartmoor Border*. Exeter, 1892.

For the Churches on the borders of Dartmoor :—

Chapter xix. of ROWE'S *Perambulation*, new edition.

For the Flora and Fauna of the moor :—

Chapters xiv.-xvii. of the same.

For the Geology of Dartmoor :—

USSHER (W. A. G.), "The Granite of Dartmoor," in *Transactions of the Devonshire Association*, 1888.

CHAPTER XI.

DARTMOOR: ITS TENANTS

DARTMOOR consists of moorland running up to heights of over 2000 feet, a great deal of the area being enclosed, forming rough grazing farms, but much of it remains to-day what it was thousands of years ago, boulder-strewn ravines, through which rush impetuous streams, rocky heights crowned with huge blocks of granite, so weather-worn and piled up as to suggest to the stranger that some Titans had so placed them to serve as castles or to add a romantic touch to already wild scenery. Great sweeps of heather and furze-clad downs run up to these elevations, and on many of these the rude stone monuments lie scattered about in all directions.

The forest of Dartmoor became the property of the Princes of Wales only so far that forest rights were granted to the Black Prince and to the Princes of Wales for ever, without prejudice to such rights as had belonged from time immemorial to all Devonshire parishes with the exception of Barnstaple and Totnes.   And the rights of Devonshire parishes were to take off the moor whatever was wanted save venison and vert, that is to say, not to cut down green trees.   As of trees there are none, or hardly any, this exception could not be very greatly felt as a grievance, and as now there are no deer, one might have supposed that Devonshire people could exercise an unlimited right over Dartmoor.   Such, however, is not the case.   The Duchy of Cornwall, vested in the Princes of Wales, has claimed and exercised the power to cut away and reject the rights of every parish except such as are immediately contiguous to the moor, and to enclose and to shut out the good people of Devon from large tracts, one of which is made over to the convicts, another to the artillery, to fire across at long range.   The tors also are given up to be hacked and quarried ; and ponies and bullocks that have found their way on to the moors and do not belong to " Venville " parishes (that is to say, such as are contiguous to the forest) are pounded, and their owners fined for trespass.   Thus the grant of forest rights, *i.e.*, rights to hunt the red deer, have been converted to very exclusive rights to everything, and the Devonians, whose right was recognised to everything save venison and vert, has been reduced to nothing at all.   But just as the Duchy encroached on the rights of all the good people of Devon, so was it also encroached upon. Before that the grant of forest rights was made to the Black Prince there were certain ancient tenements on the moor; those occupying them held under the king, and were absolutely independent otherwise. But these tenants had certain traditional rights, which they could put in force once only in their lives—on the death of the last holder the incomer might enclose ten acres of moor land, and hold it at a nominal rent. Thus these ancient tenements gradually expanded. But besides this the holders made larger enclosures, locally termed "new-takes," when the fancy came to them to do so, and they settled matters easily with the Duchy agents, to the advantage of both. Large landed proprietors managed to get slices by a little greasing of palms, and some very odd transactions took place whereby great tracts of land, and even farms, were transferred from the Duchy to other hands without the Princes of Wales being in any way benefited, or being aware that they were being robbed. But then—as the Duchy had taken from the people—had not such of the people as could contrive it a right to take back what they could?

All this is now so far a matter of the past that the Duchy is no longer robbed, it robs instead—curtailing on all sides the rights of those living in the low steamy lands to the pure air and wide wastes of that great well-head of health and life—the ancient Forest of Dartmoor.

During the abnormally dry summers of 1893 and 1897 Dartmoor proved of incalculable advantage not

to the County of Devon only, but far further afield.
When grass was burnt up everywhere, and water
failed, then the moor was green, and was twinkling
with dancing streams. From every quarter the starv-
ing cattle were driven there in thousands and tens of
thousands. Drovers came from so far east as Kent,
there to obtain food and drink unobtainable elsewhere.

Thousands and tens of thousands more might
have been sustained there but for the enclosures
that have been suffered to be made—nay, have been
encouraged.

Dartmoor is divided into four regions, and over
each region a moorman is placed. In every quarter
of the moor a special earmark is required for the
ponies that are turned out, a round hole punched
in the ear, through which is passed a piece of dis-
tinguishing tape, red or blue, white or black. The
ponies are much given to rambling; they pass from
one quarter to another in search of pasture; but
the moorman of each quarter can recognise those
turned out on his region by the earmark. Sheep
also and bullocks are turned out on the moor; but
they have to be cared for at home in the winter,
whereas the ponies brave the storms and snow.
The flocks and herds are not driven on to the moor
till summer, and are driven off at the approach of
winter.

Although every farmer round has a right to turn
out his beasts, yet the moorman expects a fee for
each horse, bullock, or sheep sent out on the downs.
Cattle, horses, and sheep sent upon the common

lands that adjoin the forest are liable to stray on to the broader expanse, and in order to detect these and exact a fine for them certain drivings are ordered, locally called "drifts." The day when a drift is to take place is kept a profound secret till it is proclaimed early in the morning. Then a messenger on a fleet horse is sent round very early to announce it. On certain tors are holed stones, and through these horns were formerly passed and blown on such occasions. There are drifts for ponies, and drifts for bullocks. A drift is an animated and striking scene. Horsemen and dogs are out, the farmers identifying their cattle, the drivers and dogs sending the frightened beasts plunging, galloping in one direction towards the place of gathering. When all the beasts have been driven together, an officer of the Duchy mounts a stone and reads a formal document that is supposed to authorise the moormen to make their claim for fees. Then the Venville tenants carry off their cattle without objection. All others are pounded, or else their owners pay fines before being allowed to reclaim them.

Now and then the Duchy endeavours to extend its right over the commons belonging to contiguous parishes. Nothing is lost by asserting a right, and something may be gained. But when a drift is carried over such commons the farmers of the parishes rise up and repel the moormen, and battles with clubs and horsewhips ensue. Blows are given and returned; it is felt, and felt rightly, that encroachment must be resisted at all cost, lest it should serve as a stepping-stone for deprivation of further rights.

An old moorman's house was a picturesque object : built up centuries ago of granite blocks unshaped, set in earth, with no lime or cement to fix them, low-browed, with the roof thatched with rushes, the windows small, looking into a small court-yard, and this court-yard entered through a door in a high blank wall. On one side the turf stacked up, the saddles, the harness; on the other, a cow-house and stable, the well-house accessible from the kitchen without going from under cover, the well being nothing other than a limpid moor stream diverted and made to flow into a basin of scooped-out granite. The door into the house gives admission into an outer chamber, where is every description of odds and ends ; where are potatoes, old barrels, infirm cart-wheels, and the poultry hopping over everything. On one side a door gives admission to the kitchen, hall, parlour, all in one, lighted by a small window looking into the court-yard. Or, again, on the one hand is the cattle-shed, on the other the kitchen, all under one roof, and beyond the kitchen the common sleeping-chamber. Rarely is there an upper storey. The object of making these ancient houses so totally enclosed was to protect the dwelling from the furious storms. They were castles, but walled up against no other enemy than the wild weather. Nowadays these ancient houses are rapidly disappearing, and new, vulgar, staring edifices are taking their places— edifices that let in wind and water at every joint and loophole.

The dry walls of these old tenements were snug places for vipers to shelter through the winter, and I have heard many an old moorman relate how, when the peat fire was glowing and the room was warm, he has seen the heads and glittering eyes of the "long cripples" shoot out from the crevices in the wall and sway, enjoying the warmth, but too sluggish to do more.

One told me that his dog was bitten by a viper, and its head was swollen shockingly. He at once got elder flowers, and put them in a caldron to boil, and held the dog's head over the steam. It cured the poor beast.

Many years ago a Manchester man with plenty of money came down to Dartmoor, and declared that it was a shame so much land should lie waste; he would show what could be done with it. So he soon came to terms with the Duchy, which allowed him to enclose thousands of acres—which means exclude the public—and to set up machine-houses for steam-engines to thrash, and for steam-ploughs to turn the soil, and so on. The whole not very far from Crockern Tor, the umbel, the centre of the moor, the seat of the ancient stannary court, *sub Dio*, under the open vault of heaven, on unhewn granite seats.

One day an old moorman met this new-fangled farmer, and said to him : " How do 'y, Muster Vowler ? I had a dream about yü last night."

" Did you, indeed ?   I am flattered."

" Hear what it is afore yü say that."

" Well, tell me."

"Well, Muster Vowler, I falled asleep, and then I saw the gurt old sperit of the moors, old Crockern himself, grey as granite, and his eyebrows hanging down over his glimmering eyes like sedge, and his eyes deep as peat water pools. Sez he to me, 'Do 'y know Muster Vowler?' 'Well, sir,' sez I, 'I thinks I have that honour.' 'Then,' sez he in turn, 'Bear him a message from me. Tell Muster Vowler if he scratches my back, I'll tear out his pocket.'"

And sure enough old Crockern did it. After a few years Dartmoor beat the scientific farmer. He had tried to drain its bogs, it had drained his purse. He had scratched its back, and it had torn out his pocket.

There existed formerly a belief on Dartmoor that it was hunted over at night in storm by a black sportsman, with black fire-breathing hounds, called the "Wish Hounds." They could be heard in full cry, and occasionally the blast of the hunter's horn on stormy nights.

One night a moorman was riding home from Widecombe. There had been a fair there; he had made money, and had taken something to keep out the cold, for the night promised to be one of tempest. He started on his homeward way. The moon shone out occasionally between the whirling masses of thick vapour. The horse knew the way better perhaps than his master. The rider had traversed the great ridge of Hameldon, and was mounting a moor on which stands a circle of upright stones—reputedly a Druid circle, and said to dance on Christmas Eve—when he heard a sound that startled him—a horn, and then past him swept without sound of footfall a pack of black dogs.

The moorman was not frightened—he had taken in too much Dutch courage for that—and when a minute after the black hunter came up, he shouted to him, "Hey! huntsman, what sport? Give us some of your game."

"Take that," answered the hunter, and flung him something which the man caught and held in his arm. Then the mysterious rider passed on. An hour elapsed before the moorman reached his home. As he had jogged on he had wondered what sort of game he had been given. It was too large for a hare, too small for a deer. Provokingly, not once since the encounter had the moon flashed forth. Now that he was at his door he swung himself from his horse, and still carrying the game, shouted for a lantern.

The light was brought. With one hand the fellow took it, then raised it to throw a ray on that which he held in his arm—the game hunted and won by the Black Rider. It was his own baby, dead and cold. This story was told by the blacksmith at Moreton Hampstead to G. P. Bidder, the calculating boy, who as a lad was fond of playing about the old man's forge. From one of Mr. Bidder's daughters I had the tale.

It would be unjustifiable to pass over the Pixies, or Pysgies as they are generally termed, who are the little spirits supposed specially to haunt Dartmoor, although indeed they leave their traces, and perform their pranks elsewhere. To be "pysgie-

led " is to go astray and become so bewildered as
not to be able to find the way at all. How entirely
one may go wrong even with the best appliances, the
following experience will show.

One morning, my friend Mr. R. Burnard, with
one of the officers of the Ordnance Survey, another
gentleman and myself, started from the Duchy Hotel,
Princetown, with the object of visiting an unregis-
tered stone row on Conies Down Tor, which at our
request the Survey was about to include in their
map. We started at 9.30 a.m., of course provided with compasses and surveying apparatus.
There was a bit of fog as we left the hotel door,
but as we heard the larks singing aloft we expected
it to clear. Mr. Burnard and the officer got ahead
of us, and disappeared in the mist before we had
gone a hundred yards—and we saw them no more
that day.

Beyond the Prisons there is a short cut across the
enclosures made by the convicts, into the main
Tavistock and Moreton road ; we took that, and on
reaching the road struck by Fitz's Well due north,
or nearly so, for Black Dunghill (Blackadun-hill).
Then I knew that by going due north we must strike
the Lych Way, the track by which corpses were
formerly carried from the centre and east side of
the moor for interment at Lydford. This Lych Way
is fairly well marked.

The mist became thicker ; we walked on, hoping
on reaching Conies Down Tor to find our friends
there. But after a bit I got completely lost ; we
came on a dip or pan in which were sheep, but no

stream; that I could in no way account for, so we set our faces to the wind, which I knew when we started blew from the south, and about one o'clock we reached Princetown again, drenched to the skin. But the Ordnance Survey officer and Mr. Burnard had taken another route, had arrived at Mis Tor, and then by a swerve to the right along Mis Tor pan—one ghastly, boggy tract to be avoided—essayed to strike the Lych Way and reach Conies Down Tor. But in the mist they went so absolutely astray, notwithstanding their scientific appliances, that when about one o'clock they reached a stream flowing north they supposed that they had hit on the Ockment and would come out at Okehampton. Nor was it till a brawling stream came foaming down on the right, and the river took a twist south-west, that it dawned on them that they were on the Tavy. About five o'clock they reached, sopped as sponges and utterly fagged, a little tavern at Mary Tavy, where, in their prostration, they asked for a bottle of champagne. The hostess stared. "Plaize, surs, be he sum'ut to ate? Us hav'n't got nort but eggs and a rasher."

That was a case of Pixy-leading out of pure mischief, to show how superior they were to all the last appliances of science.

Now, when the way is lost, there is one thing to be done, if possible—aim at running water and follow the stream. It may lead you out thirty miles from the spot you want to reach, but it will eventually lead to a roof, and "wittles and drink," and better still— dry clothes.

But there is another way—to make two marks and

pace between them till the fog rises. This is how an old farmer's wife did, living at Sheberton. She had been to Princetown to get some groceries. On her way back in the afternoon fog enveloped her, and she lost all sense of her direction. Well, she set down her basket with the groceries on the turf, and planted her gingham umbrella at ten strides from it, and spent the night walking from one to the other, addressing each now and then, so as to keep up her spirits.

To the groceries : " Be yu lyin' comf'able there, my dears? Keep dry what iver yu dü, my büties."

To the gingham : "Now old neighbour, tesn't folded yu like to be in this sort o' weather. But us can't alwez have what us likes i' this wurld, and mebbe t'aint güde us should."

To the groceries : " Now my purties, yu'll be better bym-by. Won't ee, shuggar, whan you'm put into a nice warm cup o' tay? That'll be different from this drashy, dirty vog, I reckon."

To the gingham : " Never mind. It's for rain you'm spread. It would be demeanin' of yourself to stretch out all your boans agin' drizzlin' mist, for sure."

By morning the vapour rose, and the old lady took her direction, came cheerily home, and comforted herself with a sugared cup of tea, and spread the umbrella in the kitchen to " dry hisself."

But to return to the Pysgies themselves.

What I am now about to mention is a story I have received from Mr. T. W. Whiteway, brother of Sir William Whiteway ; he was brought up on

the confines of the moor. The story is of the Fairies'
ointment, as Nurse Warren told it.

"You have many times asked me to tell you about
the Fairies' ointment. Now I don't suppose you
will believe me, but I have heard Granny say that
a very long time ago there were Pixies scattered
all over the country. The Pixies were good and
kind to some people, but to others they would play
all sorts of tricks. You must never spy on a Pixy,
for they would be sure to pay you out if you did.
Now the story I am going to tell you was told to
me by my grandmother, who died in her eighty-
seventh year, and she heard it from her mother.
So this all happened before there was any King
George. Granny used to say that she believed it
was when there was a King Henry, who had a
number of wives.

"There was a wonderfully clever midwife, called
Morada, who lived a little way out of Holne village,
close to Dartmoor. You know in those days doctors
were not so plentiful as they be now, nor so clever;
so the people all around used to send for Nurse
Morada. Now she was a widow woman and a
foreigner. Folks did say she was a witch, and a
sight of money she got, for folks was afraid to
offend her.

"One night just before harvest Nurse had gone to
bed early, for it was a dark, dismal evening, likely
for a thunderstorm, and Nurse was much afraid of
lightning.

"She had not been long asleep when she was
awakened by such a clatter at the door as if it was

being broken down, and it was thundering and lightning frightful. Nurse was greatly frightened, but lay still, hoping the knocking would cease, but it only got worse and worse. At last she rose and opened the window, when she saw by the lightning flashing, which almost blinded her, a little man sitting on a big horse, hammering at the door.

"'Come down, woman,' he said; 'my wife is ill, and wants you.'

"'Do you think I'm mad?' she called out. 'I would not go out for the queen herself such a night as this,' and was going to shut the window.

"'Stop!' he cried out; 'will you come with me for ten golden guineas?'

"Now this was a sight of money in those days, and Nurse was very greedy for money; so she told the man to wait, and she would be dressed as soon as possible.

"The man jumped down from his horse, and pointing to a shed said two words in a foreign language, whereupon the horse cleverly walked in out of the rain. The man entered the house, and when Nurse saw him she was that frightened she almost fainted away. He was not old at all, but a very handsome young man. He was small, to be sure, but he looked a real little gentleman, with such beautiful fine clothes, and eyes that fairly looked through you. He laughed to see how frightened the woman was.

"'Now listen to me,' he said in a voice as sweet as a thrush's, 'and be sure that if you do what I tell you, and never speak of what you may see or hear, no harm will happen to you, and I will give you ten guineas now and ten more when you return home. If you keep your promise all will be well, but if you do not I will punish you very severely. Now to show you what power I have, I tell you that although you say that you are a widow and call yourself Morada, that is not your name, for you never were married. Shall I tell you some more of your past life?'

"'No, sir, no!' she called out. 'I will do all that you tell me.'

"'That's right and sensible. Now the first thing I do is to blindfold you, and you must not try to take off the bandage from your eyes. Take these ten guineas and put them away.'

"This the woman did, and hid them behind the mantelpiece. They both left the house, the woman locking the door. He took the woman behind him on the horse, and tied her with a strap round her waist. Away went the horse like the wind across the moor; Nurse thought from the time they took they must have gone pretty near as far as Lydford. When he got off from the horse he made sure that she had not moved the handkerchief. Unlocking a door, he led her up through a long passage, and, unlocking another door, pulled her inside.

"'Now take off your handkerchief,' said he, and she found herself in a queer-looking place all lighted up with beautiful lamps. A little squint-eyed man came and said something the Nurse could not understand. The little gentleman then hurried off Nurse into another room, where, lying on a beautiful velvet bed, was the prettiest little lady anybody ever did see.

"Well, before many hours there was a sweet little dot of a boy born. Then the gentleman brought the Nurse a box of ointment and told her to rub some over the baby's eyelids. When nurse had done so she put the box in her pocket and forgot all about it. This got her into great trouble, as I'll tell you about presently. Nurse stayed some days with the little lady, and got to love her very much, she was that kind and good. The little lady liked Nurse, and told her that she herself was a princess; that her husband was a prince; that they lived in a beautiful country where there was no frost or snow, and that they were fairies, not Pixies. Her father was the king of all the fairies, and he was very angry because she ran away and married the prince, who was not of so high a rank as she was, although he was her cousin, and that to punish them he sent 'em both to Dartmoor for a year. That time was now up, and they were all going home in a few days.

"The fairy prince took Nurse to her home blind-folded on the big horse, in the same way as he brought her there, and on parting gave her the other ten guineas as he had promised. The next morning Nurse was in a great quandary when she found the box of ointment in her pocket. 'Well,' she thought, 'he will be sure to come for this ointment, as they will all be going away to-morrow or the next day.'

"Nurse stayed up all that night, but the prince did not come, and the next day and night passed without seeing him. Then Nurse felt certain that they were all gone, and had forgotten the ointment, and she could scarcely eat, drink, or sleep for thinking what virtue there might be in it.

"When the fourth night had passed without his coming Nurse could wait no longer, but opened the box and rubbed in a little of the ointment on her left eye; but she only felt the eye prick and sting a bit, so the woman thought the ointment must be only good for fairy babies, and she went to bed quite satisfied.

"The next morning she thought she must have died and awakened up in another world. Everything about her looked as if it had grown ever so much. The cat, which always slept in her room, looked as large as a great dog. Then remembering the ointment, she covered her left eye, and all was as it used to be. The woman now got very frightened, and started off after breakfast to go to Ashburton to consult a friend of hers, a Mr. Stranger, who was very clever about herbs.

"As she walked along she would now and again cover up her right eye, and then everything would look so grand and beautiful; and looking up, she saw stars, although the sun was shining brightly, she could see that wonderfully far off. Now, she had not gone very far when suddenly the fairy prince, sitting on his horse, appeared before her.

"'Good morning, sir,' she said, dropping a curtsy.

"'Ah!' he cried, 'the ointment! Which eye do you see me with?'

"'The left, sir.'

"Instantly she felt something like a blow on that

eye. The fairy prince vanished, and appeared again as the little man she had first seen.

"'Nurse,' said he, 'you are blinded in your left eye as a punishment for having used the ointment. I am sorry, for you were kind to my wife. Here is a present she has sent you.'

"He then gave her ten guineas, and she returned him the box. He then vanished. This is all the story that Granny told me about the fairy ointment."

A farmer on the west side of Dartmoor, having had sickness among his cattle in 1879, sacrificed a sheep and burnt it on the moor above his farm as an offering to the Pysgies. The cattle at once began to recover, and did well after, nor were there any fresh cases of sickness among them. He spoke of the matter as by no means anything to be ashamed of, or that was likely to cause surprise.

There can be little doubt that many of the Pixy stories, as well as those of ghosts, have their origin in practical jokes.

Old Joe Leaman, of Dartmeet, recently dead, had an experience with Pysgies, as he supposed.

One day, having need of fuel, he went up the Dart to cut faggots of wood in the Brimpts plantation. Whether he had leave to do so, or took it, is not recorded.

He went among the trees, cut a faggot, bound it, and carried it to a place where he purposed making a pile, which he would carry home at his leisure. But he was observed by some young fellows, and after he had deposited his faggot and had disappeared in the plantation, they went to the spot, removed and concealed the faggot, and hid themselves.

Presently Joe came from out of the wood with a second faggot on his back. On reaching the place where the first had been placed, he set down the second, looked about, rubbed his eyes, shook his head, and taking his staff drove it through the faggot, and pinned it firmly to the ground. Then he went again to the wood.

No sooner was he gone than the young fellows crept from their hiding-place and removed the second bundle, but planted his staff where he had set it.

Back came Joe Leaman bowed under a third faggot, but when he saw that the second had vanished like the first, and his stick remained, this was too much for him; down went number three, and he took to his heels, and did not halt till he reached his cottage.

Some hours later the mischievous youths came in, and saw the old fellow crouched over his peat fire.

"Well, Joe, how bee'st a?"

"A b'aint well."

"What's the matter?"

"Umph! b'aint well."

Nothing more could be got out of him.

During the night the lads brought all three faggots and his stick, and pegged them down at his door. Joe came out in the morning.

"Ah!" said he, "them Pysgies! They'm vriends wi' me again. Now I'm all right. It ud niver do,

us on the moor not to be on güde tarms wi' they.
I'm right as a trivet now."

The schools have pretty well banished superstition
from Dartmoor; none now remains, and I doubt
whether the old stories are any longer to be picked
up there.

Education, however, is not in an advanced condition. The other day I took down for preservation
the following notice I saw affixed to the church gate
at Post Bridge. It was written on vermilion-red
paper:—

> "Mary maze hencot as been and kellad
> John Webb Jack daw.
> and he got to pay 5ˢ for kellad a Jack daw."

The sense is not clear. As may be noticed, Mary
is a *he*, just as a cow is a *he*.

Here is a bit of conversation overheard between
two Dartmoor boys:—

"I zay, Bill, 'ow many cows hev your vaither?"

"Mine—oh! dree and an oss. How many 'as
yourn?"

"Mine! oh! my vaither—e's in heaven."

"Get out! mine ha' been there scöres o' times."

This is a sceptical age. The very foundations of
faith in verities and trust in authorities are shaken.
How far may be instanced by this anecdote:—

Two choir boys had been to a Christmas treat.
There was a cake with little plaster figures on it,
and two of these were presented to the aforesaid
boys, Jack and Tom, by their pastor and spiritual
father, with strict injunctions not to eat them, as

they would be most injurious, might kill them. They took the images home, and showed them to their mother, who at once perceived that they were of plaster of Paris and not edible.

"Byes!" said she, "doant ey niver go for to ate of thickey drashey things. They'll kill yu for zure-cartain, right off on end."

Here, pray note it, was the same thing inculcated by the material as well as the spiritual parent. Some hours later the mother with a shock perceived that one of the plaster figures was gone from the mantelshelf on which she had placed it.

"Tom! Tom!" she cried to the only son who was then in the house, "where be the plaister man to?"

"Plaise, mother, Jack hev aiten 'n—and if Jack be alive this arternoon, I be goin' to ate the other wan."

When such a condition of mind exists among the young, can one expect to find a belief in Pixies still present?

The only very modern case of spectres or their congeners on the moor I have heard of is that of a moor farmer, who is wont to return from market at Moreton in a hilarious condition.

"T' other day," said he, "just as I comed to a little dip in the ground t' other side o' Merripit, who shu'd I meet but the witch o' Endor. 'Muster,' sez she, 'Yu've been drinkin' and got liquor o' board.' Now how cu'd a woman a' knawed that onless her'd been a sperrit herself or a witch I'd like to knaw."

Some of those who have been brought up on the moor cannot endure to leave it. One man named

John Hamlyn, who died aged eighty years, had never in all his life been off it. Another, Jacob Gorman, aged seventy-five, had been from it only two months in all his life. At a little cot near Birch Tor, it was said that the fire had not gone out for a hundred years, as the women had never for a night left the house.

Some of the old cottages on the moor were wonderful abodes, like Irish cabins. They are gradually disappearing, but a few still remain. The influx of visitors to Dartmoor, and the money brought there, tend to their effacement. A cot that could be run up between sunrise and sunset and a fire lighted by nightfall, has been held to constitute a right for ever to the place. Some of the hovels still standing have been so erected.

The rivers on the moor are liable to freshets. In the notable storm of 1890, Merivale Bridge on the Walla, and the old bridge leading from Tavistock to Peter Tavy over the Tavy river, were swept away. But the Dart is notorious for its sudden swelling. It was due to this that the old couplet ran—

> " River of Dart, O river of Dart,
> Every year thou claimest a heart."

The river "cries" when there is to be a change of wind. " Us shall have bad weather, maister ; I hear the Broadstones a crying." The Broadstones are boulders of granite lying in the bed of the river. The cry, however, hardly comes from them, but from a piping of the wind in the twists of the glen through which the turbulent river writhes.

In Dartington churchyard there is a tombstone to the memory of John Edmonds, who was drowned in the river on August 17th, 1840. He and his intended were coming from Staverton Church, where they had been married, when a wave of water rolled down on them, and cart, horse, and bride and bridegroom were swept away. Her body was found caught in a tree a few hundred yards below, but the body of the man was not recovered for nearly three weeks afterwards; the horse and cart were carried over the weir near Totnes bridge.

About a hundred and fifty years ago there was no stone bridge at Hexworthy, only a clapper (wooden bridge). Two men were coming down the road when they heard the roar of a freshet. "Here cometh old Dart—let's run," said one. They ran, but old Dart was too quick for them; he caught them on the clapper and carried both off and drowned them; so that year he had two hearts.

A few years ago the Meavy suddenly rose and caught a man and his horse as they were crossing a ford below the village. The man was not drowned, but died of the consequences.

Up to 1702 there were on Dartmoor but thirty-five tenements in fifteen localities, some two or three being grouped together in certain places. These ancient farms are situated in the best and most favoured portions of the Forest of Dartmoor, and have been occupied from prehistoric times, as is evidenced by the quantity of flint tools that are turned up at these spots.

There is an account of the tenants of Dartmoor

as early as 1344-5, from which it appears that they
were then forty-four in number. In 1346 the forty-
four tenants depastured no less than 4700 oxen and
thirty-seven steers, a very respectable total, and one
showing that the favoured spots in the forest some
five and a half centuries ago carried considerable
herds of cattle.

The names of the ancient tenements are: Hartland, Merripit, Runnage, and Warner; Dury, Pizwell,
Bellever, Reddon, and Babenay; Princehall, Dunna-
bridge, Brounberry, Sherberton, Hexworthy, Huccaby,
and Brimpts.

Formerly all these tenements were held as customary freeholds or copyholds, but many of them
have been purchased by the Duchy.*

Where the miners lived in the old times, when tin
mining was in vigour on the moor, is not very clear,
as very few ruins of quadrangular buildings remain
that could have served as houses, and it is quite
certain that they did not inhabit the hut circles, as
they have not left their traces therein. They, in all
likelihood, lodged in the farmhouses and their out-
buildings during the week, and returned to their
homes for the Sundays.

In 1806 the vast range of prisons was erected at
Princetown, on the bleakest and one of the loftiest
sites on Dartmoor, for the accommodation of French
prisoners of war. From 1816, when peace was proclaimed, the buildings stood empty till 1850, when
they were converted into a convict establishment,

---

* For a full account of them see BURNARD (R.), *Dartmoor Pictorial
Records*. Plymouth, 1893.

and since then the prisoners have been employed in enclosing and reclaiming the moor.

As may well be imagined, many attempts at escape have been made. I remember one, especially daring, which was nearly successful, some forty years ago. A prisoner succeeded in creeping along one of the beams sustaining the roof of the hall in which were the warders eating their supper, without attracting their attention. He got thence over the wall, and next broke into the doctor's house. There he possessed himself of a suit of clothes, and left his convict suit behind. Next he entered the doctor's stable, and took his horse out. But he was unable to enter the harness-room, owing to the strength of the lock, and so was obliged to escape, riding the horse, indeed, but without saddle, and directing it not with a bridle, but with a halter.

He rode along at a swinging pace till he reached Two Bridges, where there is an ascent rather steep for a quarter of a mile, and then he necessarily slackened his pace. To his great annoyance, as he passed the Saracen's Head (the inn which constitutes the settlement of Two Bridges) a man emerged from the public-house and jumped on his horse. This was a moorman. The morrow was appointed for a drift, and he was going to make preparations to drive his quarter of the moor. He leaped on his horse and trotted after the convict, little knowing who he was.

That night was one of moonlight. The moorman saw a gentleman in black riding a good horse before him, and he pushed on to be abreast with him and have a little talk.

"Whom have I the honour of riding with at night?" asked the moorman.

"I'm the new curate," said the convict, "going round on my pastoral duties."

"Oh, indeed, without saddle and bridle?"

"I was called up to a dying person. My groom was away. For souls one must do much."

"Indeed, and your clothes don't seem to fit you," observed the moorman.

Now the doctor was a fat man, and the man who wore his clothes was lean.

"My duties are wearing to the carnal man," said the rider.

"And the horse. By ginger! it's the doctor's," exclaimed the moorman.

The convict kicked the flanks of his steed, and away he bounded. The hill had been surmounted. The moorman gave chase.

Then he recollected that the doctor's horse was an old charger, and he thundered out, "Halt! Right about face!"

Instantly the old charger stopped — instantly — stopped dead, and away over his head like a rocket shot the *soi-disant* curate.

In another moment the moorman was on him, had him fast, and said grimly, "You're a five-pounder to me, my reverend party."

Five pounds is the reward for the apprehension of an escaped convict.

The moorman got his five pounds, and the convict got something he didn't like. He forfeited all the years of his imprisonment past, and got seven in addition for the theft of the horse and clothes.

Some years ago a convict escaped and concealed himself in a mine. Impelled by hunger, he showed himself to the men there engaged. He told them that he was, like them, a toiler underground. They agreed to shelter him, and he was kept concealed in the mine till the search for him was past. Then they gave him old clothes, and each subscribed a sum of money to help him to leave the country. He got away, and some year or two after he sent back all the money he had been given, to be repaid to the men who had subscribed to get him off, and a good present into the bargain.

A very different case was this.

A man got out, escaped from the moor, and made his way to his wife's cottage. She gave him up and claimed the five pounds reward for her treachery.

A friend was spending some months at Beardown. One evening he returned late from Tavistock, and to give notice that he was arriving fired off a pistol as he crossed the little bridge over the river below. Little did he then imagine, what he learned later, that a couple of convicts who had escaped were hiding under the bridge ; they would have sprung out on him and despoiled him of his clothes and money, possibly have murdered him, but were deterred by his chance firing of the pistol. They were captured a day or two later, and this was their confession.

It is not by any means easy for a convict to escape.

When they are at work there are two rings of warders about them armed with rifles, and there is moreover a signal-station that commands where they are at work, from which watch is kept upon them.

Our criminal class costs the nation a prodigious sum. The prison population for England and Scotland is about 30,000, and the prison expenditure last year (1898) was £604,696, so that the cost annually to the country of each convict is about £20.

But there are indirect costs. If we put down :—

Law courts at	. .	£3,757,960.
Police at	. . . .	5,000,000.
Loss of property by depredation of criminals not less than	. . .	1,000,000.
	Total	£9,761,960.

and add to this the cost of the prisons, we reach the frightful expenditure of over ten millions. Surely the nation is penny wise and pound foolish. If instead of spending so much to get men *into* prison, and keep them there, it would but concern itself with keeping them *out*, there would be a great reduction in cost.

The convict is not such an utter black sheep as we might be disposed to think him. That which forms the class is the sending back among their fellows men who have been in prison. They cannot get out of the association, and consequently they return again and again to their cells.

There is indeed a society for helping prisoners on leaving to get into situations, but this is a duty that should be undertaken by the nation; and very often the only way to really give a poor fellow a chance is to move him entirely away from this country. It is a difficult problem, and we could not, of course, send them to our colonies; but all social problems are difficult, yet should be faced, and there is a solution to be found somewhere.

All that the convict really requires is a certain amount of discipline, a strong hand, and a clear head in a leader or master, and he may yet be made a man of, useful to his fellows.

"You don't think I'm such a fool as to like it, do you?" said a convicted burglar to the chaplain. "I do it because I can't help myself. When I leave prison I have nowhere else to go but to my old pals and the old diggings."

If it could be contrived to give these fellows, after a first conviction, a start in a new country, nine out of ten might be reclaimed. They are like children, not wilfully given to evil, but incapable of self-restraint, and cowards among their fellows, whose opinions and persuasion they dare not oppose.

There is one institution connected with Dartmoor that must not be passed over—Bellever Day.

When hare-hunting is over in the low country, then, some week or two after Easter, the packs that surround Dartmoor assemble on it, and a week is given up to hare-hunting. On the last day, Friday, there is a grand gathering on Bellever Tor. All the towns and villages neighbouring on Dartmoor send out carriages, traps, carts, riders; the roads are full of men and women, ay, and children hurrying to Bellever. Little girls with their baskets stuffed with saffron cake for lunch desert school and trudge to the tor. Ladies go out with champagne luncheons ready. Whether a hare be found and coursed that day matters little. It is given up to merriment in the fresh air and sparkling sun. And the roads that lead from Bellever in the afternoon are careered over by riders, whose horses are so exhilarated that they race, and the riders have a difficulty in keeping their seats. Their faces are red, not those of the horses, but their riders—from the sun and air—and they are so averse to leave the moor, that they sometimes desert their saddles to roll on the soft and springy turf.

Trout-fishing on Dartmoor is to be had, and on very easy terms, but the rivers are far less stocked than they were a few years ago, as they are so persistently whipped. The trout are small and dark, but delicious eating.

There would be more birds but for the mischievous practice of "swaling" or burning the heather and gorse, which is persisted in till well into the summer, and, walking over a fresh-burned patch of moor, one may tread on roasted eggs or the burned young of some unhappy birds that fondly deemed there was protection for them in England.

The "swaling" is carried on upon the commons round the forest as well as on the forest itself, so that the blame is not wholly due to the representatives of the Duchy.

One is disposed to think that the moor must be a desolate and altogether uninhabitable region in the winter. It is not so—at no time do the mosses

show in such variety of colour, and when the sun
shines the sense of exhilaration is beyond restraint.

To all lovers of Dartmoor I dedicate the song with
which I conclude this chapter.

THE SONG OF THE MOOR.

'T is merry in the spring time,
　'T is blithe on Dartimoor,
Where every man is equal,
　For every man is poor.
I do what I 'm a minded,
　And none will say me nay,
I go where I 'm inclinèd,
　On all sides—right of way.

　　　O the merry Dartimoor,
　　　O the bonny Dartimoor,
　　　　I would not be where I 'm not free
　　　As I am upon the moor.

'T is merry in the summer,
　When furze be flowering sweet ;
The bees about it humming,
　In honey bathe their feet.
The plover and the peewit,
　How cheerily they pipe,
And underfoot the whortle
　Is turning blue and ripe.

　　　O the merry Dartimoor, etc.

'T is merry in the autumn,
　When snipe and cock appear,
And never see a keeper
　To say, No shooting here !
We stack the peat for fuel,
　We ask no better fire,
And never pay a farden
　For all that we require.

　　　O the merry Dartimoor, etc.

'T is merry in the winter,
  The wind is on the moor,
For twenty miles to leeward
  The people hear it roar.
'T is merry in the ingle,
  Beside a moorland lass,
As watching turves a-glowing,
  The brimming bumpers pass.

  O the merry Dartimoor,
  O the bonny Dartimoor,
    I would not be where I 'm not free
  As I am upon the moor.

NOTE.—Articles to be consulted :—

COLLIER (W. F.), "Dartmoor," in *Transactions of the Devonshire Association* for 1876.

COLLIER (W. F.), "Venville Rights on Dartmoor," *ibid.*, 1887.

,,   "Dartmoor for Devonshire," *ibid.*, 1894.

,,   "Sport on Dartmoor," *ibid.*, 1895.

CHAPTER XII.

OKEHAMPTON

WHAT brought Okehampton into existence? It is not fathered by the castle, nor mothered by the church. Both have withdrawn to a distance and repudiated responsibility in the stunted bantling. It "growed not of itself," like Topsy, for it did not grow at all; it stuck.

Sourton Down on the west, Whiddon Down on the east—where the devil, it is reported, caught cold —Dartmoor on the south, shut Okehampton in. It was open only to the wintry north, where population is sparse.

Formerly, once in the day, once only did the mail coach traverse the one long street, ever on the yawn, and this was the one throb of life that ran through it. No passenger descended from the coach, no meals were taken, no lodging for the night was sought. The mails were dropped and the coach passed away.

There were, in Okehampton, no manufacture, no

business, no pleasure even, for it had no assembly balls, no neighbourhood. Okehampton was among towns what the earth-worm is in the order of animated nature, a digestive tube, but with digestive faculty undeveloped. Now all is changed. The War Office has established a summer barrack on the heights above it, and life—in some particulars in undesirable excess—has manifested itself. Trade has sprung up: a lesson in life—never to despair of any place, any more than of any man. It has an office to fill, a function to perform, if only patience be exercised and time allowed. But if Okehampton in itself considered as a town be ugly and uninteresting, the neighbourhood abounds in objects of interest, and the situation is full of beauty.

Two brawling rivers, the East and the West Ockments, dance down from the moors and unite at the town; and if each be followed upwards scenes of rare wildness and picturesque beauty will be found.

It is towered over by Yes Tor and Cosdon, two of the highest points on Dartmoor, and some of the moor scenery, with its tumbled ranges of rocky height, is as fine as anything in the county of Devon.

The Ockment (*uisg-maenic*)* or stony water, gives its name to the place; the Saxon planted his *tun* at the junction of the streams, whereas the earlier *dun* of the Briton was on the height above the East

---

* The Ock (*uisg*, water) occurs elsewhere. The Oke-brook flows into the West Dart below Huckaby Bridge; and Huckaby is Ock-a-boe. The earlier name of the Blackabrook must have been Ock, for the bridge over it is Okery.

Ockment. Baldwin the Sheriff was given a manor there, and he set to work to build a castle, in the days of the Conqueror. Some of his work may be seen in the foundations of the keep. He took rolled granite blocks out of the river bed and built with them. But later, when the neck of slate rock was cut through on which the castle stands, so as to isolate it from the hill to which it was once connected, then the stone thus excavated was employed to complete the castle keep. Baldwin de Moels, or Moules, was the sheriff, and his descendants bore *mules* on their coat armour. The castle and manor remained in the hands of the de Moels and Avenells till the reign of Henry II., when they were given to Matilda d'Avranches, whose daughter brought it into the Courtenay family.

The castle stands half a mile from the town. "Okehampton Castle," says Mr. Worth, "differs from the other ancient castles of Devon in several noteworthy features. Most of the Norman fortalices, whether in this county or in Cornwall, have round shell keeps, as at Plympton and Totnes, Restormel and Launceston, may be seen to this day. The typical Norman castles, with the true square keeps, were fewer in number, but, as a rule, of greater comparative importance. Among them, that of Okehampton occupies what may be regarded as a middle position. More important than Lydford in its adjuncts, it must have been much inferior to Exeter —Rougemont; nor in its later phases can it ever have compared with the other Courtenay hold at Tiverton, as a residence, with their present seat at Powderham, or in extent and defensive power with the stronghold of the Pomeroys at Berry. Nevertheless, in the early Middle Ages it must have been regarded as a place of no little strength and dignity, when the Courtenays had completed what the Redverses began."

The keep is planted on a mound that has been artificially formed by paring away of a natural spur of hill; it is approached by a gradual slope from the east, along which, connected with the mound by curtain walls, are the remains of two ranges of buildings, north and south. On the north is the hall, and adjoining it the cellar; on the south guard-rooms and chapel, and above the former were the lord's rooms. A barbican remains at the foot of the hill. The whole is small and somewhat wanting in dignity and picturesqueness. All the buildings except the keep were erected at the end of the thirteenth century.

In the chapel may be seen, cut in the Hatherleigh freestone, " Hic V . . . . t fuit captivus belli, 1809." In the churchyard are graves of other French prisoners. Many were buried, or supposed to have been buried, at Princetown, where the prisons were erected for their accommodation. Recently, in making alterations and enlarging the churchyard there, several of their graves have been opened, and the coffins were discovered to be *empty*. Either the escape of the prisoners of war was connived at, and they were reported as dead and buried, or else their bodies were given, privately, for dissection.

Okehampton Church was burnt down in 1842, with

the exception of the fine tower. It was rebuilt immediately after, and, considering the period when this was done, it is better than might have been expected. The chapel of S. James in the town was "restored" in a barbarous manner some thirty years later.

Finely situated, with its back against rich woods, is Oaklands House, built by a timber merchant named Atkyns, who made his fortune in the European war, and who changed his name to Saville. It is now the property of Colonel Holley. On the ridge above the station is a camp. The East Ockment should be followed up to Cullever Steps. On the slope of the Belstone Common is a circle called the Nine Maidens, but there are a good many more than nine stones. These are said to dance on Midsummer night, and to be petrified damsels who insisted on dancing on a Sunday when they ought to have been at church. The circle is no true "sacred circle," but the remains of a hut circle consisting of double facing of upright slabs, formerly filled in with smaller stone between.

One of the most interesting excursions that can be made from Okehampton is to Belstone and the Taw Marsh. This was once a fine lake, but has been filled up with rubble brought down from the tors. At the head of the marsh stands Steeperton Tor, 1739 feet, rising boldly above the marsh, with the Taw brawling down a slide of rock and rubble on the right. This is one way by which Cranmere Pool may be reached. Cranmere is popularly supposed to derive its name from the cranes that it is conjectured may have resorted to it, but as no such birds have been seen there, or would be likely to go where there is neither fish nor spawn, the derivation must be abandoned.

It is more probably derived from *cren*, Cornish " round," or from *crenne*, to quake, as the pool is in the heart of bogs. It lies at the height of over 1750 feet, in the midst of utter desolation, where the peat is chapped and seamed and is of apparently great depth. But the pool itself is nothing. Gradually the peat has encroached upon it, till almost nothing but a puddle remains.

In this vast boggy district rise the Tavy, the two Ockments, the Taw, the North Teign, and the two Darts. The nearest elevation is Cut Hill, that reaches 1981 feet, and Whitehorse Hill, 1974. Across this desolate waste there is but one track from Two Bridges to Lydford, narrow, and only to be taken by one, if on horseback, who knows the way. On each hand is unfathomed bog. Cut Hill takes its name from a cleft cut through the walls of peat to admit a passage to Fur Tor.

Even in this wilderness there are cairns covering the dead. One is led to suppose that they cover peculiarly restless beings, who were taken as far as possible from the habitations of men. I remember seeing a cairn in Iceland in a howling waste that in historic times was raised over one Glâmr who would not lie quiet in his grave, but walked about and broke the backs of the living, or frightened them to death. He was dug up and transported as far as could be into the wilderness, his head cut off and placed as a cushion for his trunk to sit on, and then reburied.

Cranmere Pool, though but a puddle, deserves a visit. The intense desolation of the spot is impressive. On such solitary stretches, where not a sound of life, not the cry of a curlew, nor the hum of an insect is heard, I have known a horse stand still and tremble and sweat with fear. Here a few plants becoming rare elsewhere may still be found.

There is a story told in Okehampton of a certain Benjamin Gayer, who was mayor there in 1673 and 1678, and died in 1701, that he is condemned nightly to go from Okehampton to Cranmere to bale out the pond with a thimble that has a hole in it.

Tavy Cleave may be visited from Okehampton or from Tavistock. There is but one way in which it ought to be visited to see it in its glory. Take the train to Bridestowe and walk thence to the "Dartmoor Inn." Strike thence due east, cross the brawling Lyd by steps to Doe Tor Farm, and thence aim for Hare Tor: keep to the right of the head of the tor and strike for some prongs of rock that appear south-east, and when you reach these you have beneath you 1000 feet, the ravine of the Tavy as it comes brawling down from the moor and plunges over a bar of red granite into a dark pool below. Far away to the north comes the Rattle Brook, dancing down trout-laden from Amicombe Hill and Lynx Tor, and to the east in like desolation rises Fur Tor, set in almost impassable bogs.

Between the Cleave rocks and Ger Tor is a settlement with hut circles well preserved, but one in a far better condition lies beyond the Tavy on Standon.

Tavy Cleave is fine from below, but incomparably finer when seen from above.

In June it is a veritable pixy fruit garden for luxuriance and abundance of purple whortleberries.

All the veins of water forming depressions have been at some remote period laboriously streamed.

Another interesting excursion may be made to South Zeal. The old coach-road ran through this quaint place, but the new road leaves it on one side. A few years ago it was more interesting than it is now, as some of the old houses have recently been removed. It, however, repays a visit. Situated at the opening of the Taw Cleave, under Cosdon Beacon, it is a little world to itself. The well-to-do community have extensive rights of common, and of late have been ruthlessly enclosing. None can oppose them, as all are agreed to grab and appropriate what they can. This has led to much destruction of prehistoric remains. There was at one time a circle of standing stones from eight to nine feet high. This has gone; so has an avenue of upright stones on the common leading to West Week. But another of stones, that are, however, small, starting from a cairn that contains two small kistvaens, is beside and indeed crosses the moor-track leading towards Rayborough Pool; and on Whitmoor is a circle still fairly intact, though three or four of the largest uprights have been broken and removed to serve as gate-posts. Near this is the Whitmoor

Stone, a menhir, spared as it constitutes a parish boundary.

In South Zeal is a little granite chapel, and before it is a very stately cross. The inn, the "Oxenham Arms," was formerly the mansion of the Burgoynes. I spent there an amusing evening a few winters ago. I had gone there with my friend Mr., now Dr., Bussell collecting folk-songs, for I remembered hearing many sung there when I was a boy some forty years before. I had worked the place for two or three days previously, visiting and "yarning" with some of the old singers, till shyness was broken down and good-fellowship established. Then I invited them to meet me at the "Oxenham Arms" in the evening.

But when the evening arrived the inn was crowded with men. The women—wives and daughters—were dense in the passage, and outside boys stood on each other's shoulders flattening their noses, so that they looked like dabs of putty, against the window-panes. Evidently a grand concert was expected, and the old men rose to the occasion, and stood up in order and sang—but only modern songs—to suit the audience.

However, the ice was broken, and during the next few days we had them in separately to sup with us, and after supper and a glass, over a roaring fire, they sang lustily some of the old songs drawn up from the bottom-most depths of their memory. There were "Lucky" Fewins, and old Charles Arscott, and lame Radmore, James Glanville, and Samuel Westaway, the cobbler. I remember one of them was stubborn; he would not allow me to take down the words of a song of his—not a very ancient one either—but did not object to the "pricking" of the tune. It was not till two years after that he gave way and surrendered the words.

The old house of the Oxenham family is in the neighbourhood, but has passed away into other hands. To this family belonged, there can be little doubt, the John Oxenham who was such an adventurous seaman and explorer in the Elizabethan days. He was one of those who accompanied Francis Drake in the expedition to Nombre de Dios in 1572, and afterwards, in an adventure on his own account, was the first Englishman who launched a keel on the Pacific Ocean, or South Sea, as it was then called. He fell into the hands of the Spaniards, and was carried to Lima, where he was executed as a pirate. His story has been worked into Kingsley's *Westward Ho!* The omen of the appearance of a white bird before death, supposed to belong to the family, is there effectively introduced.

The house of Oxenham is of the last century, and was built about the year 1714, the date which is sculptured on one of the granite pillars of the entrance gates. The family does not seem to have been qualified to bear arms in 1620, the last Herald's visitation, but the coat borne by the family is *ar. a fess embattled between 3 oxen sa.* The story is told that once upon a time a certain Margaret Oxenham was about to be married to the man of her choice. In the midst of the preparations on the wedding morn, when all was going merrily, the white bird appeared and hovered over the bride-elect.

The ceremony, however, proceeded, and at the altar of South Tawton the hapless bride was stabbed to death by a rejected lover.

There is a remarkably circumstantial printed account of some appearances of the family omen in the year 1635 in a very rare tract, entitled, *A True Relation of an Apparition in the likenesse of a Bird with a white brest, that appeared hovering over the Death-Beds of some of the children of Mr. James Oxenham, of Sale Monachorum, Devon, Gent.* Prefixed to the tract is a quaint engraved frontispiece. It is in four compartments; in each of the first three is a representation of a person lying in a bed of the four-post type, and in the fourth is a child in a wicker cradle. Over each individual is a bird on the wing, hovering. At the foot of these pictorial compartments are the names of those above whom the bird appears: John Oxenham, aged 21; Thomasine, wife of James Oxenham the younger, aged 22; Rebecca Oxenham, aged 8, and Thomasine, a babe.

This tract may have been provoked by a letter of James Howell to "Mr. E. D.," dated 3rd July, 1632, and written from Westminster :—

"I can tell you of a strange thing I saw lately here, and I believe 't is true. As I pass'd by St. Dunstans in Fleet-street the last Saturday, I stepp'd into a Lapidary, or stone-cutter's shop, to treat with the Master for a stone to be put upon my Father's Tomb; and casting my eyes up and down, I might spie a huge Marble with a large inscription upon 't, which was thus to my best remembrance :—

"'*Here lies* John Oxenham, *a goodly young man, in whose chamber, as he was struggling with the Pangs of Death, a Bird with a white brest was seen fluttering about his Bed, and so vanished.*

"'*Here lies* Mary Oxenham, *the sister of the said* John, *who died the next day, and the same Apparition was seen in the Room.*'

"Then another sister is spoke of. Then:—

"'*Here lies hard by* James Oxenham, *the son of the said* John, *who dyed a Child in his Cradel a little after, and such a Bird was seen fluttering about his head, a little before he expir'd, which vanish'd afterwards.*'

"At the bottome of the Stone ther is:—

"'*Here lies* Elizabeth Oxenham, *the Mother of the said* John, *who died sixteen years since, when such a Bird with a white Brest was seen about her bed before her death.*'

"To all these ther be divers Witnesses, both Squires and Ladies, whose names are engraven upon the Stone. This Stone is to be sent to a Town hard by Exeter, wher it happen 'it." *

There are several suspicious points about the story. No such a monument exists or has existed in South Tawton Church, nor is one such known to have been set up in any other in the county. The stone was of marble, and therefore not for the graveyard, but for the interior of the church.

According to the registers there was a John Oxenham, *senior*, died, and was buried May 2nd, 1630, but not one of the others mentioned. There were two John Oxenhams in the parish : John, son of James and Elizabeth, born in 1613 ; and John, son of William and Mary, born in 1614. Mary was

* *Epistolæ Ho-Elianæ*, 5th edition, p. 232. London, 1678.

the sister of the latter, and their father was the village doctor. But it was Elizabeth, according to Howell, who was the mother. No James, son of John, was baptised at the time at South Tawton. Elizabeth, the mother, according to Howell, died about 1616. No such a person was buried at South Tawton at any date near that.

The persons named in the tract of 1635—three years after Howell's letter—are also four, but they are of Zeal Monachorum. But the name of Oxenham does not occur at all in the registers of that parish, and in the tract, apparently, South Zeal has been mistaken for Zeal Monachorum.* In the first edition of Howell's epistles there is no date to the letter; that was supplied later, probably by the publisher. Now it is curious that in 1635 the name John Oxenham does occur as having been buried at South Tawton on July 31st, aged twenty-one. He was baptised July 10th, 1614. But there are no entries of Thomasine, wife of James, nor of Rebecca, aged eight, either baptised or buried; nor of Thomasine the babe.

In the tract we are informed that the white-breasted bird appeared when Grace, the grandmother of John Oxenham, died, in 1618.

And in fact we do find in the South Tawton registers for that date, September 2nd, 1618, Grace, the wife of John Oxenham, was buried.

* The author of the tract could not find any *parish* of Zeal in Devonshire except Zeal Monachorum, where, as he did *not* know, there were no Oxenhams, and so he converted the hamlet of Zeal in South Tawton, where the Oxenhams *were* at home, into the Zeal where they were not.

That Howell's quotation from memory refers to
the same four as are named in the tract is, I think,
probable. He had not seen the tract, or he would
have quoted the names correctly. The letter was
not written at the date added to it at a later period,
but in the same year as the tract appeared, when
he was a prisoner in the Fleet for debt. Whether
he ever saw the monument may be doubted, and
he may have merely written for publication with
mention of the story which he had from hearsay.
As to the tract, it was one of those pious frauds by
no means uncommon among the "goody-goody"
writers of that and other days, and the incident
of the white-breasted bird was an invention employed to "catch" the attention of readers, and lead
on to the moral and pious sentiments that stuff
the remainder of the tract. The trick of giving a
list of witnesses was one resorted to by the ballad
and tract mongers of the period, and it is noticeable that those whose names are appended as
witnesses never existed at South Zeal, in South
Tawton parish.

When once this pious fraud had been launched,
it rolled on by its own weight, and it became a
point of honour in the family to uphold it; and
plenty of after-apparitions were feigned or fancied
to have been seen.

The whole story of the alleged appearances of
the white bird has been gone into with thorough-
ness by Mr. Cotton, of Exeter, who to some extent
credits it; that is to say, he thinks that some real
instances of birds fluttering at the window may

have given rise to the story. But the basis is rotten, and the superstructure accordingly will not stand.*

A mine had been worked formerly above South Zeal. It had been under a "captain," of practical experience but no scientific knowledge. It yielded a small but steady profit. Then the directors and shareholders became impatient. They discharged the old captain, and sent down a fellow who had passed through the mining college, had scientific geology and mineralogy at his fingers' ends. He scouted the machinery that had been hitherto in use, sneered at the old-fashioned methods that had been pursued, boasted of what he was going to do, revolutionised the mine, reorganised the plant, had all the old machinery cast aside, or sold for old iron ; had down new and costly apparatus — then came heavy calls on the shareholders—renewed calls —and there was an end of profits, and as *finis* a general collapse.

Some years ago a great fraud was committed in the neighbourhood. It was rumoured that gold was to be found in the gozen — the refuse from the mines. All who had old mines on their land sent up specimens to London, and received reports that there was a specified amount of gold in what was forwarded. Some, to be sure that there was no deception, went up with their specimens and saw them ground, washed, and analysed, and the gold extracted. So large orders were sent up for gozen-crushing

* COTTON (R. W.), "The Oxenham Omen," in *Transactions of the Devonshire Association*, 1882.

machines. These came down, were set to work, and no gold was then found. The makers of the machines had introduced gold-dust into the water that was used in the washing of the crushed stone. I made use of this incident in my novel *John Herring*.

But to return to the singers. Here is a song of local origin, which, however, I did not obtain from these South Zeal singers. I must premise that the local pronunciation of Okehampton is Ockington.

> At Ockington, in Devonshire,
> Old vayther lived vor many a year.
> And I along wi' he did dwell
> Nigh Dartimoor 'tes knawed vull well.
> > Diddle-diddle-dee.
>
> It happ'nd on a zartain day,
> Vour score o' sheep—they rinned astray.
> Zeth vayther, Jack go arter'n, yū.
> Zez I—Be darned if ee'r I dū.
> > Diddle-diddle-dee.
>
> Purvokèd at my sāacy tongue,
> A dish o' brāath at me he flung.
> Then fu' o' wrath, as poppy red
> I knacked old vayther on the head.
> > Diddle-diddle-dee.
>
> Then drayed wor I to Ex't'r jail,
> There to be tried—allowed no bail,
> And at next Easter 'zizes I
> Condemnèd was therefor to die.
> > Diddle-diddle-dee.
>
> Young men and maydens all, I pray
> Take warnin' by my tragedy.
> Rin arter sheep when they are strayed,
> And don't knack vaythers on the 'ead.
> > Diddle-diddle-dee.

South Tawton Church is fine. The restorer has taken the monumental slabs, sawn them in half, and employed them for lining the drain round the church, thus destroying the historical records of the parish. This is the more to be regretted, as a fire that occurred in the parsonage has seriously damaged the old registers. There is a fine Wyke monument in the church.

But by far the most interesting church within an excursion of Okehampton is Bratton Clovelly, which, although not large, has a stately grandeur internally that is very impressive. Much money has been spent in "restoring" this church. The glass is good, but the new work in wood and alabaster is barely passable. North Lew Church contains very fine old oak, beside modern woodwork of poverty-stricken design.

There are some early Christian monuments near Okehampton, a well at Sticklepath with an inscribed stone by it, and another inscribed stone by the roadside from Okehampton to Exeter.

NOTE.—Books that may be consulted :—

BRIDGES (M. B.), *Some Account of the Barony and Town of Okehampton.* New edition, Tiverton, 1889.

WORTH (R. N.), "Okehampton Castle," in *Transactions of the Devonshire Association,* 1895.

CHAPTER XIII.

MORETON HAMPSTEAD

MORETON, with its whitewashed cottages and thatched roofs, has a primitive appearance, and withal a look of cleanliness. It is now the fashion to go to Chagford, which has been much puffed, but Moreton makes quite as good a headquarters for Dartmoor excursions.

It has a fine church of the usual type, that was gutted at its so-called restoration, and a remarkably fine carved oak screen was turned out, but happily secured by the late Earl of Devon, who gave it to Whitchurch, near Tavistock. A few years ago the fine screen of South Brent was thrown out when the church was made naked under the pretence of restoration, and allowed to rot in an outhouse.

Moreton undoubtedly at one time was a town in the moors, and the bold ridge that runs from Hell

Tor to Hennock to the east was till comparatively recently furze-and-heather-clad moor.

An object of singular picturesqueness in Moreton is the almshouse, with the date of 1637, with a charming arcade of granite stunted pillars. Opposite another almshouse has been erected in modern times, to show how badly we can do things now when our forefathers did things well.

In the same street is the base of the old village cross and the head of the same broken off. In the place of the cross the "Dancing Tree" has sprung up, that has been made use of by Mr. Blackmore in his novel of *Christowel*. The tree in question is un-happily now in a condition to be danced round, not any longer to be danced upon.

The tree is an elm, and it grows out of the base-ment of the old village cross, the lower steps of which engirdle the trunk; and a fragment of the head of the cross lies just below. The tree must have sprung up after the destruction of the cross, or, possibly enough, it was itself the cause of destruc-tion, much in the same way as trees have destroyed and rent in sunder the tomb of Lady Anne Grim-stone, in Tewin churchyard.

Of this latter the story goes that Lady Anne on her deathbed declared that she could not and would not believe in the resurrection of the body. Rather, she was reported to have said, will I hold that nine trees shall spring out of my dead body.

Now in process of time the great stone sepulchral mass placed over her grave split asunder, and through the rents issued the shoots of nine trees, six ash and three sycamores, together with great trunks and coils of ivy, that among them have tossed up and hold in suspense the fragments of Lady Anne's tomb. The story is of course made to account for the phenomenon.

But to return to the Cross Tree, Moreton Hampstead. The elm, grown to a considerable size, was pollarded and had its branches curiously trained, so that the upper portion was given the shape of a table. On this tree-top it was customary on certain occasions to lay a platform, railed round, access to which was obtained by a ladder, and on this tree-top dancing took place.

The following extracts taken from a journal kept by an old gentleman, a native and inhabitant of Moreton Hampstead at the beginning of this century, are interesting as giving us some actual dates upon which festivities took place on the tree.

"June 4th, 1800.—His Majesty's birthday. Every mark of loyalty was shown. In the afternoon a concert of instrumental music was held on the Cross Tree.

"August 28th, 1801.—The Cross Tree floored and seated round, with a platform, railed on each side, from the top of an adjoining garden wall to the tree, and a flight of steps in the garden for the company to ascend. After passing the platform they enter under a grand arch formed of boughs. There is sufficient room for thirty persons to sit around, and six couples to dance, besides the orchestra. From the novelty of this rural apartment it is expected much company will resort there during the summer.

"August 19th, 1807.—This night the French officers* assembled on the Cross Tree with their band of music. They performed several airs with great taste."

* Prisoners of war staying on parole at Moreton Hampstead.

Unfortunately, and to the great regret of the inhabitants of Moreton, the tree was wrecked by a gale on October 1st, 1891, when the force of the wind was so great that the ancient elm could not withstand it, and at about a quarter past two o'clock in the afternoon most of the upper part was blown down, carrying with it a large piece of the trunk, which is quite hollow. This latter has been replaced and securely fastened.

A recent visit to the Cross Tree shows that the old elm is not prepared to die yet; it has thrown forth vigorous spray and has tufted its crown with green leaves.

Moreton tree is not the only dancing tree in the West of England. On the high road from Exeter to Okehampton, near Dunsford, is a similar tree, but an oak, and this was woven and extended and fashioned into a flat surface.

The story in the neighbourhood used to be that the Fulfords, of Great Fulford, held their lands on the singular tenure that they should dine once a year on the top of the tree, and give a dance there to their tenants. But this usage has long been discontinued. The Fulfords are at Great Fulford still, notwithstanding.

Again another dancing tree is at Trebursaye, near Launceston. This also is an oak, but is now in a neglected condition and has lost most of its original form, looking merely as a peculiarly crabbed and tortured old tree. Here anciently a ghost was wont to be seen, that of a woman who had fallen from it during a dance and broken her neck, and many stories were afloat relative to horses taking fright at night and running away with the riders, or of passers-by on foot who were so scared as to be unable to pursue their journey, through seeing the dead woman dancing on the tree. At length matters became so serious that Parson Ruddle, vicar of Launceston, a notable man in his way, and famous as a ghost-layer, was induced to go to the tree at nightfall and exorcise the unquiet spirit. The ghost had so effectually frightened people that the dances on the top of the tree had been discontinued. They were never resumed.

According to tradition there was again another dancing tree on the road from Okehampton to Launceston, near the village of Lifton. This tree was held to be the earliest to put forth leaves in all the country round. Entertainments were given on it, but it has disappeared, and the only reminiscence of it remained till recently in "The Royal Oak" Inn, hard by which the old dancing tree stood.

There is yet another, the Meavy Oak, sometimes called the Gospel Oak, for it is supposed that preaching was made from the steps of the village cross that stands before it. The oak, however, is of vast age. It is referred to in deeds almost to the Conquest, and that it was a sacred tree to which a certain amount of reverence was given is probable enough. The cross was set up under its shadow to consecrate it, and probably to put an end to superstitious rites done there. Anyhow this tree till within this century was, on the village festival, surrounded with poles, a platform was erected above the tree, the top of which was kept clipped flat like a table, and a set of stairs erected, by means of which the platform could be reached.

On the top a table and chairs were set, and feasting took place. Whether dancing I cannot say, but in all probability in former generations there was dancing there as well as feeding and drinking. These trees where dancing took place are precisely the May-pole in a more primitive form. The May-pole is a makeshift for an actual tree; a pole was brought and set up and adorned with flowers and green boughs, and then danced round. There was in Cornwall, and indeed elsewhere, a grand exodus from the towns and villages to the greenwood on May Day, when the lads and lasses at a very early hour went in quest of May bushes, green boughs and flowers wherewith to decorate the improvised May tree. This was then decorated profusely, and the merry-makers danced about it; ate, drank, and rose up to play, precisely as of old did the Israelites about the Golden Calf in the wilderness of Sinai.

And most assuredly in early times, before Christianity had been established, those dances and revels about a sacred tree, whether naturally grown or whether manufactured as a May-pole, were an act of religious worship addressed to the spirit of vegetation manifesting itself in full vigour in spring.

When S. Boniface strove to bring the Saxons to the knowledge of the truth, he cast down the great oak of Fritzlar which had received divine honours. In this lived the spirit of fertility, and till it fell beneath his axe, Boniface was well aware that he could not triumph over the popular superstition.

S. Germanus, Bishop of Auxerre, who visited Britain to expose the Pelagian heresy, was himself guilty before his ordination of paying superstitious reverence to a pear tree. He had been a hunter, and it was customary for those who returned from the chase to suspend in the tree the heads and antlers of the game killed, as an act of homage to the spirit that inhabited it. The Bishop Amator remonstrated, but in vain. Then one day, when Germanus was out hunting, Amator cut the tree down.

That some lingering notion of veneration due to trees hung on, and was regarded as savouring of something not orthodox, is perhaps shown by the following incident, which is perfectly true. It was told me by the person concerned. A new parson had been appointed to a remote parish in one of the north-western dales of Yorkshire under the Fells. Not being a native of Yorkshire, but a southerner, he was eyed with suspicion, and his movements were watched. Now in the parsonage garden was a large tree, and about the roots was a bed of violets. The suspicious villagers observed the pastor as he walked round the tree and every now and then bowed to pick a violet. This proceeding took place daily. Why he bowed they could not understand, unless it were in homage to the tree, and they actually drew up a memorial to the Archbishop of York complaining of their parson as guilty of idolatrous tree-worship.

The bush hung out of a wine-shop signified that

within were drinking and dancing. The bush is but the sacred tree reduced to its smallest dimensions, and the drinking and dancing that in former times took place around the tree are now relegated to within the house, but the bush is retained to symbolise roystering and mirth. I remember the case of a gentleman who "went off his head;" his family were reluctant to allow it to transpire. But one day a climax was put to his eccentricities by his thrusting the stable broom out at an upper window, and proclaiming, "This bush is to give notice, that within I have got two marriageable daughters on sale. Sherry stood all round. Going to the highest bidder. Going—going——" His wife caught him by the shoulders, twisted him about, and said: "Gone completely—and off to the asylum you shall pack at once."

Moreton Hampstead was the birthplace of that remarkable genius George Parker Bidder. He was born in very humble circumstances, his father having been a stonemason ; and at the age of seven, when his talent first became apparent, he did not know the meaning of the word "multiplication," nor could he read the common numerical symbols.

An elder brother had taught him to count to one hundred. His great haunt was the forge of the village blacksmith, a kindly old man, about whom more presently. In his workshop neighbours would gather to prove the boy with hard questions involving figures, as it soon became known that he had an extraordinary faculty for calculation. The earliest public notice of this that has been met with is in a letter dated

January 19th, 1814, and signed "I. Isaac," printed in the *Monthly Magazine* (xxxvii. 104).

"SIR,—Having heard that George Parker Bidder, seven years of age," (he was really seven months over the seven years, as he was born June 14th, 1806) "has a peculiar talent for combining numbers, I sent for him, desired him to read a few verses of the New Testament, and found he could scarcely do it even by spelling many words; and knew not the numbers of the letters from one to ten." (Mr. Isaac then asked him several questions in the first four rules of arithmetic, to each of which he replied correctly and readily. He then proceeds to say): "I then asked him how many days are in two years. But here he was at a stand, did not know what a year is, or how many hours are in a day, but having the terms explained, he soon made out the hours in a week, in a month, in twelve months. When asked how many inches are in a square foot, he soon signified that he knew neither of the terms, nor how many inches a foot contains, but with the aid of explanation he soon made out the number 1728; and when desired to multiply this by twelve, he complained the number was too large, but having time, about two minutes, he made out the number 20,738."

His father now took him over the country to exhibit his wonderful powers. In 1815 he was presented to Queen Charlotte. He is said to have been a singularly bright and prepossessing boy. In a memoir in the *Proceedings of the Institute of Civil Engineers* (lvii. pp. 294) we read :—

"Travelling about the country, for the purpose of exhibiting his son's powers, proved so agreeable and profitable to his father, that the boy's education was entirely neglected.

Fortunately, however, amongst those who witnessed his public performances were some gentlemen who thought they discerned qualities worthy of a better career than that of a mere arithmetical prodigy. The Rev. Thomas Jephson and the late Sir John Herschel visited Moreton in the autumn of 1817, to see the 'Calculating Boy,' and they were so much impressed by his talent and general intelligence that before the vacation was over Mr. Jephson and his Cambridge friends agreed to defray the expenses of his education, and he was placed with the master of the grammar school at Camberwell. There he remained for about a twelvemonth, when his father insisted on removing him, for the purpose of resuming the exhibition of his talents. Among other places, he was taken to Edinburgh, where he attracted the notice of Sir Henry Jardine, who, with the assistance of some friends, became responsible for his education. Bidder was then placed with a private tutor, and afterwards, in 1819, he attended the classes at the University of Edinburgh."

He quitted Edinburgh in 1824, and was given a post in the Ordnance Survey. In April, 1825, he quitted the Ordnance Survey and was engaged as assistant to Mr. H. R. Palmer, a civil engineer.

It is deserving of remembrance that George Bidder's first care when starting in the world was to provide for the education of his two younger brothers, and for that purpose this lad of eighteen stinted and saved, denying himself all but the barest necessities.

In 1833 he superintended the construction of the Blackwall Wharf, and in 1834 joined George and Robert Stephenson, whom he had known in Edinburgh.

Experience showed him the importance of electric

communication between stations ; he introduced it on the Blackwall and Yarmouth railways, and became one of the principal founders of the Electric Telegraph Company.

In hydraulic engineering his chief works were the construction of Lowestoft Harbour and the Victoria Docks at North Woolwich.

"Mr. Bidder took a distinguished part in the great parliamentary contests which attended the establishment of railways. His wonderful memory, his power of instantaneous calculation, his quick perception and readiness at repartee, caused him to be dreaded by hostile lawyers, one of whom made a fruitless application before a committee in the House of Lords that Mr. Bidder should not be allowed to remain in the room, because 'Nature,' he said, 'had endowed him with qualities that did not place his opponents on a fair footing.'

"A remarkable instance of Mr. Bidder's wonderful readiness and power of mental numeration occurred in connexion with the passing of the Act for the North Staffordshire Railway.

"There were several competing lines, and the object of Mr. Bidder's party was to get rid of as many as possible on Standing Orders. They had challenged the accuracy of the levels of one of the rival lines, but upon the examination before the Committee on Standing Orders their opponents' witnesses were as positive as those of the North Staffordshire, and apparently were likely to command greater credence.

"Fortunately Mr. Bidder was present, and when the surveyors of the opposing lines were called to prove the levels at various points he asked to see their field-books, which he looked at apparently in the most cursory manner, and quietly put down without making a note or any observation, and as though he had seen nothing worthy of notice. When the surveyors had completed their proofs Mr. Bidder, who had carried on in his own mind a calculation of the heights noted in all the books, not merely of the salient points upon which the witnesses had been examined, but also of the intermediate rises and falls noted in the several books, suddenly exclaimed that he would demonstrate to the Committee that the section was wrong. He then went rapidly through a calculation which took all by surprise, and clearly proved that if the levels were as represented at one point they could not possibly be as represented at another and distant point. The result was that the errors in the levels were reported, and the Bill was not allowed to proceed."[*]

Some of his extraordinary achievements have been reported, but they are somewhat doubtful. It will be best to quote only one that is well authenticated from the *Proceedings of the Institute of Civil Engineers* (lvii. 309).

"On 26 September, 1878, being in his 73rd year, he was conversing with a mathematical friend on the subject of Light, when, it having been remarked that '36,918 pulses or waves of light, which only occupy 1 inch in length, are requisite to give the impression of red,' the friend 'suggested the query that, taking the velocity of light at 190,000 miles per second, how many of its waves must strike the eye and be registered in one second to give the colour red, and, producing a pencil, he was about to calculate the result, when Mr. Bidder said, 'You need not work it; the number of vibrations will be 444,433,651,200,000.'"

[*] Obituary Notice in *Transactions of the Devonshire Association*, 1879. See also that for 1886, pp. 309–15.

Mr. Bidder died suddenly from disease of the heart on September 20th, 1878, aged seventy-two years.

Mr. Bidder remembered many of the old stories of the moor told him by the blacksmith in whose forge he spent so many hours.

I have given one in my chapter on Dartmoor and its tenants. Here is another, as recorded by Miss Bidder, the daughter of Mr. George P. Bidder.

There was a woman, and she lived at Brennan * on the moor. And she had a baby. And one day she left her baby on the moor to play and pick "urts" (whortleberries), and she hasted to Moreton town. Now as she went she saw three ravens flying over her head from Blackiston. And she said, "Where be you a goin' to, Ravens cruel?" They answered, "Up to Brennan! up to Brennan!" She had not gone far before she saw three more flying in the same direction. And again she asked, "Where be you a goin' to, Ravens cruel?" And these three likewise answered her, "Up to Brennan! up to Brennan!" Now when she had gone somewhat further, and was drawing nigh to Moreton, again she saw three ravens fly over her head, and for the third time she put the same question and received the same answer. When in the evening she returned to Brennan Moor, there no little baby's voice welcomed her, for all that remained of her child was a heap of well-picked white bones.

Brennan is what is marked on the Ordnance Survey as Brinning, a lonely spot south of Moreton

* *Bran*, pl. *bryny*, Cornish, a crow.

Hampstead, and between it and North Bovey. It seems to me that the story needs but a touch, and it resolves itself into a ballad.

BRENNAN MOOR.

Three ravens, they flew over Blackistone,
　　Down-a-down, hey and hey !
And loudly they laughed over Moreton town,
　　Over Moreton town,
Saying, Where and O where shall we dine to-day ?
On the moor, for sure, where runneth no way.

As I sat a-swaying all in a tree,
　　Down-a-down, hey and hey !
I saw a sweet mother and her babie,
　　And her babie,
Saying, Sleep, O sleep.　I 'm to Moreton fair,
For Babie and me to buy trinkets rare.

As I was a-flying o'er Brennan Down,
　　Down-a-down, hey and hey !
I saw her a-wending her way to town,
　　Away to town.
Our dinners are ready, our feasting free,
Away to Brennan, black brothers, with me.

The babe upon Brennan, so cold and bare,
　　Down-a-down, hey and hey !
The mother a-gadding to Moreton fair,
　　To Moreton fair.
We 'll laugh and we 'll quaff the red blood free,
There is plenty for all of us, brothers three.

Three ravens flew over Blackistone,
　　Down-a-down, hey and hey !
And loudly they laughed over Moreton town,
　　Over Moreton town.
With an armful of toys, came mother, to none
Save a little white huddle of well-picked bone.

From Moreton an expedition may be made to Grimspound.

This is an enclosure, prehistoric, on the slope between Hookner Tor and Hameldon.

The circumference wall measures over 1500 feet, and was not for defence against human foes, but served as a protection against wolves. Grimslake, a small stream that dries up only in very hot summers, flows through the enclosure at its northern extremity. It passes under the wall, percolates through it for some way, and then emerges three-quarters of the way down.

The pound was constructed where it is for two reasons: one, to take advantage of the outcrop of granite that divides the waterways, and which was largely exploited for the construction of the enclosure wall and of the huts within; and the other, so as to have the advantage of the stream flowing through the pound.

The entrance is to the south-south-east, and is paved in steps. There are twenty-one huts within the pound; most of these have been explored, and have revealed cooking-holes, beds of stone, and in some a flat stone in the centre, apparently for the support of the central pole sustaining the roof. Flints and rare potsherds have been recovered.

The most perfect of the huts has been railed round, and not filled in after clearing, that visitors may obtain some idea of these structures in their original condition. This one has a sort of vestibule walled against the prevailing wind. On the hill-top above Grimspound, a little distance from the source of Grimslake, is a cairn surrounded by a ring of stones; it contains a kistvaen in the centre. On the hill opposite, the *col* between Birch Tor and Challacombe Common is a collection of stone rows leading to a menhir.

By ascending Hameldon, and walking along the ridge due south, the Great Central Trackway is crossed, in very good condition, and a cross stands beyond it.

On the left-hand side of the road under Shapley Tor, above a little hollow and stream, before reaching the main road from Tavistock to Moreton, may be seen a remarkably fine hut circle composed of very large slabs of stone. On Watern Hill, at the back of the "Warren Inn," or to be more exact, on that portion called Chagford Common, are two double rows of upright stones leading from a cairn and small menhir. The stones are small, but the rows are very perfect.

The Central Trackway to which I have alluded is a paved causeway, the continuation of the Fosseway. It runs across Dartmoor. It can be traced from Wray Barton, in Moreton Hampstead, where it crosses the railway and the Moreton and Newton road. Thence a lane runs on it to a cross-road; this it traverses, and is continued as a practicable road by Langstone—where, as the name implies, there was once a menhir—by Ford to Heytree, where is a cluster of hut circles. Then it ascends Hameldon by Berry Pound, and becomes quite distinct. From the cross on Hameldon it descends into the valley, mounts Challacombe, and aims across the upper waters of the Webburn for Merri-pit; on the marshy ground above the little field planted round with beech at Post Bridge it can be seen. Road-menders have broken up a portion of it, thus exposing a section. It traverses the East Dart, and can be distinctly traced above Archerton, whence it aims for Lower White Tor. It has been thought to be distinguished on Mis Tor, and striking for Cox Tor, but I mistrust this portion, and am inclined to think that the old Lych Way is its continuation from Lidaford Tor, where it disappears. The Lych Way, or Corpse Road, is that by which the dead were borne to burial at Lydford, till licence was granted by Bishop Bronescombe in 1260 to such people on the moor as were distant from their parish church, to recur to Widecombe for their baptisms and interments. The Lych Way is still much used for bringing in turf, and for the driving out and back of cattle. The paved causeway is fine, but in parts it has been resolved by centuries of use to a deep-cut furrow. It was said formerly that of a night ghostly trains of mourners might be seen flitting along it.

There are extensive, and in some cases very ancient, stream works at the head of the two Web-burns. Chaw Gully is an early effort in mining. The rocks were not blasted, but cut by driving wedges or cutting grooves into the stone, then filling the holes with lime and pouring water over the quicklime, when the expansion split the rock.

Great quantities of tin have been extracted from these rude works; how early and how late these are

none can say. The same heaps have been turned
and turned again.

There are good screens in the churches of Bridford, Manaton, Lustleigh—where is also an inscribed
stone — Bovey Tracey, and North Bovey; and
beautiful scenery in Lustleigh Cleave and about
Manaton.

Bowerman's Nose is a singular core of hard
granite, left standing on a hillside in the midst of
a "clitter." The way in which it was fashioned
has been already described.

The valley of the Teign is beautiful throughout;
it deserves a visit both above and below Dunsford
Bridge. Fingle has been spoken of in the chapter
devoted to Exeter. Below Dunsford the river should
be left to ascend a picturesque combe to Bridford,
in order to visit the very fine screen and pulpit.

Christow Church is good, and there is in the
porch a stone, on which is inscribed, " Nathaniel
Busell, aet. 48 yeers, clark heere, dyed 19th Feb.,
1631." Tradition asserts that he was shot where
he lies buried by the soldiers of the Parliament,
who desired to enter and deface the church; but
Busell refused to deliver up the keys. In the
churchyard are some stately yews.

Ashton possesses a screen with paintings on it in
admirable preservation. Here was the seat of the
family of that name from which came Sir George, who,
after the battle of Stratton, passed over from the side
of the Parliament to that of the king. Hence also
sprang the notorious Duchess of Kingston, the lovely
Miss Chudleigh, who was tried for bigamy in West-

minster Hall by the peers in 1776, and who was the original from whom Thackeray drew his detailed portrait of Beatrice Esmond, both as young Trix and as the old Baroness Bernstein. She has had hard measure dealt out to her, and cruellest of all was that John Dunning, a native of her own part of Devon, should have acted in the prosecution against her and insulted her before the peers, so as to wring tears from her eyes. There can be no question but that when she married the Duke of Kingston she believed that her former clandestine marriage was invalid.*

Further down the Teign, in a beautiful situation, is Canonteign, an old mansion of the Davie family, well preserved. Hence Hennock may be visited, lying high on the ridge between the Bovey and the Teign. Of this place Murray in his *Handbook* told the following story:—" It is said that when a vicar of Hennock, one Anthony Lovitt, died, his son, of the same name, took his place, although not in orders. The parishioners made no objections, and it was not until some years afterwards, when he tried to raise their tithes, that they denounced him, thinking that, ' if they were to pay all that money they might as well have a real parson.'" The story, however, is not true. There *was* a vicar, Anthony Loveys, and he had a son of the same name whom he appointed parish clerk, and the second Anthony remained on as clerk after his father's death and the appointment of a new vicar. The name continues in the place, and has become that of a yeoman family.

* I have told her story in my *Historic Oddities and Strange Events*, Methuen, 1889.

There was a very locally-famous parson of Hennock, named Harris, not yet forgotten. He was a wizard. Those who had lost goods went to him, and he recovered them for the true owners. One day Farmer Loveys went to him. " Pass'n," said he, " last night my fine gander was stolen. How can 'y help me ? "

So Parson Harris went to his books, drew a circle, muttered some words, then opened his window, and in through the casement came the gander, plucked, trussed, and on the spit, and fell at his feet.

On another occasion someone else came to him with a similar complaint, only on this occasion several geese had been carried off.

" You be aisy," said the vicar. " The man as has a done this shall be put to open shame." So next Sunday, when he got up in the pulpit, he proclaimed:—" I give you all to know that Farmer Tuckett has had three geese stolen. Now I 've read my books and drawn my figures, and I have so conjured that three feathers of thickey geese shall now—this instant—stick to the nose of the thief."

Up went the hand of one in the congregation to his nose. At once Parson Harris saw the movement, pointed to him, and thundered forth, " There is the man as stole the geese."

His maid, Polly, had a lover, as the manner of maids is. The young man took service in Exeter. Polly was inconsolable. He left on Saturday, and the girl did nothing but sob all day. " You be easy, Polly," said her master; " I 'll conjure him home to you."

So he began his abracadabra, but Sunday came and Sunday passed, and no John appeared. Polly went to bed much shaken in her belief in the powers of the master.

However, about the first glimmer of dawn there came a clatter of feet and a rapping at the door, and lo ! outside was John, in his best suit, except the coat, bathed in perspiration and out of breath. The spell had not taken effect on him all day because he had worn his best coat *with the Prayer Book in the pocket*. But so soon as ever at night he took off his coat, then it operated, and he had run all the way from Exeter to Hennock.

At Hennock are Bottor Rocks and also those of John Cann. A path at the side is called " John Cann's path." John Cann is said to have been a staunch Royalist, who was hunted by the Round-heads. He took refuge among these rocks, to which provisions were secretly conveyed for his use, and there he secreted his treasure. The " path " was worn by his pacing at night. He was finally tracked to his hiding-place by bloodhounds, taken and hanged, but his treasure, the secret of which he would not reveal, lies concealed among the rocks, and a little blue flame is thought to dance along the track and hover over the place where lies the gold.

Lustleigh Cleave is a fine rocky valley, so strewn with rocks that the river for a considerable distance worms its way beneath, unseen. From hence an ascent may be made to Becky Falls, a dribble except in very wet weather, and higher still to Manaton and to Hey Tor Rocks, bold masses of hard granite. More picturesque, though not so massive, are Hound Tor Rocks, that take their name from the extraordinary shapes, as of dogs' heads formed by the granite spires and projections.

Widecombe is a valley shut in by moor; where the people are much of a law to themselves, having no resident manorial lords over them, and having no neighbours. A sturdy and headstrong race has grown up there, doing what is right in their own eyes, and somewhat indifferent to the opinions and feelings of the outer world. In winter they are as much closed in as was Noah in the ark.

This was the scene of a terrible thunderstorm, a record of which is preserved in the church. Mr. Blackmore has worked it into his novel of *Christowel.* The tower is very fine, but the church does not come up to one's expectations. Widecombe is walled up to heaven on the west by Hameldon, and the morning sun is excluded by a bold chain of tors on the east. It was for the purpose of going to Widecombe Fair that Tom Pearse was induced to lend his old nare, which is the topic of the most popular of Devon hire songs.

> " Tom Pearse, Tom Pearse, lend me your grey mare,
>   All along, down along, out along, lee.
>   For I want for to go to Widecombe Fair,
>   Wi' Bill Brewer, Jan Stewer, Peter Gurney, Peter
>   Davy, Dan'l Whiddon,
>   Harry Hawk, old Uncle Tom Cobbleigh and all."
>
>   *Chorus.*—Old Uncle Tom Cobbleigh and all.
>
> "And when shall I see again my grey mare?"
>   All along, etc.
> "By Friday soon, or Saturday noon,
>   Wi' Bill Brewer, Jan Stewer," etc.

Then Friday came, and Saturday noon,
  All along, etc.
But Tom Pearse's old mare hath not trotted home,
  Wi' Bill Brewer, etc.

So Tom Pearse he got up to the top o' the hill,
  All along, etc.
And he seed his old mare down a making her will
  Wi' Bill Brewer, etc.

So Tom Pearse's old mare, her took sick and died,
  All along, etc.
And Tom he sat down on a stone, and he cried
  Wi' Bill Brewer, etc.

But this isn't the end o' this shocking affair,
  All along, etc.
Nor, though they be dead, of the horrid career
  Of Bill Brewer, etc.

When the wind whistles cold on the moor of a night,
  All along, etc.
Tom Pearse's old mare doth appear, gashly white,
  Wi' Bill Brewer, etc.

And all the long night be heard skirling and groans,
  All along, etc.
From Tom Pearse's old mare in her rattling bones,
    And from Bill Brewer, Jan Stewer, Peter Gurney,
      Peter Davy, Dan'l Whiddon,
    Harry Hawk, old Uncle Tom Cobbleigh and all.

  Chorus.—Old Uncle Tom Cobbleigh and all.

CHAPTER XIV.

ASHBURTON

A PLEASANT, sleepy, country town, hardly able to maintain its old-world dignity against the ruffling, modern, manufacturing Buckfastleigh. A pleasant centre, whence delightful excursions may be made, and with an old-world aroma about it, as though preserved in *pot-pourri*.

It has a beautiful church. Ashburton consisted of a royal and an episcopal manor, each with its several municipal officers. A stream divided the manors. Ashburton is the *tun* on the Ashburn. *Ash* is but another form of *Exe*, from *usk*, water. It owed its growth and prosperity to the wool trade. The proximity to Dartmoor, an unrivalled run for sheep, and the water of the stream to turn the mills, gave to Ashburton a great significance as a centre of cloth manufacture. Added to which it was a stannary town.

The old chapel of S. Laurence in the town, now converted into a grammar school, belonged to the guild of the cloth-workers, and their seal became the arms of the borough : On a mount vert, a chapel with spire, in dexter chief the sun in splendour, in sinister a crescent moon, in dexter base a teasel, in sinister a saltire. The teasel and sun and moon were emblematical of the chief staples of the place ; the woollen trade and the mining interests.

The old fulling-mills were locally termed tucking-mills, and the extent to which cloth-working was carried on in South Devon is shown by the prevalence of the surname Tucker.*

The process of manufacture given by Westcote, in 1630, is as follows :—

" First, the gentleman farmer, or husbandman, sends his wool to the market, which is bought either by the comber or spinster, and they, the next week, bring it hither again in yarn, which the weaver buys, and the market following brings that hither again in cloth, when it is sold, either to the clothier, who sends it to London, or to the merchant, who, after it hath passed the fuller's mill, and sometimes the dyer's vat, transports it. The large quantities whereof cannot be well guessed, but best known to the custom-book, whereunto it yields no small commodity, and this is continued all the year through."

The clothier was a man of some means, that bought the yarn or *abb* in the Tuesday's market from Cornish and Tavistock spinners, who kept this

* For what follows on the woollen trade I am greatly indebted to a paper by Mr. P. F. S. Amery in the *Transactions of the Devonshire Association*, 1879.

branch of the trade pretty much to themselves. The worsted was spun into " tops "—and the name Toop is common now in the neighbourhood. Tops, the combed wool so called by poor cottagers, was made by them into chains to form the warp or framework of the fabric.

One day a week the serge-maker assumed a long apron and met his weavers, the poor folk of the neighbourhood, who frequently hired their looms from him, paying him a shilling quarterly. He served out to them the proper proportions of *abb* and worsted, with a certain quantity of glue to size the chain before tying it to the loom. This they took home with them, and wove at leisure, returning it the following week and receiving the price of their labour.

These serges were then fulled at the borough tucking-mill. This was supplied with a water-wheel that gave motion to the tree or spindle, whose teeth communicated it to the stampers, which were made to rise and fall. The stampers or pestles worked in troughs in which was laid the stuff that was intended to be fulled. The cloth had already been saturated in various unsavoury liquids to prepare it for the stampers. For raising the nap after dying the dipsacus, or common teasel, was extensively grown. The heads were fixed round the circumference of a large, broad wheel which was made to revolve, and the cloth was held against it.

The cloths were then ready.

It is evident that no large capital was needed in this mode of doing business; the clothier had no operatives to look after, and only a small portion of his time was occupied in his business. A day set apart to "tend" his weavers, and an hour in the yarn market on Tuesdays was about all that was regularly required of him. Yet the business done was large, and he expended his capital in purchasing land, in enclosing commons, and in starting tanneries, above all in acting as banker to the neighbourhood.

It is really surprising to see how many of the notable heraldic families of Devon rose from being clothiers. But then the serges of the West were in request not in England only, but also abroad. Westcote says :—

"The stuff of serges or perpetuanos is now in great use and request with us, wherewith the market at Exeter is abundantly furnished of all sorts and prices ; the number will hardly be credited. Tiverton hath also such a store in kersies as will not be believed. Crediton yields many of the finest sorts of kersies. Totnes and some places near it hath had besides these a sort of coarse cloth, which they call *narrow-pin-whites*, not elsewhere made. Barnstaple and Torrington furnish us with bays, single and double frizados. At Tavistock there is a good market. Ottery St. Mary hath mixed kersies ; Cullompton, kersey stockings."

The introduction of worsted spinning-frames in the North of England early in the present century revolutionised the trade, and in 1817 Mr. Caunter started the first worsted spinning-frames in Ashburton, charging 10*d*. a pound for spinning. For a while he held the monopoly. But the Dart was now called into requisition at Buckfast, and on the site and out of the materials of the abbey a spinning factory was established.

"The next great change," says Mr. Amery, "was brought about by the fact that all the weaving was carried on in the houses of the poor. Perhaps in a social point of view it was a good thing, as the mother was always occupied at home, and had her eye on the family; but to the manufacturer it was bad, as the materials entrusted by him to the weaver were open to great peculations, for weavers could always supply themselves with yarn or *abb* sufficient to provide their families with stockings, and joiners could purchase the best glue at half price in the little shops, where it had been bartered for small goods. So great was the loss of yarn, worsted, and glue, and so various were the means taken to make up the short weight by the use of oil, water, etc., that a remedy was sought and found in the expedient of erecting large factories, fitted with the newest *spring looms;* here the weavers came and worked, and nothing was allowed to be carried off the premises."

More wool is now worked up by the aid of the power-looms and combing machines at Ashburton and Buckfastleigh than in the old prosperous times.

Ashburton's most distinguished son was John Dunning, first Baron Ashburton. He belonged to a respectable family, originally seated in Walk-hampton parish, which, though not bearing an armorial coat, was yet above the class of yeomen. His father, John Dunning, settled as an attorney at Ashburton, where the future Lord Ashburton was born in 1731.* John Dunning the elder had as one of his clients Sir Thomas Clarke, Master of

* For a memoir of John Dunning, see that by Mr. R. DYMOND, in the *Transactions of the Devonshire Association,* 1876.

the Rolls, who owned a good deal of property about Ashburton. A legal instrument drawn up by the young Dunning when only nineteen, and sent to Sir Thomas, struck the Master of the Rolls as being so well done that he undertook the charge of fitting him for a career at the bar; and under this patron's auspices young Dunning, in the twenty-first year of his age, entered the Middle Temple in 1752.

It was whilst keeping his terms that Dunning made acquaintance with Horne Tooke, who addressed to him in 1778 his *Letter on the English Particle*, which was later expanded into *The Diversions of Purley*. After four years of study Dunning was called to the bar, and for five weary years after that his prospects remained in a most unpromising condition. He was a very ugly man, stunted in growth, his limbs misshapen, and his features mean. Horne Tooke used to tell a story illustrative of his personal appearance. On one occasion Thurlow wished to see him privately, and going to the coffee-house he frequented, asked the waiter if Mr. Dunning were there. The waiter, who was new to the place, said he did not know him. "Not know him!" exclaimed Thurlow with his usual volley of oaths. "Go into the room upstairs, and if you see a gentleman like the knave of clubs, call him down." The waiter departed, and returned with Dunning.

On one occasion he was retained in an assault case, and his object was to disprove the identity of the person named by an old woman as the aggressor. Abandoning his usual overbearing demeanour towards witnesses, he commenced his cross-examination thus, mildly :—

"Pray, my good woman, what sized man was he?"

"Short and stumpy, sir; almost as small as your honour."

"Humph! What sort of a nose had he?"

"Well now, what I should ca' a snubby nose, like your own, sir, only not quite so cocked up like."

"Humph! His eyes?"

"He'd gotten a bit o' a cast in 'em, sir, like your honour's squint."

"Go down, woman. That will do."

Presently affairs took a turn. Dunning worked his way into notice by adopting violent radical or democratical views, and became the friend of the notorious Wilkes, who also had a squint, and he acted as junior counsel in the famous prosecution of the publishers of No. 45 of the *North Briton*, which contained strictures on the speech from the throne, at the close of the session of 1763. It was in this case that Dunning firmly established his reputation as a close and subtle reasoner, and he could ever calculate on being employed by his party. From this date no member of the bar obtained a larger number of briefs. I have already told, in my *Old Country Life*, a story illustrative of the way in which he managed the defence of a man on trial for murder. In 1766 he won the recordership of Bristol, he was appointed Solicitor-General in 1767, and in the general election of 1768 he was elected member for Calne.

"Among the new accessions to the House of

Commons at this juncture," writes Lord Mahon, "by far the most eminent in ability was John Dunning. . . . He was a man both of quick parts and strong passions; in his politics a zealous Whig. As an orator, none ever laboured under greater disadvantages of voice and manner; but these disadvantages were most successfully retrieved by his wondrous powers of reasoning, his keen invective, and his ready wit. At the trial of the Duchess of Kingston for bigamy, when he appeared as counsel against her Grace, Hannah More, who was present, thus describes him : ' His manner is insufferably bad, coughing and spitting at every word, but his sense and expression pointed to the last degree. He made her Grace shed bitter tears.'" The mode in which he used his hands was absurd as it was peculiar. He drew them whilst speaking up close together to the height of his breast, where he rested his wrists, and kept up a continual paddling with his outspread palms, moving them with a rapidity corresponding to the motion of his tongue. It was said that he looked on such occasions like a flat fish hung up in a fishmonger's shop, the body rigid, but the fins in front vibrating up and down unceasingly.

In 1769 Dunning bought the manors of Spitchwick and Widecombe. "Manors in Devonshire!" exclaimed Jack Lee. "A pity, Dunning, you should have them there, and should bring no manners with you to Westminster."

In 1770 he resigned his position as Solicitor-General, and resumed his old position outside the bar, but with a professional income estimated at the then unprecedented sum of £10,000 per annum.

He was now on the Opposition benches in the House. In the hot debates on the American War, Dunning steadfastly advocated a policy of conciliation. An instance of Dunning's sharpness of repartee was afforded when Chatham moved an address to the Crown in favour of this policy. The motion was upheld by Lords Shelburne, Camden, and Rockingham, and they were supported by the vote of the Duke of Cumberland. His Royal Highness was one day complimenting Dr. Price on a pamphlet he had written in favour of the Americans. "I sat up reading it last night," said he, "till it had almost blinded me." "On the rest of the nation, your Royal Highness," said Dunning, who stood by, "the pamphlet has had the opposite effect. It has opened their eyes."

John Dunning was nearly fifty years old when he married. His choice was Elizabeth Baring, daughter of John Baring, of Larkbeare, one of the many woollen merchants then flourishing in Exeter, and sister of the founders of the great house of Baring Brothers. He was married to her in 1780.

His honeymoon must have been short, for exactly one week after his marriage Dunning brought forward in Committee of the House of Commons his famous motion, "That it is the opinion of this Committee that the influence of the Crown has increased, is increasing, and ought to be diminished." After a fierce debate he succeeded in carrying his motion by a majority of eighteen.

On the 15th March, 1782, a motion of want of confidence, though negatived by a majority of nine, proved fatal to the Administration, and the Premier resigned. Then, after twelve years passed in "the cold shade of opposition," the Whigs were again in power; and one of the first steps taken by the Marquess of Rockingham, who now became Prime Minister, was to reward John Dunning with a coronet. His patent of nobility bore date April 8th, 1782, and thus the misshapen but clever son of the little Ashburton attorney became the first Baron Ashburton. None when in opposition had denounced more vigorously, and with greater display of righteous indignation, the bestowal of pensions on a large scale; but no sooner had he passed out of the Opposition into place than he exacted for himself the enormous pension of £4000 per annum, a sum to him quite unnecessary, as he had amassed a huge fortune.

By this time, however, his health had begun to fail, and he died on August 18th, 1783, of paralysis, leaving a son, Richard Barré Dunning, to succeed him in the title, and to inherit a fortune of £180,000. The second Lord Ashburton married a daughter of William Cunninghame, of Lambshaw, and through her became allied with the Cranstoun family, to whom a large portion of his ample possessions passed at his death without issue in 1823.

Ashburton, in the Tudor period, seems to have possessed a school of wood-carving. The Church-wardens' Book shows that much work was done in

the church between 1515 and 1525. An Exeter
man named John Mayne was then employed in
wood-carving, but there were Ashburton workmen
as well. There was then erected a very fine screen.
The rood-loft was removed in 1539, but not the
screen itself till last century, when portions of it
became the property of private persons, and others
were laid as foundations to the galleries.

The side chapels seem also to have been screened
in ; and there was one Thomas Prideaux who was
a liberal contributor to the beautification of the
church. In one of the side chapels was a rich,
canopied altar-piece with wings. When the chan-
tries and chapels were destroyed, this was carried
away by the son, Robert Prideaux, and employed
for the decoration of his room. The central piece
of the triptych has been lost, but the wings and
the canopy remain. Some of the wood-carving of
Henry the Seventh's reign in and about Ashburton
is of the very finest quality, quite unsurpassed in
its style. Work by apparently the same hand may
be seen at Fulford in the hall.

In Ashburton stands a quaint slated house-front
with the pips on cards cut in slate ornamenting the
front. The old ring to which the bull was attached
for baiting still remains where was the ancient bull-
ring of the town. Ashburton was, as already said,
originally composed of two manors—one royal, the
other episcopal—and each had its portreeve. The
King's Bridge united them, and the river divided one
from the other. This was a relic of pre-Saxon times,
when the chief of the land and the ecclesiastical

chief had their separate establishments. At a later period Ashburton passed wholly into the hands of the Bishop of Exeter. Bishop Oldham, 1504–1519, was a benefactor to the church, and gave it a lectern with an owl, his symbol, supporting the desk. This owl was sold to Bigbury, along with the handsome pulpit. Holne pulpit is very similar to that formerly in Ashburton.

The church of Ashburton has been renovated, and is now very stately and beautiful. It is to be regretted that the architect, the late Mr. Street, was superior to restoring the screen from the fragments that remained, and instead evolved one out of his inner consciousness, quite out of character with the church, and entirely different in feeling from the work common throughout the neighbourhood, which is exquisite in beauty of design and in detail. But such is the way with architects. The Arlers of Gmünd designed Milan Cathedral, but were not allowed to complete it; it was given to sixteen different Italian architects to meddle with and to muddle it; the result is that the exterior is a bit of miserable frippery in marble. Happily the original design for the interior was not interfered with.

But something incomparably worse may be seen near Ashburton, in the interior of Bickington.

Ilsington Church retains a few poppy-head benches of rich work, unique in the county.

In Ilsington is Ingsdon, once the seat of the Pomeroy family, but no relics of the ancient house remain. According to tradition, the Pomeroy ancestor was jester to Robert the Magnificent, father of William the Conqueror. He was a dwarf, full of comical movements as well as of quips and quirks. As he came in with the dessert he was called Pomme-roy, the Apple King. His son became a faithful servant of William, and was rewarded by him with large manors in Devon and Somersetshire. A junior branch was settled at Ingsdon. The tradition is of course groundless, as the family derived from a place Pomeraye in Normandy, near Bayeux. It probably originated with a family tendency to jest, and to a certain grotesqueness of appearance. It is told by Miss Strickland in her *History of the Queens of England.* But the odd circumstance about it is that there are Pomeroys now in and about Ashburton of humble degree—the children, the plague of the schoolmaster and mistresses, as they are born humourists, and withal have such a droll appearance and expression as to inevitably provoke mirth.

Holne Church has a good painted screen, and the parsonage is the house in which Charles Kingsley was born. The view of the winding of the Dart from the parsonage garden is beautiful.

Dean Prior was long the place to which poor Robert Herrick was banished. He did not love it, nor did he relish the rude ways of his parishioners. It is to be feared he did not labour very hard to better them. He was buried here in the churchyard in 1674. Here also was laid his servant "Prue," recorded in his poems. Her burial is entered in the register as that of "Prudence Balden, an olde maid," and Herrick's trust that the violet might blossom on her grave is perhaps not unfulfilled, although her grassy mound is not now known.

The Abbey of Buckfast is within an easy walk, and should on all accounts be visited. It is the earliest foundation in Devon, going back to long before the Conquest, in fact no documents exist to show when it was founded. " Mr. Brooking Rowe has suggested that Buckfast Abbey probably existed before the coming of the Northmen; that would be before A.D. 787. It may be so, but, at least, it must be grouped with Bodmin and Glastonbury Abbey as one of a trio of monastic churches which had property in Devon before King Edgar's time, and is probably, with the exception of Exeter, the only monastery before that time existing in the county. Its extreme antiquity may be inferred from the fact that Buckfast itself was never assessed." That is, at the taking of Domesday.

Now I have an idea concerning it. Two of its churches were Harford and South Brent, and both are dedicated to S. Petrock. We find S. Petrock again, further down the Dart, at its mouth. Where we find a Celtic dedication, there we may be pretty certain that either the saint founded the church, or that it was given to him, not necessarily in his lifetime.

In Celtic monasteries, when a grant was made, it was not made to the community, but to the saint personally, who was supposed never to die, and all the lands and churches granted became his personal property. Now, as we find two of the churches belonging to this venerable abbey bearing S. Petrock's name, I think it quite possible that the original abbey may have been, like that of Padstow, a foundation of S. Petrock. When, however, the abbey was re-endowed and recast, and occupied by monks belonging to the Latin orders, S. Petrock would be ignored at Buckfast, and the only indication left of his having once owned the whole territory of Buckfast would be the lingering on of his name in some of the churches that belonged to that same territory.

I am not sure that we have not hard by traces of other Celtic saints, S. Wulvella in Gulwell, a Holywell at Ashburton, and her brother S. Paul of Leon at Staverton, though now supplanted by Paul the Apostle.

Buckfast Abbey, after having been given over to the wreckers, has been purchased by French Benedictines, expelled from France in 1882, and they are carefully rebuilding the abbey on its old lines, following all the details as turned up among the ruins. The foundations of the church have been uncovered, and show that it was of great size. It was pulled down in 1806, and the materials employed in the construction of a factory.

Staverton Church is deserving a visit because of its superb screen, that has been most carefully restored. It exhibits a screen complete in all its parts, a thing very rare. Most of these lack what was their crowning glory, the upper member. Indeed there is but one completely intact in the county—Atherington, if we except the stone screen at Exeter.

There are other screens in the neighbourhood; that of Buckland has on it some unexplained paintings.

The Celt was never a builder. His churches were rude to the last degree of rudeness. But what he delighted in was wattle-work, interlacing osiers into the most intricate and beautiful and varied designs. We may conjecture that our Celtic forefathers did not concern themselves much about the stonework of their churches, and concentrated all their efforts on a screen dividing chancel from nave, which with platting and interweaving they made into a miracle of loveliness. And this direction given to decoration hung on in Devon and Cornwall, and resulted in the glorious screens. For them, to contain them, the shells were built. Everything was sacrificed to them, and when they are swept away what remains is nakedness, disproportion, and desolation.

Of the excursions in the neighbourhood of Ashburton to scenes of loveliness I will say but little. Yet let me recommend one of singular beauty—it is called Dr. Blackall's Drive. The Tavistock road is taken till the Dart is passed at New Bridge, then after a steep ascent the highway is abandoned before Pound Gate is reached, and a turf drive runs above the Dart commanding its gorge, the Holne coppice, and Benjie Tor, and the high road is rejoined between Bell Tor and Sharp Tor. This excursion may be combined with a drive through Holne Chase, if taken on a day when the latter is open to the public.

Holne Chase, however, should be seen from both sides of the Dart, as the aspects are very different on the two sides.

Hembury and Holne Chase camps are both fine,

and deserve investigation. They commanded and defended the entrance to the moor from this side. Widecombe has been spoken of under the head of Moreton.

Bovey should be visited, with its fine church and screen and painted and gilt stone pulpit, and with the Bovey Heathfield potteries.

Bovey was one of the manors of the De Tracy who was a principal hand in the murder of Thomas à Becket, and it is to this ambitious and turbulent prelate that the church is dedicated. The story goes that William de Tracy built the church at Bovey as penance for his part in the murder; but the church constructed by him was burnt about 1300, and was rebuilt in the Perpendicular style. The story was diligently propagated that De Tracy died on his way to the Holy Land, in a frenzy, tearing his flesh off his bones with his teeth and nails, and shrieking, " Mercy, Thomas, mercy! " But, as a matter of fact, no judgment of God fell on the murderers. Within four years after the murder, De Tracy was justiciary of Normandy. The present Lord Wemyss and Lord Sudeley are his lineal descendants. The pedigree, contrary to all received opinions on the subject of " judgments " on sacrilege, exhibits the very singular instance of an estate descending for upwards of seven hundred years in the male line of the same family. Fitzurse, another of the murderers, went to Ireland, and became the ancestor of the McMahon family.

There are some curious pictures on the Bovey screen which are supposed to have reference to the story of Becket and his quarrels with the king.

Chudleigh is at some distance, but it is worth a visit, partly because of the good screen in the church, but mainly because of the very pretty ravine through which the Kate (*Cad*, fall) tumbles. The rock here is of limestone, a fine and beautiful marble, and in its face is a cavern supposed to be haunted by the Pixies, with a stalagmite floor that was broken up by Dr. Buckland in 1825, and the soil beneath it examined in the slip-shod, happy-go-lucky style usual with explorers of that period. It deserves to be reinvestigated systematically.

NOTE.—Books and articles on Ashburton :—

WORTHY (C.), *Ashburton and its Neighbourhood*. Ashburton, 1875.

AMERY (P. F. S.), Articles already noticed in the *Transactions of the Devonshire Association*, 1876 and 1896.

CHAPTER XV.

TAVISTOCK

CERTAIN towns tell you at a glance what was
their *raison d'être;* Tavistock has clustered
about its abbey, that lay low near its fish-ponds,
whereas Launceston clings about its castle, that
stood high to command the country round.

Very possibly the original Saxon stockade was
where still some earthworks remain, above the South
Western Railway, but the centre of life moved thence
on account of the fancy coming into the head of
Ordulf, Earl of Devon, to found an abbey by the
waterside in the valley beneath him. The legend,
as told in a cartulary summarised in Dugdale's
Monasticon, is that, in the reign of Edgar, Ordulf
was one night praying in the open air, when he saw
a pillar of fire brighter than the sun at noon hovering
where now anyone, on any day, may see a lowering
cloud of smoke. That same night an angel bade

him go forth at dawn and explore the spot where
he had seen the fire, and then build an oratory to
the four evangelists. I think I can explain the vision.
The farmer was " swaling." At a certain period a
good many pillars of fire may be seen about
Tavistock, when either the furze is being burnt, or
the farmers are consuming the " stroil "—the weeds
from their fields. So I do not reject the story
as altogether fabulous, but as " improved." What
Ordulf had a mind to do was to establish a monastery for the comfort of his soul, having, I doubt not,
bullied and maltreated the poor Britons without com-
punction. His father had had a mind the same way,
but had died without performing what was his intent.

Next day Ordulf went to the spot where he had
seen the fire, and there beheld four stakes, marking
out the ground, and this fact confirms me in my
opinion. For it was the custom of the natives thus to
indicate the bounds of their fields. The stakes were
called *termons*. In like manner miners indicated their
setts by cutting four turves annually at the limits
of their grounds.

Ordulf now set to work and erected an oratory
with buildings for an abbot and brethren, and he
gave them of his inheritance Tavistock, Milton,
Hatherleigh, Burrington, Rumonsleigh, Linkinhorne,
Dunethem, and Chuvelin, which I cannot identify.
He also bestowed on the monastery his wife's dower.

When the monastic church was built he moved
to it the bones of his father, mother, and brother,
and after his death was there laid himself.

However, before he graced it with his own relics,

he transferred to it the remains of S. Rumon or Ruan (960), who, if we may judge from some place-names, had been there at a considerably earlier period as a missionary; for there is near Meavy a Roman's cross, and between Tavistock and Bere Ferrers is Romansleigh, and on the Tamar Rumleigh.

The saint reposed in the church of Ruan Lani-horne (Llan-ruan) in Cornwall, but Ordulf did not scruple to rob a mere West Welsh church to give honour and glory to one of his own founding.

Rumon was by no means a saint with a name and not a story. He had been a convert of S. Patrick, a Scot of Ireland. As I shall say something con-cerning him when we come to his field of labours in the Lizard district, I will say no more about them here.

Ordgar, Earl of Devon, was father of the beautiful Elfrida, who accordingly was sister of Ordulf. Her story, though tolerably well known, must not be passed over here.

King Edgar was a little man, but thought a good deal of himself—a merciful dispensation of Provi-dence accorded to little men to make up for their lack of inches. He was of a warm complexion. He once carried off a nun from her convent, and was repri-manded for it by S. Dunstan, who forbade him for this disreputable act to wear his crown for seven years. His first wife was Ethelfleda, called the Duck —Duckie, doubtless, by her husband—and after her death he looked out for another, as is an infirm way that widowers have.

Edgar, hearing that Elfrida, daughter of Ordgar,

was the loveliest woman in England, with a true
Devonshire complexion of cream and heather-bloom,
sent Ethelwald, Earl of the East Angles, to interview
her before he committed himself. Ethelwald no
sooner saw her than he was a "gone coon," and
he asked the hand of Elfrida from her brother.
Having received his consent, he hurried back to the
king and told him that the lady was much over-
rated, that her chief beauty lay in her wealth ; as her
only brother Ordulf was childless, she had expectations of coming in for his fortune when it should
please Providence, and so on.

So, as though looking only to her expectations,
Ethelwald asked the king to give him the lady.
Edgar yielded his consent, and Ethelwald married
Elfrida, and became by her the father of a boy whom
he persuaded the king to take as his god-child, and
to whom he gave the name of Edgar. Then Ethelwald was glad, for he knew that according to the
laws of the Church, they had contracted a spiritual
relationship which would prevent the king from ever
marrying Elfrida and removing himself, the obstacle
which stood in the way should he contemplate an
union.

Now the report reached the king that he had been
"done," done out of the loveliest woman in Christendom, and the little man ruffled up and became fiery
red, and vowed he would a-hunting go, and hunt in
the royal chase of Dartmoor. So he sent word to
Ethelwald that he purposed visiting him at his Castle
of Harewood, and solicited a bed and breakfast.

Harewood is situated on a tongue of land about

which the Tamar makes a great loop—at one time assuredly a very strong camp ; then it became a gentleman's place, now it is a ruin.

Ethelwald felt uneasy. He told his wife the story of the deception he had practised, which shows how soft and incapable of dealing with women he was. Then he went on to ask of her the impossible—to disguise her beauty. As if any woman would do that !

But when Elfrida knew the story she also ruffled up, not a little, and made a point of dressing herself in her most costly array, braiding her lovely hair with jewels, and washing her pretty face in milk and *eau de*—elder-flowers. Edgar became madly enamoured, and to boot furious with the man who had deceived him.

As they were together one day hunting, and were alone, the king smote Ethelwald with a javelin so that he died, and he took Elfrida to be his wife ; and to expiate his peccadillo, erected a convent in the Harewood forest.

Edgar died in 975, and he was but thirty-two years old when he died.

Now, is there any truth in this story ?

The tale comes to us from Geoffrey Gaimar and from William of Malmesbury, and their accounts do not quite tally, for Gaimar makes the king send off the obnoxious husband to the wars, to fall by the hand of the rebels in Yorkshire, and this looks like a cooking-up of the story of David and Uriah. On the other hand, William of Malmesbury's tale smells somewhat of an English version of the story in the Nibelungenlied of Sigurd and Kriemhild.

Both historians certainly drew from ballads, but these ballads were the vehicle through which history in early times was preserved. It has been supposed that the Harewood in question was Harewood near Leeds, in Yorkshire, but surely Elfrida would be on her inheritance in the West. Another difficulty is that there was no convent of nuns near the place. But this may have been thrown in as a sort of moral to the tale—if kings or other men do naughty things, they will have to pay for it.

Tavistock Abbey had some men of rare ability to rule over it. One was Aylmer, chosen in 981, who lived in difficult times, when the Vikings came and harried the coasts, ran up the rivers, and plundered and burned wherever they went. When the Danes were spoiling the land, driving off the cattle and burning the farms, he gave out of the revenues of the abbey a double danegeld or contribution for the relief of those in distress. But presently his own abbey was surrounded, pillaged, and burnt. This was in 997, by a horde that had first landed at Watchet, and then returned round the Land's End, and had run up the Tamar. They went as far as Lydford, and burnt and slew everything and every person they could lay hands on.

But a far abler man was Lyfing, afterwards Bishop of Worcester, and at the same time of Devon and Cornwall.

Another admirable man was Aldred, who succeeded Lyfing in the see of Worcester in 1046, after having been Abbot of Tavistock fourteen years ; and he was made Archbishop of York in 1060, and died in 1069, broken-hearted at the misery that came in the wake of the Conquest. The lives of both these men, showing how to steer a difficult course in a troubled sea among many rocks, are worth a study, and for that I refer the reader to Mr. Alford's *Abbots of Tavistock*. (Plymouth, 1891.)

The Abbey Church of Tavistock was second only to Exeter for size and dignity in the West. It has completely disappeared, and the road in front of the Bedford Hotel now runs over what was the nave of the great church.

Where now stands the hotel was in ancient days the Saxon school; it was pulled down in 1736, when the inn, then the house of the Dukes of Bedford, was erected on its site and out of its materials.

The parish church is large, in the Perpendicular style, and somewhat uninteresting. But it must be remembered that the Devon and Cornish churches were built with intent to have their chancels and side chapels cut off by a very rich screen. Such a screen did once exist at Tavistock, and were it in place and complete, the church would at once appear well proportioned. It looks now unfurnished, like a railway station. It was repaired in 1845, and for the period the work was really marvellously well done. The carved oak benches were faithful copies of those in Bere Ferrers Church, and there was no scamping in the material. The new glass in the windows ranges from very good to execrably bad. Some objects of interest connected with the history of the church, among these the reputed thigh-bones of Ordgar and Ordulf, are preserved.

There is a fine monument to John Fitz, who died in 1590. Opposite it is one of Judge Glanville, Serjeant-at-Law in 1589 and Justice of Common Pleas in 1598. He died July 27th, 1600. He had by his wife a fair family. Now here comes in a question of some interest.

The current tradition is that one of Glanville's daughters, Eulalia by name, was married to a John Page, whom she murdered, and for the crime she was sentenced to be burned alive; which sentence was carried into effect in 1590 at Barnstaple.

I will give the story as contained in a letter by Mr. Daniel Lysons, author of the *Magna Britannia*, in 1827 :—

"The Judge's daughter was attached to George Stanwich, a young man of Tavistock, lieutenant of a man-of-war, whose letters, the father disapproving of the attachment, were intercepted. An old miser of Plymouth, of the name of Page, wishing to have an heir to disappoint his relatives, who perhaps were too confident in calculating upon sharing his wealth, availed himself of this apparent neglect of the young sailor, and settling on her a good jointure, obtained her hand. She took with her a maidservant from Tavistock, but her husband was so penurious that he dismissed all the other servants, and caused his wife and her maid to do all the work themselves. On an interview subsequently taking place between her and Stanwich, she accused him of neglecting to write to her, and then discovered that his letters had been intercepted. The maid advised them to get rid of the old gentleman, and Stanwich at length, with great reluctance, consented to their putting an end to him.

Page lived in what was afterwards the Mayoralty House (at Plymouth), and a woman who lived opposite hearing at night some sand thrown against a window, thinking it was her own, arose, and looking out, saw a young gentleman near Page's window, and heard him say, 'For God's sake stay your hand!' A female replied, ''T is too late; the deed is done.' On the following morning it was given out that Page had died suddenly in the night, and as soon as possible he was buried. On the testimony, however, of his neighbour, the body was taken up again, and it appearing that he had been strangled, his wife, Stanwich, and the maid were tried and executed. It is current among the common people here that Judge Glanville, her own father, pronounced the sentence."

That sentence would be one for petty treason, burning alive. It was not till 1790 that the law requiring women to be burnt alive for putting to death their husbands or their masters was repealed. A woman was so burnt in 1789. A poor girl of fifteen was burnt at Heavitree, near Exeter, on July 29th, 1782, for poisoning her master. Eulalia Page and her servant were actually executed at Barnstaple and George Stanwich was hanged. All that is certain. But the question about which a difficulty arises is— Was Eulalia a daughter of Judge Glanville?

There is a contemporary tract that contains an account of the transaction, which was reprinted by Payne Collier.* From this we learn that Mrs. Page having failed in an attempt to poison her husband, prevailed on one of her servants, named Robert Priddis (Prideaux), to assist her, and on the other

* *Bibliographical Catalogue of Early English Literature*, 1865, ii. pp. 83-6.

side Strangwich (Standwich) hired one Tom Stone
to assist in the murder.

The deed was accomplished about ten o'clock on
the night of February 11th, 1591, and all four were
tried at Barnstaple, whither the assizes had been
moved from Exeter because the plague was raging
in the latter city, and were executed on March 20th
following. Philip Wyot, town clerk of Barnstaple,
kept a diary at the time, extracts from which have
been printed. He gives some particulars:—"The
gibbet was sat up on the Castle Green and xviij
prisoners hanged, whereof iiij of Plimouth for a
murder." These four were the murderers of Page.
How it was that Ulalia was hanged instead of being
burnt, in contravention of the law, does not appear,
and we may doubt the statement. Three of those
hanged were buried in the churchyard at Barnstaple,
but Ulalia Page was laid in that of Bishops Tawton.
Now as to the statement that Judge Glanville sentenced his own daughter.

In the first place, *was* she his daughter? It
appears not; for from the tract already referred to,
"in the town of Testock (Tavistock) . . . there
dwelled one Mr. Glandfield (Glanville), a man of
good wealth and account as any occupier in that
cuntrie," whose daughter Eulalia was; and she set
her affections on George Strangwich, who was in
her father's employ. Mr. Glanville, of Tavistock,
almost certainly was a near relative of the judge.
The Glanvilles were tanners of Whitchurch, in trade,
but the family was respectable. They have been
given a fanciful pedigree from a Norman Lord of

Glanville near Caen, but it is deficient in proof.
What is clear is that the family occupied a respectable position near Tavistock in the reign of
Elizabeth; they had their tan pits, and they went
into trade without scruple. In fact, John Glanville,
father of the judge, was himself a merchant, *i.e.*,
shopkeeper in Tavistock. That Eulalia was a *sister*
of the judge is possible enough. That her name
was not inserted in the pedigree as recorded in the
Herald's Visitation may easily be understood.*

The next point is—Did Judge Glanville preside
at the trial?

Now we are informed by E. Foss (*Biographia
Juridica*, 1870, p. 303) that Glanville "was promoted
to the bench as a Justice of the Common Pleas on
June 30th, 1598." Consequently he was not a judge
at the time that Eulalia Page was tried. The judge
who tried the case, as we learn from Wyot's diary,
was Lord Anderson. Nevertheless, Glanville was
present at Barnstaple at the assizes, for Wyot men-
tions him as Serjeant Glandye, who was one of the
principal lawyers present, and he had been "called
to the degree of the coif," Ford records, two years
before. So, as far as we can discover :—

1. Eulalia was very probably *sister* of Judge
Glanville, she being daughter of a merchant Glanville, of Tavistock, as he was son of one.

2. That she really was executed for the murder
of her husband, Page, along with her lover, George
Strangwich, and two assistants.

* Glandfeelde is the same as Glanville ; so in the Tavistock register,
Grenville is entered as Greenfeelde.

3. That Strangwich had not been in the Navy, but was a shop assistant of Mr. Glanville.

4. That John Glanville, Serjeant - at - Law, presumably her brother, was present at the trial, but was not judge at the time.

The tragic story was not only turned into ballads, but also was dramatised by Ben Jonson and Decker. In Halliwell's *Dictionary of Old English Plays* (1860) is this entry :—

"Page, of Plymouth. A play by Ben Johnson and Decker, written in 1599, upon the story of the murder of one Page at Plymouth."*

A little way out of the town on the Plymouth road, by the Drake statue, is the gateway of old Fitzford House. About this a good deal of both history and legend hangs.

The house was that of old John Fitz, whose splendid monument is in Tavistock Church. Late in life he had a son of the name also of John, an only child, whose story is tragical. The heir was fourteen only when he lost his father. John Fitz, who was "a very comely person," was married before he had attained his majority to a daughter of Sir William Courtenay. Of this marriage one child, Mary, was born in 1596, when her father was just twenty-one years old.† The young gentleman being now of age, and finding

* Dr. Brushfield has sifted the whole story in the pages of *The Western Antiquary*, ix., p. 35.

† The story of John Fitz and of Lady Howard has been worked out very carefully by Mrs. George Radford, to whose paper in the *Transactions of the Devonshire Association*, 1890, I am much indebted for what follows.

himself free from all restraint, began to live a very rackety life for three years, when an incident happened that ought to have sobered him. What follows is quoted, condensed, from *The Bloudie Booke: or The Tragical End of Sir John Fitz.* London, 1605.

" Meeting (June 4th, 1599) at Tavistocke a dinner wyth manie of his neighbors and friends, with great varietie of merriments and discourse they outstript the noontide. Amongst other their table-talk Sir John (he was not knighted at the time) was vanting his free Tenure in holding his lande, boasting that he helde not a foote of any but the Queene in England ; to whoome Mayster Slanninge replyed, that although of ceurtesie it were neglected, yet of dewe hee was to paye him so muche by the yeere for some small lande helde of him ; uppon which wordes Sir John told him with a great oath he lyed, and withall gave fuell to his rage, offering to stab him. But Maister Slanning with a great knife warded the hazard."

Friends intervened and the quarrel was patched up, so that presently Slanning left and departed for his home at Bickleigh. He had not gone very far before, dismounting, he bade his man take the horses along the road, whilst he walked by a short cut across the fields.

At that moment he heard the tramp of horses, and saw John Fitz and four more galloping after him. So as not to seem to be running away Slanning remained on the spot, and on John Fitz coming up asked what he wanted. Fitz drew his sword and raved that he would revenge the insult offered him, and Slanning was forced to defend himself. He was wounded, and someone struck Slanning from behind, whereupon he staggered forwards and Fitz ran him through the body. Local tradition, and Prince in his *Worthies*, will have it that the affray took place at Fitzford Gate.

Nicolas Slanning was buried in Bickleigh Church, which, when " restored " and made desperately uninteresting, lost the great feature of Slanning's monument, which was fine, though of plaster. Now the inscription alone remains :

" Great was the lamentation that the country side made for the death of so beloved a Gentleman as Maister Slanning was."

John Fitz, then aged twenty-four, fled to France, where he remained until, by his wife's exertions, a pardon was procured for him, December 16th, 1599.

He returned home, and for a year or two led a blameless life — at least he did not murder any more of his friends—and at the coronation of King James I. was knighted.

Whether the honour conferred on him was too much for him, or whether there was a mad strain in his blood, cannot be said, but on his return from London he broke out into wild ways again. Finding the presence of his wife and only child a restraint on him, he turned them out of the house, and surrounded himself with dissolute companions, chief among whom was " Lusty Jacke, one whose deedes were indeed meane, whose good qualities altogether none."

In the summer of 1605 he received a summons to London to appear before the courts, in answer to a claim of compensation for their father's death made by the children of Nicolas Slanning. He set out attended by a single servant. He was a prey to terrors, particularly afraid of his father-in-law, Sir William Courtenay, who he knew was very incensed with him because of his behaviour to his wife, the daughter of Sir William. He had moreover been squandering money which had been settled on her by deed. Every day his fancies got more disordered, till he put up at Kingston-on-Thames, his last resting-place before reaching London ; but there, a prey to alarms and fancies, he would not lie, and rode on to Twickenham, where he stopped at "The Anchor," a small hostelry kept by one Daniel Alley, whom he roused out of his bed about 2 a.m. The host, to accommodate him, was forced to surrender to him his own bed, and send his wife to sleep with the children. But the knight could not rest after he had lain down, and was heard crying out that he was pursued by enemies.

Very early, the host rose that he might go out and mow a field, but his wife entreated him not to leave the house. He laughed at her alarms, but she persisted, and a neighbour who was going to help in the mowing came in. Sir John Fitz started out of sleep on hearing voices, and persuaded that his fears were verified, rushed from his room in his nightgown, with his sword, and ran Alley through the body. He then wounded the unhappy wife, and finding the error into which he had fallen, finally mortally wounded himself. A doctor was sent for, but he tore off the bandages, and so died, lamented of none save Lusty Jack.

No sooner was he dead than the Earl of Northumberland hastened to buy the wardship of the little
heiress, Mary Fitz, then nine years and one week old.
At the time the Crown became the guardian of
orphans whose lands were held *in capite* or direct
from the Crown, and was wont to sell the wardships
to the highest bidders. The guardian had complete
control, to the exclusion of the mother, over the
ward, and he could marry the ward as he liked, this
also being generally an affair of money. As soon as
Mary Fitz was twelve, the Earl, as she was a desirable heiress, disposed of her to his brother, Sir Allan
Percy, aged thirty-one; she did not, however, live
with her husband, but was placed under the charge
of Lady Hatton. Sir Allan died in November, 1611,
three years after, and then it was said:—"Sir Allan
Percy is gone the way of all flesh, dying, his lady the
way of all quicke flesh, having stolen out of my Lady
Eliz. Hatton's house in London, in the edge of an
evening, and coupled herself in marriage with Mr.
Darcy, my lord Darcye's eldest son." This was
on December 18th, 1611, just about a month after
the death of husband number one. He was of her
own age, and no doubt she found him to her liking;
however, he lived only a few months after his
marriage, and Lady Mary was again a widow, and
was imposed (1612), hardly by her own choice, on
Sir Charles Howard, fourth son of Thomas, Earl
of Suffolk. So she had number three when scarcely
sixteen. Sir Charles died in 1622; consequently they
were together for ten years. She had two daughters
by Sir Charles Howard, and a son, George Howard,

is mentioned, but there is some doubt as to his parentage. In 1628 she took a fourth, Sir Richard Grenville, the younger brother of the gallant Sir Bevil. He was a very disreputable, bad-tempered, altogether ill-conditioned fellow. Lady Howard took good care, before accepting number four, to have her property well tied up to herself, so that he could not touch it. When he discovered this he was furious, and treated her with insolence and violence. By him she had two daughters, Elizabeth, who died early, and Mary.

The condition of family broil became at last so intolerable that she was forced to appeal to the justices of peace against him, and finally to endeavour to obtain a divorce, 1631–2. The re-velations then made on both sides are not pleasant reading. If he was abusive, she did not keep her tongue shut behind her teeth.

The story of her further troubles during the Civil War, of Sir Richard's playing fast and loose with one party and then the other, of his masterful seizure of her house at Fitzford and her estates in Devon, need not here be told at length. She lived in London, and was put to desperate shifts for money. At last Sir Richard was thrown into prison, but escaped to France, 1646. Lady Grenville, or as she now called herself—for she held herself to be divorced—Lady Howard, at once returned to Fitzford, found it gutted and in a wretched condition, and set to work to cleanse, repair, and refurnish. Her son, George Howard, managed her business for her till his death in September, 1671, without issue. His mother, at this date very old, was probably bedridden ; the shock of her son's death was too much for her, and she died a month later. Knowing her to be ill, her first cousin, Sir William Courtenay, hastened to her bedside, and, probably with the connivance of a trusted maid, Thomasine Wills, persuaded the old lady to make over to him all her landed estates, to the exclusion of her two daughters, who were alive and married. It was an infamous piece of roguery, and it brought no luck on the Courtenays.

Popular feeling was outraged and has revenged itself on her, who really was not so much to blame as Sir William Courtenay, in painting her in the blackest colours. She is popularly represented as having murdered her first three husbands, as conceiving a deadly hatred against her daughter Elizabeth, who apparently died early, but cannot be traced, and as not exactly *walking* but *riding* after death. When the clock strikes twelve every night she is supposed to start in a coach made of bones from the gateway of Fitzford House, drawn by headless horses ; before the carriage runs a sable hound with one eye in the middle of his forehead. The spectral coach makes its way to Okehampton, where the hound plucks a blade of grass from the castle mound, and then the *cortège* returns to Fitzford, where the blade is laid on the threshold of the gate. This is Lady Howard's penance, and it will last till every blade of grass on the mound of Okehampton Castle hill has been plucked, which will not be till the crack of doom, as the grass grows faster than the hound can carry it off.

I frequently heard of the coach going from Oke-hampton to Tavistock when I was a boy; and there was a ballad about it, of which I was able to recall a few fragments, which I completed and published along with the original air in my *Songs of the West*. As a child I remember the deadly fear that I felt lest I should be on the road at night, and my nurse was wont to comfort me by saying there was no fear of the "Lady's Coach," except after midnight.

In the vicarage garden are some very early in-scribed stones collected from the neighbourhood. There is no token on them that they are Christian. Their inscriptions are :—

1. Neprani fili Condevi
2. Sabini fili Maccodecheti
3. Dobunii Fabri fili Enabarri.

This latter has on it also in oghans *Enabarr*. The second has the test word *Mac* for *Map* or *Mab*, indica-tive of Irish occupation. Moreover Dechet was a name, probably of a *sept* or tribe in Kerry, where several stones inscribed with the same name are found.*

The third is interesting, for Dobun was a *faber* or smith. In Celtic organisation every *tuatha* or tribe had its chief smith, and every *fine* or clan had its smith and forge as well, all whose rights and dues were determined by law; moreover, the head smith of the tribe was a man of very considerable consequence, social and political.

* A member of the same clan or tribe was buried at Penrhos Llygwyin, Anglesea—"*Hic jacet Maccudecheti*."

Dobuni, in the third, is the Latin for the genitive *Douvinias*, also a Kerry name. A stone at Ballintaggart bears an inscription to a son of Dobunus, MUCCOIDOVVINIAS. Another stone of another son is at Burnham, also in Kerry, in Lord Ventry's collection. Here, then, we have written and engraven in stone for our learning the record of an Irish settlement from Kerry in the neighbourhood of Tavistock. If S. Rumon preached there he could preach in Gaelic and be understood.

Of the abbey of Tavistock there are but poor remains. Betsy Grimbal's tower in the vicarage garden was a gate-house, and takes its name from a woman who was murdered there by a soldier. A porch into the refectory or abbot's hall is the dairy of the "Bedford Inn." Some fragments of the monastic buildings are united and converted into library and municipal buildings, but they are dominated and oppressed by an architectural monstrosity—an absurd Town Hall in nondescript style.

The Drake statue is of bronze, and fine, in front of the Fitzford gate, and possesses the bas-reliefs on the base, in which the *replica* on Plymouth Hoe is deficient. Sir Francis Drake was born at Crowndale, the first farm down the Tavy valley. The old house has been destroyed. The Drakes were of yeoman origin in Whitchurch, nothing more. They laboured to prove a kinship to the ancient family of Drake of Ash, but failed, and Sir Francis Drake was granted an entirely new coat of arms.

The story is told that Sir Francis and Sir Bernard, —the latter the head of the Ash family—had a heated quarrel over the matter in the presence of Queen Elizabeth, Sir Bernard objecting to the navigator assuming the wyvern gules.

"Well," said Bess, "I will give Sir Francis a new coat, a ship in full sail, with the wyvern turned head over heels at the poop."

But Sir Bernard was too important a man to be offended; she thought better of it, and gave Sir Francis the noble coat of a fess wavy between two pole stars.

The story is pronounced to be apocryphal.

Sir Francis became possessor by purchase of Buckland Abbey (1581), which is not only beautifully situated, but is interesting. It is, in fact, the cruciform abbey church converted into an Elizabethan mansion. The nave has been floored, and the drawing-room upstairs is in it; the hall below is also in part therein. There is here some splendid plasterwork. The choir was pulled down and a kitchen wing built at right angles. In the grounds are some remarkably fine tulip trees.

Buckland Monachorum Church is large, Perpendicular, but cold, and has a naked, unfurnished look internally from being without its screen.

There are two points on no account to be missed by a visitor to Tavistock, and both can be combined in one drive or walk—the Raven Rock above the Virtuous Lady Mine, opposite the point where the Walla falls into the Tavy; the other the better known Morwell Rocks. The former, hardly inferior to the other, but less known, is reached from the Bere Alston road.

At Morwell is the hunting - lodge of Abbot Courtenay, cousin of Bishop Grandisson, and appointed by him to Tavistock Abbey. It was a very unsatisfactory appointment. He alienated the property of the abbey, and allowed its buildings and discipline to fall into decay, and got the monastery into a debt equivalent to twenty thousand pounds of our money. All he cared for was sport, like the jolly monk in Chaucer's *Prologue*.

The quadrangle, which was in a singularly untouched condition, with hall and butteries and kitchens, was somewhat wantonly mutilated some fifty years ago and turned into farmhouse and cottages.

From Tavistock Lydford can be visited with ease. This was a very strong place at one time, a sort of inland cliff-castle, situated in a fork between ravines, with mounds and trenches drawn across the neck. The castle, an uninteresting ruin, occupies a natural mound artificially shaped; it was long the Stannary prison. The waterfall is graceful rather than fine, a steep slide of seventy feet in height in the midst of woods. From this the river Lyd should be ascended for three miles by a path through a ravine that grows in grandeur till it is spanned by a bridge. The ascent may well be continued to Kits Steps, another fall of a totally different character, much spoiled by refuse-heaps from an abandoned mine. From Lydford a visitor should take a walk across the shoulder of Hare Tor to the rocks of Tavy Cleave, perhaps the grandest scene on Dartmoor.

Another excursion is to be made to Brent Tor, a subaqueous volcanic cone, crowned by a little church. The base of the hill has been fortified. The banks are most perfect on the east. The view from the top of the tor is remarkably extensive and fine. Endsleigh, the country seat of the Duke of Bedford, is almost unsurpassed in England for beauty of scenery. Mary Tavy Church has a good new screen, and Peter Tavy a scrap of an old one and remains of a magnificent early Tudor pew, wantonly demolished.

From either Whit Tor may be ascended, a tor of gabbro, or volcanic traplike formation. The summit has been fortified. On Peter Tavy Moor is a fine circle of upright stones, and a menhir. Peter Tavy Combe should on no account be passed over unseen.

NOTE.—Books on Tavistock :—

ALFORD (Rev. D.), *The Abbots of Tavistock.* Plymouth, 1891.

BRAY (Mrs.), *The Borders of the Tamar and the Tavy*, 2 vols. new edition. London: Kent and Co., 1879. A valuable book for old stories and superstitions. Mr. Bray was also the first to explore Dartmoor for its antiquities. But all the rubbish about Druids must be put aside. When written in 1832 antiquaries knew no better; they talked and wrote nonsense on such subjects.

EVANS (R.), *Home Scenes; or, Tavistock and its Vicinity.* Tavistock, 1846; now not easily procured.

TORQUAY

THIS pleasant winter residence is now stretched
from Paignton on one side to Marychurch on
the other, with different climates in its several parts.
Torquay is backed by a high ridge against the east,
and consequently is sheltered from cutting winds
from that quarter. S. Marychurch is on the top of
the cliffs, and catches every wind. Paignton looks
across the bay due east, and is therefore exposed
to the most bracing of all winds. In Frying Pan
Row, Torquay, one may be grilled the same day
that at Paignton one may have one's nose and fingers
turned blue.

A century ago Torquay was a little fishing village,
numbering but a few poor cottages.

Torquay has benefited largely from the Palk family,
but then the Palks also have benefited largely by
Torquay.

A cloud of dust has been stirred up to disguise

the humble, but respectable, origin of the family; and even Foster in his *Peerage* (1882), who is always accurate when he had facts placed before him, commences with "Sir Robert Palk, descended from Henry Palk, of Ambrook, Devon (Henry VII., 1493–4)." But Ambrook, which is in Staverton, never did belong to the Palks; it was the property first of the Shapcotes, and then of the Nayles. Sir Bernard Burke, in addition to the Ambrook myth, states that Walter, seventh in descent, married Miss Abraham, and had Robert, Walter (who was member for Ashburton), and Grace. The late Sir Bernard Burke was not remarkable for accuracy, and here he has floundered into a succession of blunders. The descent from Henry Palk, of Ambrook, is apocryphal; and Walter Palk never was member for Ashburton, or for anywhere else. Another false assertion made has been that the family are descended from a Rev. Thomas Palk, of Staverton, a "celebrated" Nonconformist divine, who died in 1693. Wills proved in the Court of the Dean and Chapter of Exeter disprove this.

The real facts are these.

Walter Palk, of Ashburton, married Grace Ryder, and by her means came in for a petty farm called Lower Headborough, close to Ashburton. He died in 1707, when his personal estate was valued at £160 10s. 5½d. His son Walter married Frances, daughter of Robert Abraham, a farmer in Woodland, and his pack-horses carried serge from Ashburton over Haldon to Exeter. This is probably the origin of the story commonly told that the first Palk was a carrier between Exeter and Ashburton. He had two sons : Walter, whose son, the Rev. Jonathan Palk, vicar of Ilsington, described his father as a "little farmer with a large family." The second son, Robert, born in 1717, was sent as a sizar to Oxford, by the assistance of his uncle Abraham. He was ordained deacon, and became a poor curate in Cornwall. On Christmastide he walked to Ashburton to see his father, and as he was returning on his way home, he stood on Dart Bridge, looking down on the river, when a gentleman riding by recognised him, drew up, and said, "Is that you, Palk?" He had been a fellow-student at Oxford. Palk had a sad story to tell of privation and vexation. The other suggested to him to seek his fortune under John Company in India, and volunteered an introduction. He went out, acting as chaplain to the *Stirling Castle*, and during the time he was in India, attracted the attention of General Lawrence, who in 1752 obtained for him an appointment as paymaster to the army, of which he had then assumed the command. But already by clever speculation Mr. Palk had done well; the new position enabled him to vastly enlarge his profits.

He next embarked in trade, and this also proved remunerative. He came back to England for the first time in 1759. Subsequently a difficulty arose in India. The Company were debating it at the old East India House in Leadenhall Street. What capable man could they find to do the difficult work before them? At last one of them exclaimed, "Gentlemen, you forget that we have Mr. Palk at home." "The very man!" He was sent out as Governor of Madras in 1763. In 1775 General Lawrence died, and left £80,000 to his old *protégé*.

The acquisition of the property about Torquay, at the time when it was a place of no consideration, was a shrewd stroke of business. Mr. Palk was created a baronet, and elected to represent Devon in Parliament. Subsequently, when the Rev. John Horne Tooke, a Jacobin, as it was the fashion to call Radicals of that day, was returned to Parliament, the House settled that it would not allow of clerical members being admitted, and this would have excluded Sir Robert Palk as well as Horne Tooke, but that Palk was only in deacon's orders.

Sir Robert did much for Torquay. Sir Lawrence continued to promote the material welfare of the place in every way available.

He constructed the outer harbour and new pier, which were completed in 1870, at an outlay of £70,000. Further attractions were afforded to visitors by the provision of recreation grounds and public walks. He also gave sites for new churches, and the modern town of Torquay has risen into a place full of beauty and attraction.

"Robert Palk's touch seemed to turn everything into gold. He realised it for himself, for his children, for his relatives, for his friends, and for his surroundings. He was an ancestor to look back upon, a forefather of whom any family might reasonably be proud."*

* WORTHY, *Devonshire Parishes*, 1889, vol. ii., p. 335. Mr. Worthy has worked out the Palk pedigree from extant wills and registers.

The other family attached to Torquay to which it must look is that of Cary, as ancient and noble as that of Palk is modern and humble. The nest of the family is Cary, on the river of the same name in S. Giles-in-the-Heath, Devon, but on the borders of Cornwall. It can be traced back like those of most men to an Adam—but an Adam Cary in 1240.

Torbay is noted as the place where Dutch William arrived in 1688. He landed at Brixham on November 4th, and, as the tide was out, he called for someone to carry him ashore, whereupon a little man named Varwell volunteered.

The local story is that the good folk of Brixham presented their illustrious visitor with the following address :—

> "An' please your Majesty, King William,
> You're welcome to Brixham Quay,
> To eat buckhorn and drink Bohea
> Along wi' we,
> An' please your Majesty, King William."

But the story is of course apocryphal, as the prince was not a king, and tea was at a fabulous price.

The subsequent history of the "little man" who carried the king ashore is rather singular. Having a short ambling pony, he rode bare-headed before the prince to Newton and afterwards to Exeter, and so pleased him with his zeal that the prince bade him come to court, when he should be seated on the throne, and that then he would reward Varwell. The prince also gave him a line under his hand, which was to serve as a passport to the royal presence. In due time accordingly the little man took his course to London, promising his townsmen that he would come back among them a lord at least. When, however, he arrived there, some sharpers, who learned his errand at the tavern where he put up, made Varwell gloriously drunk, and kept him in this condition for several successive weeks. During this time one of the party, having obtained the passport, went to court, with the "little man's" tale in his mouth, and received a handsome present from the king. Our adventurer, recovering himself afterwards, went to the palace without his card of admission and was repulsed as an impostor, and returned to Brixham never to hold up his head again.

It is fair to say that the Varwell family entirely repudiate the latter part of the tale, and say that the "little man" did see the king and got a hundred pounds out of him.

The troops with the prince were obliged to encamp in the open air, but William got a lodging in one of the cottages.

Whitter, who was one of the attendants on the Dutch adventurer, has left a graphic account of the landing and subsequent march :—

"It was a cold, frosty night, and the stars twinkl'd exceedingly; besides, the ground was very wet after so much rain and ill weather; the soldiers were to stand to their arms the whole night; and therefore sundry soldiers went to fetch some old hedges and cut down green wood to burn therewith and make some fire. Those who had provision in their gnap-sacks did broil it at the fire, and others went into the villages thereabouts to buy some fresh provisions for their officers, but, alas! there was little to

be gotten. There was a little ale-house among the fishermen's houses, which was so extremely thronged that a
man could not thrust in his head, nor get bread or ale
for money. It was a happy time for the landlord, who
strutted about as if indeed he had been a lord himself."

The little ale-house is probably that now entitled
the "Buller Arms." It was there William is said
to have slept, and to have left behind him a ring that
remained in the possession of the taverner's family
till it came to one Mary Churchward, who died
about 1860. It was stolen from her one night by
a thief who entered her room whilst she slept, and
it was never recovered.

On the morrow William and his Dutchmen with a
few Scots and English marched to Paignton, and
many people, mostly Nonconformists, welcomed
him.

A gentleman, very advanced in age, in 1880
says :—

"There are few now left who can say as I can, that they
have heard their fathers and their wives' fathers talking
together of the men who saw the landing of William the
Third at Torbay. I have heard Captain Clements say
he, as a boy, heard as many as seven or eight old men
each giving the particulars of what he saw ; then one said
a shipload of horses hawled to the Quay, and the horses
walked out all harnessed, and the quickness with which
each man knew his horse and mounted it surprised them.
Another old man said, 'I helped to get on shore the horses
that were thrown overboard, and swam on shore, guided
by only a single rope running from the ship to the shore.'
My father remembered one Gaffer Will Webber, of
Staverton, who lived to a great age, say that he went

from Staverton as a boy with his father, who took a cart-load of apples from Staverton to the highroad from Brixham to Exeter, that the soldiers might help themselves to them, and to wish them 'God-speed.'

"I merely mention this to show how easily tradition can be handed down, requiring only three or four individuals for two centuries." *

What was done by the country folk was to roll apples down the slopes from the orchards to the troops as they passed.

The prince spent the second night at Paignton in a house near the "Crown and Anchor Inn," where his room is still shown.

Next day he with his troops marched to Newton, and he took up his quarters in Ford House, belonging to Sir William Courtenay, who prudently decamped so as not to compromise himself. A room there is called the Orange Room, and is now always papered and hung with that colour. At Newton the prince's proclamation was read on the steps of the old market cross, not by the Rev. John Reynell, rector of Wolborough, as is stated on a stone erected on the spot, but by a chaplain, no doubt the fussy and pushing Burnet. Reynell had also made himself scarce. From Newton the prince marched to Exeter.

One can tell pretty well what were the political leanings of squires and parsons at the period of the Jacobite troubles, for where there was zeal for the House of Stuart, there Scotch pines were planted;

* WINDEATT (T. W.), "The Landing of the Prince of Orange," in *Transactions of the Devonshire Association*, 1880.

where, however, the Dutchman was in favour, there lime trees were set in avenues.

In Torquay Museum is an interesting collection of relics from Kent's Cavern. This is a cave in the limestone rocks that was first explored in 1824, when Mr. Northmore, of Cleve, near Exeter, visited it with the double object, as he stated, "of discovering organic remains, and of ascertaining the existence of a temple of Mithras," and he declared himself happy to say that he was "successful in both objects." An amusing example this of the egregious nonsense that was regarded as antiquarianism at the beginning of this century. He was followed by Mr. (afterwards Sir) W. C. Trevelyan, who was the first to have obtained any results of scientific value.

The Rev. J. MacEnery, a Roman Catholic priest, whose name must be for ever associated with the Cavern, visited it in the summer of 1825. The visit was a memorable one, for, devoting himself to what he conjectured to be a favourable spot, he found several teeth and bones; and he thus sums up his feelings on the occasion :—

"They were the first fossil teeth I had ever seen, and as I laid my hands on them, relics of extinct races and witnesses of an order of things which passed away with them, I shrank back involuntarily. Though not insensible to the excitement attending new discoveries, I am not ashamed to own that in the presence of these remains I felt more of awe than joy."

He communicated his discovery to Dr. Buckland, and from time to time dug into the deposits. At

that and a long subsequent period the proper
method of studying deposits of this kind was not
understood, and the several layers were not
distinguished. Trenches were cut that went through
beds separated in age by many centuries, perhaps
thousands of years, and no distinction was made
between what lay near the surface and what was
found in the lowermost strata. A proper examination began in March, 1866, and was continued
without intermission through the summer of 1880
under the able direction of Mr. W. Pengelly, at a
cost of nearly two thousand pounds.

Kent's Cavern gives evidence of a double occupation by man at a remote distance of time the one
from the other. The upper beds are of cave-earth.
Below that is the breccia, and in the upper alone are
traces of the hyena found. In the lowest strata of
crystalline breccia are rude flint and chert implements
of the same type as that found elsewhere in the river-
drift. In association with these were the remains of
the cave-bear, and a tool was found manufactured
out of an already fossilised tooth of this animal. The
chert and flint employed were from the gravels that
lie between Newton Abbot and Torquay.

Above the breccia is the cave-earth, in which
flint implements are by far more numerous,
and are of a higher form, some being carefully
chipped all round. The earlier tool was fashioned
by heavy blows dealt against the core of flint,
detaching large flakes. But the tools of the second
period are neatly trimmed. The flakes were detached, very often by pressure and a jerk, and then

the edges were delicately worked with a small tool. A bone needle was also met with, and bone awls, and two harpoons of reindeer antler, the one barbed on one side and the other on both.

Rude, coarse pottery has also been found, but only quite near the surface, and this belongs to a later period.

There are other caves in the same formation, at Anstis and at Brixham, that have rendered good results when explored.

The two deposits are separated from each other by a sheet of crystalline stalagmite, in some places nearly twelve feet thick, formed after the breccia was deposited, and before the cave-earth was introduced. After the stalagmite had been formed, it was broken up by some unknown natural agency, and much of it, along with some of the breccia, was carried out by water from the cave, before the deposition of the cave-earth began.

"From these observations it is evident that the River-drift men inhabited the caves of Devonshire, Derbyshire, and Nottinghamshire in an early stage of the history of caverns, and that after an interval, to be measured in Kent's Hole by the above-mentioned physical changes, the Cave-men (those of the Second Period) found shelter in the same places. The former also followed the chase in the valley of the Elwy and the vale of Clwydd in North Wales, and the latter found ample food in the numerous reindeer, horses, and bisons then wandering over the plains extending from the Mendip Hills to the Quantocks, and the low, fertile tract now covered by the estuary of the Severn and the Irish Sea. When all these facts are taken into consideration, it is difficult to escape Mr. Pengelly's conclusion that the two sets of implements represent two distinct social states, of which the ruder is by far the most ancient." *

We have, in the caves of France, evidence of the successive layers of civilisation, one superposed on the other, down to the reindeer hunter, who ate horses, represented by the cave-earth man of Kent's Hole; and in this latter we have this same man superposed on the traces of the still earlier man of the river-drift. To make all plainer, I will add here a summary of the deposits.

Neolithic	Modern, Roman, etc. Iron Age, Celtic, bronze ornaments. Bronze weapons, Ivernian, flint tools. Flint and pottery.	Fauna, as at present.
Palaeolithic	Flint and bone tools, cave-men. Rudest flint tools, river-drift men.	Hyena, cave-bear, reindeer, mammoth.

There are remains of a cliff castle at Long Quarry Point; from its name one may conjecture that a church stood in Celtic times on Kilmarie. Almost certainly this was a cliff castle, but the traces have disappeared.

The old church of Tor Mohun is dedicated to S. Petrock, as is shown by a Bartlett will in Somerset House, in 1517. Tor Abbey has been crowded into a narrow space by encroaching buildings. Cocking-

* BOYD DAWKINS, *Early Man in Britain*, 1880, p. 197.

ton House and church deserve a visit, as forming
a charming group. Paignton Church contains a very
fine but mutilated tomb with rich canopy and screenwork, showing that there must have been in the
fifteenth century a native school of good figure
sculptors. Marldon Church is also interesting, and
in that parish is the curious Compton Castle, of
which history has little to say. Haccombe, the seat
of the Carews, has a church crowded with fine monumental effigies. The mansion is about the most
hideous that could be conceived. It is said that a
Carew pulled down his fine Elizabethan mansion and
went to Italy, leaving instructions to an architect
to build him a handsome house in the Georgian
style.

When he returned and saw what had been erected :
" Well," said he, " I believe that now I may take to
myself the credit of possessing the very ugliest
house in the county." The situation is of exquisite
beauty. How lovely must have been the scene with
a grave old Elizabethan manor-house, mottled with
white and yellow lichen, embowered in trees, above
which rose the hills, the evening sun glittering in
its many mullioned windows, while the rooks wheeled
and cawed about it.

The little combes that dip into the estuary of the
Teign, rich with vegetation growing rank out of
the red soil, are very lovely. Stoke-in-Teignhead
not only has a good screen, but it is a parish that
has never had a squire, but has been occupied
from the sixteenth century by substantial yeomen,
who have maintained themselves there against en-

croaching men of many acres. Combe-in-Teignhead
has a very fine screen and equally good old benches.

Wolborough has a good church occupying a site
that was once a camp, and contains an excellent
screen, well restored and glittering with gold and
colour. East Ogwell has also a screen, and the old
manor mill is a picturesque object for the pencil.
Denbury is a strong camp.

Torbrian, situated in a lovely spot, has fine screenwork and monuments of the Petres. The three
Wells, Coffinswell, Kingskerswell, and Abbotskerswell, lie together. At Kingskerswell are some
old monumental effigies of the Prowse family. At
Abbotskerswell are a screen, and a large statue of the
Blessed Virgin in a niche of the window splay. This
latter had been plastered over into one great bulk;
when the plaster was removed the statue was revealed.
The very fine Jacobean altar-rails were removed at
the "restoration," to make place for something utterly
uninteresting. Here there is an early and interesting
church-house. The church-house was the building
in which the parishioners from a distance spent
a rainy time between morning service and vespers.
The house was divided by a floor into two storeys,
that above for women, that below for the men.
Here were also held the church ales, that is to say,
the ale brewed by the wardens and sold to defray
church expenses. The ale was also supplied on
Sundays by the clerk to those who tarried for even-
song, and so, little by little, most of these old church-
houses degenerated into taverns.

Abbotskerswell is the seat of the Aller pottery

art manufacture, started by the late Mr. John Phillips, with the object of providing the village young men with remunerative work at their own homes. But about this presently. The story of the inception of the work is interesting.

Coffinswell still possesses its holy well, that is called the "Lady Well," used by young girls for fortune-telling.

At some little distance from this spring lies a nameless grave in unconsecrated ground, where is buried a lady banished holy ground for her sins. Every New Year's morn, after the stroke of midnight, she rises and takes "one cock's stride" towards the churchyard, which, when she reaches, she will find rest, and her hope is to be found therein—at the crack of doom.

The three well-parishes lie about the stream of the Aller (W. *allwy*, to pour forth, to stream), that flows into the Teign below Newton Abbot. But it was not always so. At some remote period, when the great Dartmoor peaks "stood up and took the morning," far higher than they do now, the mountain torrents that swept the detritus of quartz from Hey Tor and Rippon Tor not only filled the lake of Bovey with pure white china clay, till they had converted a basin into a plain, but they also poured between red sandstone and limestone cliffs into the sea at Torbay. Then came a convulsion of nature; these latter formations rose as a wall across the bed of the torrent, and the spill of the granite upland passed down the Teign valley. Then the little Aller was formed of the drainage of the combes of the upraised barrier, and, blushing at its insignificance, it stole through the ancient bottom, cutting its modest way through the beds of quartz clay left by the former occupant of the valley, and, of course, flowing in a direction precisely the reverse of the former flood. The deposits of the earlier stream remain in all the laps of the hills and folds of the valley. They consist of quartz clay, somewhat coloured by admixture of the later rocks that have been fretted by lateral streams.

The first to discover these beds were the gipsies. They were our early potters. These wandering people were wont to camp wherever there was clay, and wood suitable for baking the clay. They set their rude wheels to work, and erected their equally primitive kilns, and spent one half the year in making pots, and the other half in vending them from place to place. When the wood supply was exhausted, then the Bohemians set up their potteries on another spot that commended itself to them, to be again deserted when the wood supplies failed once more.

The reason why the potteries at Burslem and elsewhere in Staffordshire have become permanent is, that there the coal is ready at hand, and that there the native population has taken the trade out of the desultory hands of the gipsies, and has worked at it persistently, instead of intermittently. The old stations, the rude kilns, the heaps of broken and imperfectly baked crocks of the ancient potters, are often come upon in the woods of Aller vale, and among the heather and gorse brakes of Bovey Heathfield.

The Aller vale opens into the Teign, as already said, below Newton Abbot, and extends about four miles south to the village of Kingskerswell, that stands on the crest of the red rocky barrier which diverted the course of the flood from Dartmoor. A branch of the valley to the west terminates at a distance of two miles at the picturesque village of Abbotskerswell, and another branch to the east leads up to the village of Coffinswell. The deepest deposit of clay is at the point where the three parishes converge.

Just nineteen years ago the idea of an art school was mooted in the district. It was enthusiastically taken up by the village doctor at Kingskerswell, in association with an institute for the labourers and young men of the parish, and after a little difficulty he succeeded in getting hold of some premises for the purpose. This earnest-hearted and energetic man, Dr. Symons, did not live to see more than the initiation of his scheme. By many the idea of an art school among village bumpkins was viewed with mistrust, even with disfavour. It was argued, and with truth, that art schools had been started in country towns, and had failed to reach a class below the middle order. Sons and daughters of artisans and labourers would have none of it. Such had been the experience in Newton, such in Torquay. If the intelligent artisan of the town turned his back on the art school, was it likely that Hodge would favour it? When people have satisfied their minds that a certain venture is doomed to failure, they are very careful not to lend their names to it, nor to put out their finger-tips to help it in any way. It was so in this case.

The managers of the Board School, when asked to lend the room for the purpose, refused it. The promoters, failing in every other direction, turned to a poor widow left with two sons, struggling hard to keep soul and body together in a modest "cob" (clay-walled) cottage with thatched roof. She was asked the loan of her kitchen, a room measuring 21 feet by 18 feet, lighted by two small latticed windows, with low open-boarded and raftered ceiling of unhewn timber. Glad to earn a few pence, she consented, and the art classes were started on a career of unexpected success.

The school of art began with a few pupils. A Sunday-school teacher persuaded his class to go to the art school, and perhaps to humour him, rather than with any anticipation of profit, the boys accepted the invitation. The widow's kitchen was whitewashed and clean. On the hearth a log fire blazed. A few simple pictures hung on the walls, and a scarlet geranium glowed in a pot in the window. A couple of trestles supported a plank for a table, and a pair of forms served to seat the pupils. The ploughboy, with his stiff fingers, was set to draw straight lines, and wonderful were his productions. The lines danced, trembled, wriggled, halted, then rushed off the page. They were crackers in their gyrations at first, and then rockets. By degrees the lines became less random, more subdued and purposeful, and finally a crow of delight proclaimed to the whole class that the curly-headed

ploughboy had succeeded in producing a musical
bar of five fairly parallel lines. Then, with both
hands plunged into his pockets, young Hodge
leaned back and went off into a roar of laughter.
It had dawned on his mind that he could draw a
line with a pencil on paper as true as he could with
a ploughshare in a field. He had come to the
school for a lark, and had found that the self-
satisfaction acquired by the discovery of his powers
was a lark better than he had expected. The question presented itself from the outset—How was the
art school to be maintained? The fires must be
kept in full glow, the lamps must be supplied with
oil, the widow must be paid to clean her floor after
the boys had brought over it the red mud from the
lanes. As so much mistrust as to the advantage
and prospect of success of the classes was entertained, it was from the first resolved by the
promoters not to solicit subscriptions. The whole
thing was to be self-supporting. This was represented to the pupils, and they readily accepted the
situation. They undertook to organise and keep
going through the winter a series of fortnightly
entertainments; they would invite some outsiders,
but for the most part they would do their best
themselves to entertain. The evenings would be
made lively with recitations, readings, and songs.
Doubtful whether such performance would deserve
a fixed charge for admission, the young fellows on
putting their heads together determined to make
none, but to hold a cap at the door when the
"pleasant evening" was over, and let those who

had been entertained show their appreciation as they chose.

These fortnightly cottage entertainments became a recognised institution and a source of profit, besides serving as a means of interesting and occupying the pupils. A thing that begins in a small way on right principles, a thing that "hath the seed in itself," is bound to succeed.

Adjoining the widow's cottage was another untenanted, like it consisting of a single apartment on the ground floor. It became necessary to rent this, knock a door through the wall, and combine the cottages. The second room was turned into a workshop, with a carpenter's bench and a chest of tools.

Out of the first art school in the one well-parish grew two others, one in each of the other well-parishes. Coffinswell has but a population of a hundred souls, nevertheless its art school has been frequented by as many as twelve pupils. Sixty is the highest number reached by the three together, which are now combined to maintain an efficient art instructor.

It fell out that a stoneware pottery in the Aller vale was burnt down in 1881, and when reconstructed the proprietor, who had cordially promoted the art classes, resolved on converting what had been a factory of drain and ridge tiles into a terra-cotta manufactory, in which some of the more promising pupils might find employ, and in which the knowledge and dexterity acquired in the class might be turned to practical uses. A single experienced potter was engaged, a gipsy, to start the affair, as there was no local tradition as to the manufacture of crocks upon which to go.

The classes were from the outset for boys and girls together, and though recently there has been a change in this arrangement, the young women coming in the afternoon, and the young men in the evening, this alteration has been made owing to increase of numbers, not in consequence of any rudeness or impropriety, for such there had not been in the ten years of the career of the school. In this case the experience has been precisely the same as that of the mixed schools and colleges of the United States.

There is one thing that a visitor to Torquay is certain to carry away with him if he has made excursions on foot about it—some of its red soil. The roads, in spite of the County Council, are bad, for the material of which they are made is soft. But what a soil it is for flowers and for fruit! Anything and everything will grow there and run wild. Stick a twig into the earth, and it is bound to grow. As for roses and violets, they run riot there. And, taken on the whole, the visitor who has been to Torquay is almost sure to carry away with him something beside the red mud, something quite as adhesive—pleasant memories of the place and its balmy air.

CHAPTER XVII.

TOTNES

WHAT a pity it is that the dear old legends
that lie at the root of history have been
dissipated! That we can no longer believe in
Romulus and Remus and the she-wolf — no, not
even when the Lupercale remains on the side of
the Palatine Hill, after the palaces of Augustus,
of Tiberius, of Caligula, of Septimius Severus, have
been levelled with the dust.

How cruel, too, that the delightful story of Alfred
and the cakes, that also of Edwin and Elgiva, are
relegated to the region of fables; that we are told
there never was such a person as King Arthur, and
that S. George for Merry England never was a
gallant knight, and certainly slew no dragon, nor
delivered fair maid!

Dust we are, but is it absolutely necessary that all
human history, and the history of nature, should
spring out of dust? that the events of the childhood of our race should have been all orderly and un-
romantic, as if every nationality had been bred in trim-
ness as a Board School scholar? Now, what if we could

believe that old gossiping—I am afraid I must add lying—historian, Geoffrey of Monmouth! Why, the transformation scene at a pantomime would be nothing to the blaze of wonders and romance in the midst of which the England of history steps on to the stage.

Ah! if we could but believe old Geoffrey, or the British book which he saw and translated, why, then, Totnes would be the most revered spot in England, as that where the first man set his foot when he landed in an uncultivated, unpeopled island. Is there not on the Palatine the Lupercale, the very den in which the she-wolf suckled Romulus and Remus, to prove the tale? Are there not Arthur's Seats enough in Cornwall, Wales, Cumberland, Scotland, to show that there must have been an Arthur to sit in them? And is there not the stone in the high street of Totnes on which Brut, when he landed, set his foot to establish against all doubters the existence of Brut and the fact of his landing there?

The story is this.

As it fell upon a day there was a certain king called Sylvius in Italy, and when he was about to become a father he consulted a magician, who by the stars could tell all that was to be. Now this magician read that the child that was to be born to Sylvius would be the death of his father and mother.

In course of time the child was born, and at his birth his mother died. "He's a Brute," said King Sylvius, and so that was his name.

But King Sylvius did not have his child exposed to wild beasts; he gave it to be nursed by a good woman, who reared the "Brute" till he was fifteen.

Now it fell out that one day King Sylvius went a-hunting in the merry greenwood with horn and hounds, and the little "Brute," hearing the winding of the horn and the music of the hounds, picked up the bow he himself had made, and with the arrows he himself also had winged, forth he went to the chase. Alas! it so fell out that the first arrow he shot pierced his father's heart.

On this account Brute had to fly the country.

"And away he fared to the Grecian land,
    With a hey! with a ho! and a nonny O!
And there he gathered a stalwart band,
    And the ships they sail on the blue sea O!"

Now the mother of Brute had been a Trojan, so all the refugees, after the destruction of Troy, gathered about the young prince, and formed a large body of men. Brute took to wife Ignogne, daughter of Pandrasos, King of the Greeks, and resolved to sail away in quest of a new country. So the king, his father-in-law, gave him ships and lading, and he started. A fair wind swelled his sails, and he sailed over the deep blue sea till he reached a certain island called Loegria, which was all solitary, for it had been wasted by pirates. But Brute went on shore, and found an old deserted and ruinous temple, and there he lit three fires, and he sacrificed a white hart, and poured the blood mingled with wine on the broken altar, and he sang :—

"Sweet goddess above, in the light of love,
    That high through the blue doth sail,
O tell me who rove in the woodland grove,
    O tell me, and do not fail,
Where I shall rest—and thine altar dressed,
    Shall finish this wandering tale."

These words he repeated nine times, after which he took four turns round the altar, and laid himself down on the skin of the white hart and fell asleep. About the third hour of the night he saw a beautiful form appear with the new moon in her hair, and a sceptre with the morning star shining on its point, and she said to him :—

> " Far, far away in the ocean blue,
>   There lieth an island fair,
> Which giants possessed, but of them are few
>   That linger to haunt it there.
> O there shalt thou reign, in a pleasant plain
>   Shalt found thee a city rare,
> From thee shall a line of heroes divine
>   Carry triumph everywhere."

When Brute woke he was much encouraged by the vision, and he returned to his ship, hoisted the mainsail, and away, away, before the wind the ship flew, throwing up foam from her bows, and leaving a track as milk in the sea behind. He passed through the Straits of Gibraltar and coasted up Aquitaine, and rounded the Cape of Finisterre, and at length, with a fair wind, crossed the sea, and came to the marble cliffs of Dunan Dyffnaint, the land of deep vales, and in the cliffs opened a great rift, down which flowed a beautiful river, and he sailed up it. And lo! on either side were green pastures spangled with buttercups, and forests of mighty oaks and beech, and over his head the white gulls screamed, and in the water the broad-winged herons dipped ; and so he sailed, and before him rose a red cliff; and now the tide began to fall. So he ran his ship up against the cliff and leapt ashore, and where he leaped there his foot made its impress on the red rock, which remains even unto this day. Then, when Brute had landed, he sat himself down and said :—

> "Here I sit, and here I rest,
> And this town shall be called Totnes."

Which shows that Brute had not much idea of rhyme, nor of measure in his rhyme.

It must be told that the very spot where Brute sprang ashore is half-way up the hill from the river Dart, up which he sailed; but then the river was much fuller in those days, or men's legs were longer.

Totnes, in fact, occupies a promontory of red sandstone rock, round which the river not only winds, but anciently swept up a creek that ran for two miles. In fact there was a labyrinth of creeks there; one between Totnes and the sea, another between Totnes and the mainland, so that the town was accessible on one side only, and that side was strongly fortified by castle and earthworks. The creek to the south still fills with water; its mouth is below Sharpham, and the tide now rises only as far as Bow Bridge. Formerly it ran quite a mile further up. The town of Totnes, in fact, occupies one point alone in a ness or promontory that was formerly, when the tide rose, flushed with water on the three sides. It has, however, been supposed that the term Totnes applies to the whole of that portion of South Devon to the coast; some even assert to the whole peninsula of Devon and Cornwall. The creeks have silted up with the rich red mud, and with the washings from the tin mines on Dartmoor, to such an extent that the true ness character of the little district of Totnes and the villages of Ashprington and Harberton has not been recognised. It is a hilly district, and the clefts which formerly filled with water are natural dykes fortifying it.

The Ikenild Street, which was a British trackway, passed through Totnes, which is the old Durium of the Itineraries. The river Dart is the Dour, that comes out as Durium in Latin, and is simply the Celtic word for water. We have it again in Doro-vernia, Dover, and in Dorchester, the castle or camp on the water.

The name Totnes is probably Saxon, from *tot*, *toten*, "to project," as in Tothill, Tottenham; and we have it again in a promontory on the coast, as Dodman's Nose, which is peculiar, for this is a combination of three languages. *Dod* is the Saxon, *man* is the Celtic *maen*, stone or rock, and *ness* is the Scandinavian nose or headland.

The railway station and line to Plymouth now occupy the old creek, up which barges, and undoubtedly smuggled spirits, went to Dartington. Anyone standing on the Dartington side and looking across at Totnes will see at once what was the old character of this headland. The town occupies a long ridge, which reached to the river by one street that ran its entire length. The magnificent church of red sandstone, with its grand tower and pinnacles, occupies the centre, and on the land side, the only side assailable, towered up the castle on a mound that was thrown up in prehistoric times.

The castle is now ruined; the circular "mote" re-

mains, and a few crumbling walls and great elm trees
full of rooks' nests rise in the place of towers and
battlements. The grounds about the ruins have been
nicely laid out, and what remains of the castle is
saved from further disintegration. The character was
very much that of other castles in the West, as Rougemont, Plympton, and Launceston. There was no
square keep, but a circular drum, and a large yard
surrounded by walls that stood on earlier earthworks.
A picturesque gate gives access to the town near the
castle. The town itself is quaint and full of interesting relics. A great number of the houses date
from Elizabethan times, and belonged to the wealthy
merchants of Totnes, which was a great place for
the manufacture of woollen cloth. Indeed in the
twelfth and thirteenth centuries it was already
famous.

Totnes is one of the oldest boroughs in the
country. Its earliest charter dates from 1205,
and I believe I am right in saying that at a dinner
at the Mansion House given by a Lord Mayor of
London within the last few years to the mayors of
England, precedence was given to the representative
of the borough of Totnes over all others.

The houses of the merchants of Totnes have been
sadly tampered with. The requirements of modern
trade exact large shop-fronts, and to satisfy the
demand of the public to see at a glance what is
to be sold within, the venerable houses have been
transformed externally, at all events on the ground-
floor. But let anyone interested in such things go
within and ask to be shown the panelled rooms and

plaster ceilings, and he will see much to interest and
delight. A peculiarly fine piece of plaster-work is
in the parlour of the local bookseller, and if the
visitor desires to have his hair cut he can have it
done in a chamber of the local barber, where the
woodwork is of the sixteenth century.

Totnes preserves its old piazzas, or covered ways
in High Street, very much like those of Berne or an
Italian city, or, indeed, of the *bastides* or free cities
built by our Edward I. in his duchy of Guyenne,
of which Montpazier, Beaumont, St. Foye are notable
examples, and seem to show that piazzas were a
common feature of English towns and of towns
built under English influence in the thirteenth century.
The same sort of thing is found at Chester, but not,
that I am aware, in any other English towns. If in
Italy these covered ways are an advantage, in that
it allows those who walk along the streets to look in
at the shop windows with comfort when the sun is
shining, in Totnes it allows them the same advantage
when the rain is falling ;

"And the rain it raineth every day."

One unpardonable outrage has been committed at
Totnes. There existed in front of the churchyard
and in continuation of the piazza, a butter market,
which consisted of an enlarged piazza, supported on
granite pillars of the beginning of the seventeenth
century. The vulgar craving to show off the parish
church when so many pounds, shillings, and pence
had been spent on its restoration ; the fear lest
visitors should fail to see that the shopkeepers of

Totnes had put their hands into their pockets to do up their church, made them destroy this picturesque and unique feature.

The church itself is a very fine building. It was originally a Norman structure of the eleventh century, but was rebuilt in the thirteenth, and is, as it now stands, a structure of Perpendicular work of the fifteenth century. It is of red sandstone, of a warm and pleasant colour. In the tower are niches containing figures of saints of lighter colour. The church has gone through a restoration more or less satisfactory, or unsatisfactory, at the hands of the late Sir G. Gilbert Scott, who had no feeling for Perpendicular work. It is a stately church; its chief glory is a superb rood-screen of carved stone, erected in 1460, and richly coloured and gilt. This supported a wide gallery that extended over half the chancel, and access to this gallery was obtained by a splendid carved and gilt newel staircase in the chancel. The top of the screen is delicately spread into fan-work, intended to sustain the beam of the gallery. In the so-called restoration of the church the entire gallery was removed, consequently the stair leads to vacancy and the screen supports nothing. Moreover, one of the most striking effects of the church was destroyed. A broad belt of shadow was designed to cross the chancel, behind the screen, throwing up, on one side, the gilded tracery of the screen, and on the other, the flood of light that bathed the sanctuary and altar. All this is gone, and the effect is now absolutely commonplace. There are screens near Totnes of extraordinary richness—at Great Hempston, Ipplepen, Harberton, and Berry Pomeroy—covered with gold and adorned with paintings. But none are perfect. A screen consisted of three parts. The lower was the sustaining arcade, then came the fan-groining to support the gallery, above that, the most splendid feature of all, the gallery back, which consisted of a series of canopied compartments containing paintings representing the gospel story. This still exists in Exeter Cathedral ; the uppermost member is also to be seen at Atherington, as has been already stated, but everywhere else it has disappeared.

Formerly there stood a reredos at the east end of the chancel of Grecian design, singularly out of character with the building, but hardly worse than the contemptible concern that has been erected in its place.

At the east end of the church, on the outside, the apprentices of Totnes were wont to sharpen their knives, and the stones are curiously rubbed away in the process.

The registers of Totnes are very early and of great interest, as containing much information concerning the old merchant families and the landed gentry of the neighbourhood with whom they married.

The nearest great manorial house is that of Dartington, which was a mansion of the Hollands, Dukes of Exeter, and now belongs to the Champernownes. It possesses ruins of the splendid hall, of the date of Richard II., whose device, a white hart chained, appears repeated several times. On the opposite side of the river is the most interesting and unique

parsonage of Little Hempston, a perfectly untouched
building of the fourteenth century, exactly the priest's
house of the time of Chaucer. The house consists
of a structure occupying four sides of a tiny quadrangle. It has a hall, buttery, kitchen, and solar.
Every window, except that of the hall, looks into the
little court, which is just twenty feet square, and the
rooms accordingly are gloomy. The late John Keble,
who was often a visitor at Dartington Parsonage,
would, when missing, be found there, dreaming over
the life of the parish priest in the Middle Ages.

A very singular circumstance is connected with
the old Champernownes of Dartington. Gawaine
Champernowne was married to the Lady Roberta,
daughter of the Count de Montgomeri, leader of the
Huguenots. On account of her misconduct she was
divorced in 1582, by Act of Parliament passed for
the purpose. However, oddly to relate, no sooner
were they divorced than they patched up their quarrel
and continued to live together as husband and wife,
and had a large family. Happily the eldest son and
heir was born before the Act was passed, or in all
certainty he would have been illegitimate in the eye
of the law. But the two younger sons and three
daughters were the issue after the divorce.

The old south gate of Totnes still remains, and at
one time the chamber over it was a public-house.
It has since been converted into a reading-room, and
contains some good wood-carving of the Tudor age
and a fine plaster cornice.

On the north side of the church are the remains of
the old priory of S. Mary, founded by Judael, Earl

of Totnes, at the Conquest. These have been transformed into guildhall, prisons, and sexton's houses. The priory must have been a modest building. It stood just within the old town walls, which may be traced in fairly good preservation thence to the south gate. The church of Totnes is a vicarial church, as Judael granted it to the Benedictine Abbey of Saints Sergius and Bacchus at Angers.

The priors had the right of presentation to the parish church up to the time of the dissolution of the religious houses, except during the wars with France, when the Crown appointed, this being an alien priory.

In 1414 there was a quarrel in the church between the prior and one John Southam, what about we do not know. They seem to have punched each other's nose, so as to bring blood; whereupon the church was closed till the bishop could hold investigation whether the sacred edifice had been desecrated thereby. Bishop Stafford did hold inquiry, and in ecclesiastical language, and with proper gravity, pronounced that the case was "fudge," that the matter had been made a great deal more of than there was occasion, and that the vicar was to recommence services in the church.

Torbrian Church, picturesquely situated in a glen, has been already alluded to. This parish is the cradle of Lord Petre's family.

The splendid ruins of Berry Pomeroy Castle are within a walk or drive, and will repay a visit, not only from the interest of the remains, but also from the beauty of the situation on the brow of rock overhanging the water.

Below the town of Totnes is the quay, at which the steamboat may be entered for the beautiful descent of the Dart to Dartmouth.

On all sides, peeping out of woods, above smooth lawns, backed by orchards, appear numerous smiling villas. It would seem that many well-to-do people have come to the same conclusion as did Brute, and have made Totnes their seat, saying :—

"Here I sit—and here I rest."

And the visitor will think that old Brute was no fool when he said that, and will wish that he could do the same.

NOTE.—Books on Totnes :—

COTTON (W.), *Graphic and Historical Sketch of the Antiquities of Totnes.* London : Longman, 1850.

WINDEATT (E.), "An Historical Sketch of Totnes," in the *Transactions of the Devonshire Association*, 1880.

DYMOND (R.), "Ancient Documents relating to the Civil History of Totnes," in the *Transactions of the Devonshire Association*, 1880.

CHAPTER XVIII.

DARTMOUTH

A first visit to Dartmouth—Descent of the Dart—The Church of S. Saviour—John Hawley—The Butter Row—Slate-covered houses —The Ship Inn—Walk to the sea—Warfleet—S. Petrock's—The Castle—Attacks on Dartmouth—The Golden Strand—Kingswear —Burying under foundations—Newcomen—Sir Walter Raleigh and his pipe—Slapton Lea—Dame Juliana Hawkins—Visits to be made—What not to be done.

I WILL tell you how I first saw Dartmouth before I proceed to say anything about it, and then the reader will perhaps understand the peculiar affection with which I write about it.

It happened early one June that I had made every arrangement to go with a friend a walking tour among the Dolomite Alps. We were to meet in town and cross the Channel together to Antwerp.

At the last moment some particularly vexatious business cropped up which detained me, and I had to wire to my friend that I could not be with him on the day fixed, but would, if possible, meet him in Cologne. In two days I saw it was all up with my Continental excursion, and I was obliged to telegraph to Cologne that my friend must go on his way by himself.

Now when a man has been slaving at his desk

all winter, and has been planning out every stage of his tour, and has thought, talked, written, dreamed of it for months—then to see his hope blasted is enough to make him cross. Cross accordingly I was; so cross, that the best and most long-suffering of wives advised me to go somewhere. "Somewhere," thought I; "why, I have never been down the Dart, have never seen Dartmouth." So I took the advice given me and started.

What a day that was when I spun along the Great Western Railway from Plymouth to Totnes The day was resplendent with sun, and yet not too hot. The orchards everywhere were a mass of flowers, from white to pink. I had hit precisely on the time and train whereby a number of English officers, just landed from the Soudan at Plymouth, were dispersing to their homes. In the same carriage with me was a young officer who had bought a number of *Funny Folks* and was immersed in it. A brother officer came to the carriage-window, after we had reached a second station, and addressing my fellow-traveller through the window exclaimed, " I say, did you ever see the like of this, old chap? We are going through waves of colour, a sea of flowers. I never saw anything to equal it—and after the sands of Egypt, old boy!" The bell rang and he had to run back to his carriage. "Yes; all right," was the response of the man in my compartment, and down went his head and thoughts among *Funny Folks*.

At the next station the second officer was again at our window, and again addressing the reader of

the periodical, "I say, Jones! talk of Araby the
Blessed, it isn't worth mention in the same day
with ten thousand times more lovely, blessed, dear
old England. By George! old chap, I want to look
out of both windows at once. I can't see enough
of it. I feel as if I could cry, it is so beautiful!"

"Ah! indeed," responded the reader, and down
went his head into his paper, and did not look
off it again. "Truly," I thought, "what a blessing
to publishers that all men have not the sense of
beauty; and what a blessing it is to men like
myself that we are not addicted to the grotesque."

The descent of the Dart should be made as I
made it then, on an early summer evening when
the sun is in decline, and the lawns are yellow
with buttercups, when the mighty oaks and beeches
are casting long shadows, and the reaches of the
river are alternately sheets of quivering gold and
of purple ink.

As I went down the river, all dissatisfaction at
my lot passed away, and by the time Dartmouth
came in view I could no longer refrain myself, but
threw my cap into the air, and barely caught it
from falling overboard as I shouted, "Hurrah for
merry England! Verily it has scenes that are unrivalled in the whole world."

Indeed now, in gravity, as I write this, I cannot
think that I have ever seen any sight lovelier than
Dartmouth on an evening in early summer, with
Kingswear opposite, the one bathed in soft sweet
shadow, and the other glittering and golden in the
sun's declining rays.

The sea is not visible from Dartmouth, which is hemmed in by hills that rise to a great height on every side, shutting in the basin of water that is the port of Dartmouth, and shutting out all winds. The town itself is full of picturesque bits. The church, dedicated to S. Saviour, is really a chapelry in the parish of Townstal, the church of which, set as a beacon on a hill, is two miles distant, and reached by a scramble. The church of Dartmouth was built at the end of the fourteenth century, and has happily escaped the reckless restoration which has befallen Totnes. What has been done has been reparative, and all in the best taste. The church contains a magnificent painted and gilt wood screen, and a pulpit of the same character, with the royal badges of later date on its sides. A gallery runs round three sides of the church, over the aisles; that is of Elizabethan date, and the panels in front are emblazoned with the arms of the merchant princes of the town at the time of its prosperity. A curious door, covered with iron-work of very rich description, representing lions impaled on an oak tree, bears the date 1631, but this merely represents the restoration of the woodwork of the door. In the floor of the church is the brass of John Hawley, merchant, who died in 1408, and his two wives, Joan, who died in 1394, and Alice, who died in 1403; there can be little doubt as to which of the wives he loved best, for he is represented holding the hand of the first. This is the Hawley, merchant of Dartmouth, mentioned by old Stow in his *Annals*, who, in 1390, "waged the navie of shippes of the ports of his own charges, and took 34 shippes laden with wyne to the sum of fifteen hundred tunnes." The visitor may compare the costume worn by the ladies on the brass with the description given by Stow of the fashion that then set in : " This time was used exceeding pride in garments, gownes with deepe and broad sleeves, commonly called peake sleeves, whereof some hung downe to their feete, and at least to the knees, ful of cuts and jagges."

Among the old houses in the town, unhappily fast disappearing, must be noted those in Butter Row, a short piazza like that at Totnes, and in one of these is a very fine carved oak chimney-piece, that merits examination.

Other old houses are in Fosse Street and the Shambles. A peculiarity of the old Dartmouth houses is that they are covered with small slates, cut into various devices, and forming elegant patterns, that cover them as a coat of mail against the rain. Forty years ago there were many of these picturesque old houses, they are now woefully reduced in numbers.

The "Ship Inn" is an old-fashioned hostel, very comfortable, and though modernised externally, yet has much that is characteristic of an old inn in the inside. I was dining there one evening when the train from town had arrived, and launched its passengers into Dartmouth. Among these happened to be a German, who was on his way by the Donald Currie boat to the Cape. He came into the dining-room of the "Ship," seated himself at a table at a little distance from me, and signed that he wanted something to eat.

The courteous, elderly waiter bowed and said, "What will you have, sir, soup?"

"Yesh! yesh!"

"There is vermicelli."

"Yesh! yesh!"

"And Julienne."

"Yesh! yesh!"

"And ox-tail."

"Yesh! yesh!"

"And mulligatawny."

"Yesh! yesh!"

"And fish, sir. Would you like some?"

"Oh, yesh! yesh!"

"There is some turbot."

"Yesh! yesh!"

"And a nice pair of soles."

"Yesh! yesh!"

"And some brill."

"Oh, yesh! yesh!"

"And perhaps you would like, sir, a mayonnaise of lobster?"

"Oh, yesh! yesh!"

It was time for me to interfere. I jumped up and hastened to the assistance of the poor German, and said in his own tongue: "I beg your pardon for my interference, sir, but *are* you ordering dinner for yourself or for the entire crew? You will, I know, excuse me, but I thought it advisable to speak before it came to the wine list."

"Ach, du lieber Herr!" gasped the German. "I

know but one English word, and that is Yesh. Will you be so merciful as to order dinner for me?"

I at once entered into consultation with the waiter, and settled all matters agreeably.

A charming walk may—no, must, be taken from Dartmouth to the sea; the street, very narrow, runs between houses for a long way, giving glimpses of the water, of old bastions and towers, of gardens hanging on the steep slopes, of fuchsias and pelargoniums running riot in the warm, damp air, of red rock and green foliage, jumbled together in the wildest picturesqueness, of the blue, still water below, with gulls, living foam-flakes swaying, chattering over the surface. Then the road has to bend round Warfleet, a lovely bay bowered in woods, with an old mill and a limekiln, and barges lying by, waiting for lime or for flour. When this has been passed, and, alas! a very ugly modern house that disfigures one of the loveliest scenes in South Devon, a headland is reached by a walk under trees, and all at once a corner is turned, and a venerable church and a castle are revealed, occupying the rocky points that command the entrance of Dartmouth Harbour.

The church undoubtedly served as chapel to the castle, but is far older in dedication than any portion of the castle, for it is dedicated to the purely British Saint Petrock, who lived in the sixth century.

The church is small, much mutilated, and contains a number of old monuments, and some brasses to the Roope and Plumleigh families. On the opposite side of the estuary is another castle.

The castle that adjoins is supposed to date from

the reign of Henry VII., but one existed in the same spot at an earlier date. Edward IV., in 1481, covenanted with the men of Dartmouth to pay them annually £30 from the customs of Exeter and Dartmouth, on condition of their building a "stronge and myghtye and defensyve new tower," and of their protecting the harbour with a chain. Certainly, the men of Dartmouth earned their money cheaply, for "the myghtye tower" is a very small affair.

For their own interest one would have supposed they would have erected a greater fortress, as Dartmouth suffered severely at times from pirates and French fleets. In 1377 it was plundered by the French, who in the same year swept our shores from Rye to Plymouth. In 1403 it returned the visit of the French; in 1404 a French fleet succeeded in putting into Black Pool, a little to the right of the entrance to the Dart, but the Dartmouth men armed and came down the steep sides of the bay upon the French, killed their leader, and forced them to regain their vessels and put off to sea. The French lost four hundred men and two hundred prisoners in the engagement.

On the attempted invasion by the Spanish Armada, in 1588, two vessels, the *Crescent* and the *Haste*, were fitted out, and the former is said to have been engaged with one of the Spanish vessels. In 1592, the *Madre de Dios*, one of the great Indian "carracks" or plate ships, was taken on her way to Spain, and was brought into Dartmouth. She was a floating castle of seven decks, and was laden with silver, spices, rare woods, and tapestries. The neighbouring gentry and townsmen of Dartmouth began to clear the prize for the adornment of their own houses, and commissioners were sent from London to recover as much of the spoil as was possible.

There is a bay near Black Pool which goes by the name of the Golden Strand, because a vessel was wrecked there laden with treasure, and to this day gold coins are occasionally picked up on the beach. In the basement of the tower of Dartmouth Castle are still the traces of where the iron chain or boom was fastened that could be stretched across the entrance to the harbour in time of war.

That smuggling was carried on to a very large extent on this coast in former times cannot be doubted. Indeed, the caves artificially constructed for the purpose of holding "run" goods still exist in several places; and many capital stories are told of the good old smuggling days, and the way in which the revenue officers were cheated.

Immediately opposite Dartmouth is Kingswear, situated on the steep slope of rock that runs precipitously to the sea. There is a curious circumstance connected with the church. In 1845, the church was pulled down, when under the foundation was discovered a cavity cut in the rock filled with infant bones and quicklime. There is but too much reason to believe that we have here one of the many instances that remain of the old heathen belief that no building would stand unless a man or child were buried under the foundation. A few years ago, when the parish church of Wickersley, Lincolnshire, was rebuilt by Sir G. Gilbert Scott, on raising the foundations the complete skeleton of a man was found laid lengthwise under the masonry. At Holsworthy, North Devon, in the same way, a skeleton was discovered with much lime about it in the wall, as if to hasten decomposition. The custom still exists in the East. In 1860, the King of Burmah (father of Theebaw) rebuilt Mandalay. On that occasion fifty-three individuals were buried alive, three under each of the twelve gates, one under each of the palace gates, and four under the throne itself. In 1880 the virtue was supposed to have evaporated, and Theebaw proposed to repeat the ceremony with one hundred victims, but I believe the actual number sacrificed was about twenty-five. The Burmans believe that the nals or spirits of the persons buried guard the gates and attack persons approaching with hostile intentions. Precisely similar convictions were common all over Europe.

In S. Saviour's, Dartmouth, in the chancel, is buried the skull of Sir Charles McCarthy, who was for a while Governor of Sierra Leone, and was killed at Accra, in an encounter with the Ashantees, January 21st, 1824; the skull was greatly prized by the Ashantees, who had possessed themselves of it, and with it they decorated the war-drum of the king. The skull was happily recovered in 1829, and was brought to Dartmouth, where it was buried with some ceremony.

Dartmouth was the birthplace of Newcomen, who introduced a notable improvement in steam engines. According to the first form of his discovery, the

steam was condensed by sending a current of cold
water on the outside of the cylinder, an arrangement
that required a boy to be always at hand with a
bucket of water. Watt's improvement of employing
steam to drive down the piston was invented whilst
he was repairing one of Newcomen's engines. Newcomen was baptised at Dartmouth in 1663 ; he died
in 1729. His house was removed in 1864, but some
of the old carved oak has been utilised in Newcomen
Cottage, Townstal, as well as the "clovel" or
wooden lintel over the fireplace at which Newcomen
sat watching the steam puffing from his mother's
kettle, and first conceived the idea of employing
steam as a force for propelling engines. A chimney-
piece of plaster, representing Shadrach, Meshach,
and Abednego before Nebuchadnezzar, is at Brook-
hill House, on the Kingswear side of the river.
This same handsome chimney-piece, of oak, came
from Greenway, up the Dart, where lived Sir
Walter Raleigh, and it is said that it was before the
fire kindled under this chimney-piece that the great
navigator indulged in the first pipe of tobacco he
ever smoked in England. There is a story told of
Sir Walter being called in with his pipe for a very
novel purpose at Littleham. There lived there a
gentleman of Dutch or German extraction, named
Creveldt, who had been at deadly feud with a neighbour, Sir Roger de Wheelingham, and the latter died
without any reconciliation. Thenceforth, Creveldt
was tormented from sunset to sunrise by the ghost
of his enemy. He could not rest ; he could not eat,
and, worst of all, he could not drink. The days for

exorcising ghosts were over.   He called in the parson,
but the parson could do nothing.   Matters were in
this condition when an Exeter trading vessel, commanded by Captain Izaaks, anchored near Exmouth.
The captain heard of Creveldt's trouble ; he was
under some obligation to him, and he at once visited
him.   He heard his piteous tale, and said: " In
ancient times I have been told that incense was
used against stubborn ghosts.   I have heard that now
Sir Walter Raleigh has introduced a novel sort of
incense much more efficacious.   Let us send for him."

Accordingly, Sir Walter was invited.   He in-
structed Creveldt how to smoke tobacco ; and the
fumes of the pipe proved too much for the ghost.
The spirit departed, coughing and sneezing, to the
tobaccoless world.

No visitor should fail to visit Slapton Lea—a bar
of pebble and sand tossed up by the sea, over which
runs the coach-road to Kingsbridge—an excursion
well meriting being made.   The streams descending
from the land are held back from entering the sea
by this ridge, and form a lake that not only abounds
in fish, and attracts water birds, but also contains
water plants.

At Slapton lived Sir Richard and Dame Juliana
Hawkins, in a house called Pool.

Dame Juliana was a haughty woman, and the
story is told that she would not go to church except
on a carpet.   Accordingly, when she went to Slapton
Church to pay her devotions, a couple of negro
servants proceeded before her unrolling a carpet of
red velvet.

On the river is Dittisham, and how the salmon do congregate in the pool there! It is a great place for figs and plums, and should be seen when the plum trees are in flower. The view from the parsonage garden, commanding two reaches of the river, is exquisite. But for loveliness of situation, Stoke Gabriel in a lap or creek, facing the sun, shut away from every wind, is the most perfect.

A good picturesque modern house has been erected at a point commanding Dartmouth, on the opposite side at Maypool (F. C. Simpson, Esq.), that is a real feature of beauty in the landscape.

At Stoke Fleming is a fine brass.

The time when Dartmouth may be seen to advantage—I am not speaking now of the river—is at the autumn regatta. Then the quaint old place is *en fête*. The little square that opens on to the quay is devoted to dancing. Lights flare, flags wave, music peals forth, and the Mayor opens the ball in the open air. It is a sight not to be seen elsewhere in England—when viewed from the river it is like a scene on the stage.

There is one thing you must do at Dartmouth, because you cannot help doing so—enjoy yourself. But there is one thing you must on no account do — offend a single, though the most insignificant, member of the town. If you do, the whole population is out on you like a hive of angry bees—for in a place so shut in by hills and water everyone is related.

Sir Charles McCarthy, as already related, has left his head at Dartmouth. As the visitor leaves by the little steamer to remount the Dart, and looks at the lovely estuary, the hills embowered in trees, the picturesque old town—he feels, perhaps, like myself, as if he had left his heart there.

NOTE.—Works on Dartmouth :—

KARKEEK (P. Q.), " Notes on the Early History of Dartmouth," in the *Transactions of the Devonshire Association*, 1880.

KARKEEK (P. Q.), " The Shipping and Commerce of Dartmouth in the Reign of Richard II.," *ibid.*, 1881.

NEWMAN (Dr.), " On the Antiquity of Dartmouth," *ibid.*, 1869.

CHAPTER XIX.

KINGSBRIDGE

KINGSBRIDGE is a curious town, having a name that is a misnomer, for it possesses no bridge, there being no river. The estuary that runs some five to six miles in, at the head of which Kingsbridge stands, is a creek into which no river discharges, only brooks. It has several lateral branches—to Gerston, Frogmore, and South Pool, and at the mouth is Salcombe, a flourishing place, much in resort on account of the mildness of the climate, surpassing Torquay in this respect, and nearly as warm as Falmouth. The drawback to Salcombe is its distance from a railway.

In Kingsbridge itself there is not much to be seen. The church is interesting, with a central tower and spire, and is curious as having been enlarged at various times, making the interior very inconvenient for the hearing of the preacher.

Kingsbridge is actually in Churchstow. The town has drifted down from the high ground where was the fortified "stoke" to the quay, the "brig." The church in the town is a chapelry, and the erection took place in 1310. It is dedicated to S. Edmund the king and martyr, but why in the world they should have gone to the East Saxons for a patron I am at a loss to know. Churchstow belonged to the Abbey of Buckfast.

One half of Kingsbridge is in the parish of Dodbrooke, where there is a good church with a fine old screen.

There is a local ballad preserved relative to the departure of some troops for America quartered in the place in 1778–80, and there are old men in Kingsbridge who can recall the time when a detachment of military was there. The ballad runs :—

"On the ninth day of November, at the dawning in the sky,
　Ere we sailed away to New York, we at anchor here did lie.
　O'er the meadows fair of Kingsbridge, there the mist was lying grey ;
　We were bound against the rebels, in the North America.

"O so mournful was the parting of the soldiers and their wives,
　For that none could say for certain, they'd return home with their lives.
　Then the women they were weeping, and they curs'd the cruel day
　That we sailed against the rebels in the North America.

"O the little babes were stretching out their arms with saddest cries,
　And the bitter tears were falling from their pretty, simple eyes,
　That their scarlet-coated daddies must be hurrying away,
　For to fight against the rebels in the North America.

" Now God preserve our Monarch, I will finish up my strain ;
Be his subjects ever loyal, and his honour all maintain.
May the Lord our voyage prosper, and our arms across the sea,
And put down the wicked rebels in the North America."

There are a good many objects of interest in the neighbourhood. Combe Royal is an old house much modernised, where lemons and oranges are golden in the open air, and the blue hydrangeas lie in masses under the trees.

Fallapit has been entirely rebuilt. It was the seat of the Fortescues, and their monuments crowd the parish church of East Allington. During the civil wars, the castle at Salcombe was held for the king by Sir Edmund Fortescue. After having sustained two sieges, probably of short duration, it was summoned by General Fairfax on January 23rd, 1645, and after a long siege of nearly four months, surrendered on honourable terms to Colonel Weldon, the governor of Plymouth. Sir Edmund was allowed to march out with the garrison, bearing their arms, to Fallapit, and take with him the key of the castle he had so gallantly defended.

When Fallapit was sold, among other things put up by the auctioneer was this very key, and it was knocked down for half a crown.

A charming excursion may be made to the cell of Lee Priory, an almost perfect monastic building. The chapel has been destroyed, but the gateway and refectory and the dormitories remain intact. It is situated in a peaceful, umbrageous dell away from the world among green lawns and pleasant woods, an idyllic spot.

At South Milton in the church is an interesting rood-screen, with paintings of saints on the panels. Screens are, indeed, numerous in this district, some very fine. Crass stupidity has occasioned the destruction of those of Malborough and West Alvington. The clergy should be the guardians, not the ravagers, of their churches, but *quis custodiet custodes?*

A delightful row down the estuary will take to Salcombe, a modern place. Opposite, up a tremendous scramble, is Portlemouth, a settlement of S. Winwaloe, the great Brittany saint. He is locally called Onolaus or Onslow. Winwaloe was the son of Gwen of the Three Breasts, and her husband, Fragan or Brechan, cousin of Cado, Duke of Cornwall. Although Gwen is represented on monuments in Brittany as a woman with three breasts, yet in Celtic the epithet means no more than that she was twice married, and had children by both husbands. Winwaloe was educated by S. Budoc, and founded Landevenec in Finisterre. At one time, fired with enthusiasm at what he had heard of the achievements of S. Patrick in Ireland, he desired to go there, but was advised to remain and devote himself to the education of his own people. He accordingly gave up his life to ministering to the spiritual necessities of the Britons who came to Armorica, either as a place for expansion, finding Britain too strait for them, or driven there by dynastic revolutions.

Whether Winwaloe ever came into Devon and Cornwall we are not told in his Life, but it is not improbable, as he was closely related to the reigning princes.

His biographer gives us a somewhat minute account of his personal appearance and habits. He was of a moderate height, with a bright, smiling countenance ; he was very patient with the perverse, and gentle in his dealings with all men. He was usually clothed in a goat's skin. He never seated himself in church, but always stood or knelt.

He died about 532. In Portlemouth Church, which has been barbarously " restored," he is represented on the screen holding the church in his hand. He is the third figure from the north. The first is partly effaced; the second is probably his sister, Creirwy ; the sixth is Sir John Schorne, a Buckinghamshire rector, who died in 1308, and was supposed to have conjured the devil into a boot. He was venerated greatly as a patron against ague and the gout. There is a jingle relative to him :—

> " To Maister John Schorne, that blessed man born,
>   For the ague to him we apply,
> Which judgeth with a bote ; I beshrew his heart's rote
>   That will trust him, and it be I."

His shrine was at North Marston in Bucks, and was a great resort up to the time of the Reformation. At one time the monks of Windsor contrived to get his body removed to their church, but though they advertised him well he did not " take on " in that quarter, and they returned the body to North Marston. There are representations of him on the screens of Wolborough and Alphington, and one or two in Norfolk. The screen at Portlemouth is of a richer and better design than is general in the county. In the " restoration " of the church the

level of the chancel has been raised to an excessive
height, so as to give a ludicrous appearance to those
occupying the stalls. But altogether the restoration
has been a piece of wanton barbarity. The carving
of the screen is of a high quality. At South Huish
was another beautiful little screen. This has been
saved from the hand of desecration by being removed
to the Chapel of Bowringslea, a grand old Tudor
mansion that has been carefully and conscientiously
restored by Mr. Ilbert, the proprietor.

At South Pool is a screen with arabesques on it,
well restored ; also an Easter sepulchre.

Stokenham Church stands up boldly above a spring
that gushes forth and forms a pool below the churchyard wall. This, there can be little doubt, must have
at one time been regarded as a holy well. The
church within is stately, and contains a good screen
with paintings of saints on it, and a stone pulpit
absurdly painted with Freemason symbols. What
stained glass there is, is mediocre. Sherford, attached
as a benefice to Stokenham, has another good screen,
with apostles painted on it. Slapton has a very
fine screen, but without paintings. The church was
originally attached to a college founded in 1350 by
Sir Guy de Brian, standard-bearer to Edward III.;
the gate tower alone remains.

Some fine rocky headlands and pleasant coves
are to be visited, notably Bolt Head and Bolt Tail,
and Prawle Point, with the sweet nooks where the
brooks descend to the sea, or the cliffs give way
to form a sunny, sleepy lap, lined with sand. At
Bolt Tail is a prehistoric cliff castle. At Portle-

mouth may be traced the entrenchments cast up by the Parliamentarians in the siege of Salcombe Castle.

The river Avon, that runs down from Dartmoor, is followed by the branch line of the Great Western Railway to Kingsbridge. A station is at Gara Bridge (*Garw*, Celtic for rough). The river passes under Loddiswell (Lady's Well), and then, unable to reach the Kingsbridge estuary on account of an intervening hill 370 feet high, turns sulkily to the right and enters Bigbury Bay far away to the west. Clearly Kingsbridge Harbour was made to receive it, but the river, like the life of many a man, has taken a twist and gone astray. But where the river went not, there goes the train by a tunnel.

The Avon enters the sea under Thirlstone, a parish that takes its name from a rock that has been " thirled " or drilled by the waves, on the beach. The church contains a few fragments of the screen worked up to form an altar.

An interesting expedition may be made from Kingsbridge to the mouth of the Erme. Above where the river debouches into the sea is Oldaport, the remains, supposed to be Roman, of a harbour commanded by two towers. One of the latter has of late years been destroyed.

The ancient port occupying two creeks remains silted up. There is absolutely no record of its having been used in mediæval times, and this leads to the supposition that it is considerably earlier. It is a very interesting relic ; but the two towers have been destroyed, and all that remains is a wall that cut off the spit of land, and a deep moat.

Modbury, a little market town, was a great seat of the Champernowne family. It has always been a musical centre. In the reign of Henry VIII. Sir Philip Champernowne, of Modbury, went up to Windsor, taking with him his company of musicians on rote and tabor and psaltery and dulcimer, and all kinds of music, and they performed before King Henry, to that huge monarch's huge content. So pleased was he with their "consort of fine musicke," that he bade Sir Philip remain with his company at Windsor, to play to him whenever the evil spirit was on him ; but forgot to say that this was to be at royal charges. The entertaining of his band of musicians at court by Sir Philip during many months proved so great an expense that when he returned to Modbury he was a wiser and a much poorer man, and had to sell a manor or two to meet his liabilities.

In 1558 good Queen Bess mounted her father's throne ; and one day bethought her of the Modbury orchestra. So with her royal hand she wrote down to Henry Champernowne, grandson of Sir Philip, to bid him bring up to court his "consort of fine musicke," for that she desired greatly to hear it.

Henry was tactless, and he replied that the visit to Windsor previously had cost his grandfather two of his best manors, and that he really could not afford it. Queen Bess was highly incensed, and found occasion against Henry Champernowne to mulct him of four or five fine manors, as a lesson to him not to return such an answer to a royal mistress again. This marked the beginning of the decline of the Champernowne family at Modbury. The manor passed from them in 1700. But although the Champernownes are gone, the band is still there. It has never ceased to renew itself, and Modbury prides itself as of old on its "consort of fine musicke."

Bigbury takes its name from some great camp or bury that has disappeared under the plough. In the church is a very fine carved oak pulpit, like that of Holne, given by Bishop Oldham to Ashburton Church in or about 1510. At the same time he presented an owl as lectern to Ashburton Church, the owl being his badge. In 1777 the wiseacres of Ashburton sold pulpit and owl to Bigbury for eleven guineas. When the Bigbury folk saw that they had got an owl instead of an eagle, they were disgusted, sawed off the head and sent it to Plymouth, with an order for an eagle's head of the same dimensions. Accordingly, now the lessons are read in the church from a lectern that has an owl's body with an eagle's head. But really—as in the puzzle pictures—one is disposed to ask, "Where is the owl?" and to look for it first among the Ashburton folk who sold their bird, and secondly among the Bigbury folk who objected because he was an owl. There are some brasses in the church to the Burton family, into which married the De Bigburys.

At S. Anne's there are an old chapel and a holy well. S. Anne did not come into fashion as a saint till the fifteenth century, and there are no early representations of her, or dedications to her. But Anne was the mother of the gods among the Celts, and the name was given to several notable women, as the mother of S. Samson, and the daughter of Vortimer, king of the Britons, mother of S. Wenn, who married Solomon, king of the Dumnonii; and a suppressed cult of the old goddess went on under the plea of being directed to these historic women, till the great explosion of devotion to Anne, mother of the Blessed Virgin—known to us only through the apocryphal gospels.

Ane or Anne was the mythical mother of the Tuatha de Danan, the race found in our peninsula, in Scotland from the Clyde to the Firth of Forth, and throughout Ireland, called by the classic writers Dumnonii. They were subdued in Ireland by the Gaels or Scots. Undoubtedly throughout Devon and Cornwall there must have been a cult of the great ancestress. She has given her name to the Paps of Ane in Kerry and to S. Anne's (Agnes') Head in Cornwall, and as surely the holy wells now attributed to S. Anne were formerly regarded as sacred fountains of the great mother of the race, whose first fathers were gods.

There is a rock at sea, reached at low tide, called Borough Island, on which is a little inn. It was formerly, judging by the name, a cliff fortress.

Ringmore, the adjoining parish to Bigbury, has a church and village nestling into a pleasant, wooded combe. The church has a small spire, and the basement serves as a porch. Anent this tower is a tale.

During the civil wars, a Mr. Lane was rector,

as also incumbent of the adjoining parish of Aveton
Gifford. He mustered the able-bodied men of his
parish, drilled them, obtained some cannon, and
formed a battery manned by his fellows, to command the bridge below Loddiswell, by which Parliamentary troops were marching to the siege of Salcombe Castle, and caused them such annoyance that
during the siege of Plymouth by the Parliamentary
forces, several boats full of armed men were despatched from Plymouth to capture and shoot the
sturdy rector. Forewarned, Mr. Lane took refuge
in a small chamber, provided with a fireplace,
in the tower of the church, and there he remained
in concealment for three months, secretly nourished
by his parishioners. His most painful experience at the time was on the Sundays, when the
minister intruded by the Parliament harangued from
the pulpit in terms audible in his secret chamber.
Then Mr. Lane could hardly contain himself from
bursting forth to refute his heresies and denounce
his disloyalty.

The soldiers are said to have landed at Ayrmer
Cove and proceeded to the rectory, which they
thoroughly ransacked, but although they searched
the neighbourhood, they were unable to find the man
they were sent to capture.

The old historic parsonage has been demolished,
and its site is marked by a walled garden, but the
secret chamber in the tower remains.

At Aveton Gifford is a fine screen, carefully restored. Walter de Stapledon was rector of this parish,
and was raised thence to be Bishop of Exeter in

1307, and in 1314 he was the founder of Exeter College, Oxford. He was for several years High Treasurer to Edward II. His story is really worth giving in short. On the vacancy of the see, the king sent down *congé d'élire* on October 6th, 1307. The chapter sat. Of twenty-three canons fifteen chose Stapledon, three selected the Dean, three the Archdeacon of Totnes, and two voted for the Dean of Wells. When the result of the counting was announced, then another voting was proceeded with, and Stapledon was elected unanimously.

The result was announced to the king and he gave his assent on December 6th. But meanwhile a troublesome fellow, Richard Plymstoke, Rector of Exminster, had sent an appeal to the Pope against nine of the canons, whom he pronounced to be disqualified for election, and one of these was Stapledon. Here was an unpleasant intervention, only too sure to be eagerly seized on by the Roman *curia* for the sake of extorting money. To make matters worse, the Pope had suspended the Archbishop of Canterbury, and he had gone to France, to Poitiers, to meet the Pope and solicit, and buy, his relief. On January 18th the Archbishop, who had been restored and empowered to investigate the complaint of Plymstoke, issued his commission ; and on March 10th poor Stapledon wrote a bitter letter to the Cardinal, Thomas Joce, to complain of the condition of poverty into which he had been reduced. " It is hard on me ; at the present moment I am destitute even to nakedness."

To make matters worse, the queen, Isabella, wrote

to him requiring him to find a prebendal stall and a revenue for her chaplain—a foreigner with an outlandish name—Jargono. He replied that he could not give a canonry to this stranger, and as to finding him an income, he said that he was overwhelmed with debt, on account of the intolerable burden of costs incurred by the appeal to Rome, and in preparing for his consecration.

And it was not till October 13th, 1308, nearly a year after his election, that he was consecrated. His registers, carefully preserved at Exeter, prove him to have been a hard-working, high-principled, and altogether estimable prelate. He it was who erected that masterpiece of woodwork, the bishop's throne, in Exeter Cathedral.

Stapledon was one of the foremost statesmen of his day, and he was the trusted friend and adviser of King Edward II. Hence his frequent and prolonged sojourns in the Metropolis, and his occasional absences from England on missions of importance.

In 1323 the troubles with the Despensers, the king's favourites, began.

Charles IV., king of France, seized the Agenois and threatened Guienne. Edward sent his queen, Isabella, to Paris to negotiate with her brother. The treaty which she made was so humiliating for England that the king's council refused to discuss it. Another suggestion was then made from the French court, that if Edward would bestow Guienne on his eldest son, the king himself would not be required to do homage to the Crown of France. The Despensers urged Edward to accept this. The queen now refused to return to England; she had made a favourite and paramour of Lord Mortimer, and, out of spite against the king, favoured the Lancastrian party. Charles IV. was at last obliged to send her out of his dominions. She retired to the court of Hainault, where, under the direction of Mortimer, she prepared for the invasion of England. At the close of 1326 Isabella landed at Orwell in Suffolk, with a small but well-appointed army of Hainaulters and exiles. The Lancastrians immediately hastened to her standard. It was generally supposed that her object was simply the removal of the Despensers. After a vain attempt to rouse the Londoners in his cause, Edward fled with the two Despensers to the Welsh marches.

The king's flight and the successful advance of the queen's forces towards London encouraged the citizens to break out into open rebellion against the Government. Before leaving, Edward had made Stapledon guardian of the city. Walsingham, in his *History*, says :—

"Continuing their rage, the citizens made a rush for the house of the Bishop of Exeter, and, setting fire to the gates, quickly forced an entrance. Not finding the bishop they carried off his jewels, plate, and furniture. It happened, however, that in an evil hour the bishop returned from the country, who, although he had been forewarned, felt no manner of dread of the citizens. So he rode on with all boldness, till he reached the north door of St. Paul's, where he was forthwith seized by the raging people, who struck at and wounded him, and finally, having dragged him from his horse, hurried him away to the place of execution. Now the bishop wore a kind of armour, which we commonly calle *aketone ;* and having stripped him of that, and of all his other garments, they cut off his head. Two others, members of his household, suffered the same fate. Having perpetrated this sacrilegious deed, they fixed the bishop's head on a stake. As to the corpse, they flung it into a small pit in a disused cemetery."

Another chronicler says :—

" The naked body, with only a rag given by charity of a woman, was laid on a spot called *le lawles chirche*, and, without any grave, lay there, with those of his two esquires."

" Those," says Dr. Oliver, " who attend to the springs and principles of actions must award the tribute of praise and admiration to this high-minded bishop and minister ; they will appreciate his zeal and energy to sustain the declining fortunes of his royal master, and venerate him for his disregard of self, and for his incorruptible honour and loyalty under every discouragement."

His body was finally brought to Exeter, where it lies in the Cathedral under a beautiful canopied tomb in the north-east bay of the choir, close to the high altar.

And now, one word to the angler.

What streams these are that flow through the South Hams ! What pools under deep banks, in which the trout lurk ! To him who can obtain permission to fish the Erme, the Avon, can be assured days to be never forgotten, of excellent sport in lovely scenery.

CHAPTER XX.

PLYMOUTH

WHEN a sailor heard the song sung, to which this is the refrain :—

"O dear Plymouth town ! and O blue Plymouth Sound,
O where is your equal on earth to be found ?"

he said, "Them's my opinions, to the turn of a hair."

About Plymouth town I am not so confident, but as to the Sound it is not easily surpassed. The Bay of Naples has Vesuvius, and above an Italian sky, but lacks the wealth of verdure of Mount Edgcumbe, and has none of those wondrous inlets that make of Plymouth Sound a figure of a watery hand displayed, and of the Three Towns a problem in topography which it requires long experience to solve.

The name of the place is a misnomer.

Plym is not the name of the river which has its

mouth where the town squats. Plym is the contrac-
tion for Pen-lynn, the head of the lake, and was given
originally to Plympton, where are the remains of a
castle, and where are still to be seen the iron rings to
which vessels were moored. But just as the Taw-ford
(*ridd*) has contributed a name to the river Torridge,
above the ford, so has Pen-lynn sent its name down
the stream and given it to Plymouth. Pelynt in
Cornwall is likewise a Pen-lynn.

What the original name of the river was is doubtful. Higher up, where it comes rioting down from
the moor, above the Dewerstone is Cadover Bridge,
not the bridge *over* the Cad, but Cadworthy Bridge.
Perhaps the river was the Cad, so called from *caed*,
contracted, shut within banks, very suitable to a river
emerging from a ravine. A witty friend referring
to " the brawling Cad," the epithet applied to it by
the poet Carrington, said that it was not till the
institution of chars-a-bancs and early-closing days in
Plymouth that *he* ever saw " the brawling cad " upon
Dartmoor ; since then he has seen a great deal too
much of the article.

Plymouth as a town is comparatively modern.
When Domesday was compiled nothing was known
of it, but there was a Sutton—South Town—near
the pool, which eventually became the port of old
Plymouth.

It first acquired some consequence when the
Valletorts had a house near where is now the
church of S. Andrew.

There was, however, a *lis* or enclosed residence
of a chief, if we may accept the Domesday manor

of Lisistone * as thence derived. And there have been early relics turned up occasionally. But no real consequence accrued to the place till the Valletorts set up house there in the reign of Henry I.

The old couplet, applied with variations to so many places in the kingdom, and locally running:

> " Plympton was a borough town
> When Plymouth was a vuzzy down,"

was true enough. Plympton at the time of the Conquest was head of the district, and there were then canons there in the monastery, which dates back at least to the reign of Edgar, probably to a much earlier period. The priors of Plympton got a grant of land in Sutton, which they held as lords of the manor till 1439. It was not till the end of the thirteenth century that the name of Plymouth came to knowledge and the place began to acquire consequence. But it was not till the days of good Queen Bess that the place became one of prime importance.

" In the latter half of the sixteenth century," says Mr. Worth, " Devonshire was the foremost county in England, and Plymouth its foremost town. Elizabeth called the men of Devonshire her right hand, and so far carried her liking for matters Devonian, that one of the earliest passports of Raleigh to her favour was the fact that he talked the broadest dialect of the shire, and never abandoned it for the affected speech current at court." †

---

* Now Lipson.

† WORTH (R. N.), *History of Plymouth*, 1890, p. 39. I shall quote much from this admirable work, not only full of information, but written in a charming style.

The importance of Plymouth as a starting-point for discovery, and as the cradle of our maritime power, must never be forgotten.

Old Carew says :—

"Here have the troops of adventurers made their *rendezvous* for attempting new discoveries or inhabitances, as Thomas Stukeleigh for Florida, Sir Humfrey Gilbert for Newfoundland, Sir Richard Grenville for Virginia, Sir Martin Frobisher and Master Davies for the North-West Passage, Sir Walter Raleigh for Guiana."

It is indeed no exaggeration to say that in the reign of Elizabeth Plymouth had become the foremost port in England.

"If any person desired to see her English worthies, Plymouth was the likeliest place to seek them. All were in some fashion associated with the old town. These were days when men were indifferent whether they fought upon land or water, when the fact that a man was a good general was considered the best of all reasons why he should be a good admiral likewise. '*Per mare per terram*' was the motto of Elizabeth's true-born Englishmen, and familiar and dear to them was Plymouth, with its narrow streets, its dwarfish quays, its broad waters, and its glorious Hoe."

The roll of Plymouth's naval heroes begins with the Hawkins family, and one looks in vain in modern Plymouth for some statue to commemorate the most illustrious of her sons.

These Hawkinses were a remarkable race. "Gentlemen," as Prince says, "of worshipful extraction for several descents," they were made more worshipful by their deeds.

" For three generations in succession they were the master-spirits of Plymouth in its most illustrious days; its leading merchants, its bravest sailors, serving oft and well in the civic chair and the Commons House of Parliament. For three generations they were in the van of English seamanship, founders of England's commerce in South, West, and East, stout in fight, of quenchless spirit in adventure—a family of merchant statesmen and heroes to whom our country affords no parallel." *

The early voyages of Sir John Hawkins were to the Canary Isles. In 1562 he made his first expedition in search of negroes to sell in Hispaniola, so that he was not squeamish in the matter of the trade in human flesh. But in 1567 he made an expedition ever memorable, for his were the first English keels to furrow that hitherto unknown sea, the Bay of Mexico. He had with him a fleet of six ships, two of which were royal vessels, the rest were his own, and one of these, the *Judith*, was commanded by his kinsman, Francis Drake. Whilst in the port of S. Juan de Ulloa Hawkins was treacherously assailed, and lost all the vessels, with the exception of two, of which one was the *Judith*. When his brother William heard of the disaster he begged Elizabeth to allow him to make reprisals on his own account; and on the return of John " it may fairly be said that Plymouth declared war against Spain. Hawkins and Drake thereafter never missed a chance of making good their losses. The treachery of San Juan de Ulloa was the moving cause of the series of harassments

* WORTH.

which culminated in the destruction of the Armada.
For every English life then lost, for every pound
of English treasure then taken, Spain paid a hundred
and a thousand fold."

In the following year, at Rio de la Flacho, whilst
getting in supplies, he was attacked by Michael de
Castiliano with a thousand men. Hawkins had but
two hundred under his command; however, he
drove the Spaniards back, entered the town, and
carried off the ensign, for which, on his return, he
was granted an addition to his arms—on a canton,
gold, an escalop between two palmers' staves, sable.

In 1573 Hawkins was chosen by the queen "as
the fittest person in her dominions to manage her
naval affairs," and for twenty-one years served as
Controller of the Navy. It was through his wise
provision, by his resolution, in spite of the niggard-
liness wherewith Elizabeth doled out money, that
"when the moment of trial came," says Froude, "he
sent her ships to sea in such condition—hull, rigging,
spars, and running rope—that they had no match in
the world."

About the Armada presently.

In 1595 Hawkins and Drake were together sent
to the West Indies in command of an expedition.
But they could not agree. Hawkins wanted at
once to sail for America, Drake to hover about
the Canaries to intercept Spanish galleons. The
disagreement greatly irritated old Sir John, unaccustomed to have his will opposed. Then he
learned that one of his vessels, named the *Francis*,
had been taken by the Spaniards. Grief at this,

and annoyance caused by the double command, brought on a fever, and he died at sea, November 15th, 1595.

Old Prince says, in drawing a parallel between him and Drake, "In their deaths they were not divided, either in respect of the cause thereof, for they died both heart-broken; the one, for that being in joint commission with the other, his advice and counsel was neglected; the other, for the ill success with which his last voyage was attended. Alike they were also in their deaths; as to the place, for they both died on the sea; as to the time, they both expired in the same voyage, the one a little before the other, about the interspace of a few months; and lastly, as to their funerals, for they were both buried in the ocean, over which they had both so often rid in triumph."

The elder brother of Sir John, William, the patriarch of the port, was Mayor of Plymouth in the Armada year. William's son, Sir Richard Hawkins, sailed in 1593 from Plymouth with five vessels to the South Seas, and was taken by the Spaniards. From various causes the fleet was reduced to the single vessel the *Dainty*, which he himself commanded. Manned by seventy-five men only, she was assailed by eight Spanish vessels with crews of 1300. Nevertheless, like Sir Richard Grenville, of the *Revenge*, he showed lusty fight, which was kept up for three days, and he did not surrender till he had himself been wounded six times, and then only when he had secured honourable terms, which the false scoundrels broke, by sending their prisoners to Spain, instead of allowing them, as was undertaken, to return to England.

He is one of those to whom the ballad is supposed to relate :—

> "Would you hear of a Spanish lady,
> How she wooed an English man ?"

But it is also told of a member of the Popham family, by whom the lady's picture, and her chain and bracelets, mentioned in the ballad, were preserved.

Next to the Hawkins heroes we have Drake, a Plymothian by adoption, the son of a yeoman near Tavistock. Camden calls him, "without dispute the greatest captain of the age."

Many strange stories are told of him, as that he brought water to Plymouth by pronouncing an incantation over a spring on Dartmoor, and then riding direct to the seaport, whereupon the water followed him, docile as a dog. When he was building Buckland Abbey, every night the devils carried away the stones. Drake got up into a tree and watched. When he saw the devils at work he crowed like a cock. "Dawn coming ?" exclaimed a devil. "And there comes the sun !" cried out another, for Drake had lit his pipe ; and away they scampered.

Another story is, that he left his wife at Lynton, and was away for so long that she believed him dead, and was about to be married again, when Sir Francis, who was in the Bristol Channel, fired a cannon-ball, that flew in at the church window and fell between her and her intended "second." "None

could have done that but Sir Francis," said the lady
with a sigh, and so the ceremony was abruptly
broken off.

Drake was brought up at sea under Hawkins,
and accompanied him on the voyage of 1567, which
ended so disastrously. His first independent expedition was in 1572, when he made his memorable
expedition to Nombre de Dios.

Four years later Drake started on his voyage of
circumnavigation, with five vessels. Disaster and
disaffection broke up the little fleet, but he perse-
vered, and on September 26th, 1580, brought the
Pelican safely back to Plymouth again; the first
English captain who had sailed round the world.
Plymouth turned out to welcome him, headed by
the Mayor, and S. Andrew's bells rang a merry peal.

The *Pelican* was crammed with treasure. Drake
went to the Thames in her, and was received
graciously by the queen. "His ship," says Camden,
"she caused to be drawn up in a little creek near
Deptford, as a monument of his so lucky sailing
round the world. And having, as it were, consecrated it as a memorial with great ceremony, she
was banqueted in it, and conferred on Drake the
honour of knighthood."

Singularly enough the Spanish Ambassador complained, on the part of his Government, of Drake
having ventured into the Pacific; but the queen
spiritedly replied that she did not acknowledge
grants of strange lands, much less of foreign seas
made by the Pope, and that, sail where they might,
her good mariners should enjoy her countenance.

In 1585 Drake, with a fleet of twenty-five sail, made another expedition to the West Indies; and his next exploit, performed in 1587, was what he called "singeing the King of Spain's beard." With his fleet he ravaged the coast of Spain, and delayed the sailing of the Armada for a year. The Invincible Armada, as the Spaniards designated it in their pride, set sail from the Tagus on May 29th. It consisted of 130 vessels of all sizes, mounting 2431 guns, and carrying, in addition to the mariners, nearly 20,000 land troops, among whom were 2000 volunteers of the noblest families in Spain. But the fleet was overtaken by a storm off Coruña, and four large ships foundered at sea; on hearing which, that stingy old cat, Elizabeth, at once ordered the admiral, Lord Howard of Effingham, to lay up four of his largest vessels, and discharge their crews. The admiral had the spirit to disobey, saying that rather than do that he would maintain the crews at his own cost. On July 19th, one named Fleming, a Scottish privateer, sailed into Plymouth, with intelligence that he had seen the Spanish fleet off the Lizard. At the moment most of the captains and officers were on shore playing bowls on the Hoe. There was instant bustle, and a call to man the boats. "There is time enough," said Drake, "to play the game out first, and thrash the Spaniards afterwards."

Unfortunately the wind was from the south, but the captains contrived to warp out their ships. On the following day, being Saturday, the 20th of July, they got a full sight of the Armada standing

majestically on, the vessels drawn up in the form of
a crescent, which, from horn to horn, measured some
seven miles.

Their great height and bulk, though imposing
to the unskilled, gave confidence to the English
seamen, who reckoned at once upon having the
advantage in tacking and manœuvring their lighter
craft. The miserable parsimony of Elizabeth, who
did not allow a sufficiency of ammunition to the
fleet, interfered sadly with the proceedings of the
defenders of the English shores. But the story of
the Armada belongs to general English history, and
need not be detailed here. It is a story, read it often
as we may, that makes the blood dance in one's
veins.

It has served as the topic of many lines. I will
give some not usually quoted, by John O'Keefe,
which were set to music by Dr. Arnold :—

> " In May fifteen hundred and eighty-eight,
>   Cries Philip, 'The English I 'll humble ;
> I 've taken it into my Majesty's pate,
>   And the lion, Oh ! down he shall tumble.
> The lords of the sea !' Then his sceptre he shook ;
>   ' I 'll prove it all arrant bravado,
> By Neptune ! I 'll sweep 'em all into a nook,
>   With th' Invincible Spanish Armado.'
>
> " This fleet started out, and the winds they did blow ;
>   Their guns made a terrible clatter.
> Our noble Queen Bess, 'cos her wanted to know,
>   Quill'd her ruff, and cried, 'Pray what 's the matter?'
> ' They say, my good Queen,' replies Howard so stout,
>   ' The Spaniard has drawn his toledo.
> Odds bobbins ! he 'll thump us, and kick us about,
>   With th' Invincible Spanish Armado.'

" The Lord Mayor of London, a very wise man,
    What to do in the case vastly wondered.
Says the Queen, ' Send in fifty good ships, if you can,'
    Says the Lord Mayor, ' I'll send you a hundred !'
Our fire ships soon struck every cannon all dumb,
    For the Dons ran to *Ave* and *Credo ;*
Don Medina roars out, ' Sure the foul fiend is come,
    For th' Invincible Spanish Armado.'

" On Effingham's squadron, tho' all in abreast,
    Like open-mouth'd curs they came bowling ;
His sugar-plums finding they could not digest,
    Away they ran yelping and howling.
When Britain's foe shall, all with envy agog,
    In our Channel make such a tornado,
Huzza ! my brave boys ! we're still lusty to flog
    An Invincible . . . . Armado."

And here the dotted line will allow of Gallic, Russian, or German to be inserted. Of Spanish there need be no fear. Spain is played out.

A fine bronze statue of Sir Francis by Boehm is on the Hoe, the traditional site of the bowling match, but it is only a *replica* of that at Tavistock, and lacks the fine bas-reliefs representing incidents in the life of Drake ; among others, the game of bowls, and his burial at sea. On the Hoe is also a ridiculous ter-centenary monument commemorative of the Armada, and the upper portion of Smeaton's Eddystone light-house.

This dangerous reef had occasioned so many wrecks and such loss of life, that Mr. Henry Win-stanley, a gentleman of property in Essex, a self-taught mechanician, resolved to devote his attention and his money to the erection of a lighthouse upon the reef, called Eddystone probably because of the swirl of water about it. He commenced the erection in 1696, and completed it in four years. The structure was eminently picturesque, so much so that a local artist at Launceston thought he could not do better than make a painting of it to decorate a house there then in construction (Dockacre), and set it up as a portion of the chimney-piece. The edifice certainly was not calculated to withstand such seas as roll in the Channel, but Winstanley knew only that second-hand wash which flows over miles of mud on the Essex coast, which it submerges, but above which it cannot heap itself into billows.

Winstanley had implicit confidence in his work, and frequently expressed the wish that he might be in his lighthouse when tested by a severe storm from the west. He had his desire. One morning in November, 1703, he left the Barbican to superintend repairs. An old seaman standing there warned him that dirty weather was coming on. Nevertheless, strong in his confidence, he went. That night, whilst he remained at the lighthouse, a hurricane sprang up, and when morning broke no lighthouse was visible ; the erection and its occupants had been swept away. Three years elapsed before another attempt was made to rear a beacon. At length a silk mercer of London, named Rudyard, undertook the work. He determined to imitate as closely as might be the trunk of a Scotch pine, and to give to wind and wave as little surface as possible on which to take effect. Winstanley's edifice had been polygonal ; Rudyard's was to be circular. Commenced in 1706 and completed in 1709, entirely of timber, the shaft weathered the storms of nearly fifty years in safety, and might have defied them longer but that it was built of combustible materials. It caught fire on the 2nd December, 1755. The three keepers in it did their utmost to extinguish the flames, but their efforts were ineffectual. The lead wherewith it was roofed ran off in molten streams, and the men had to take refuge in a hole of the rock. When they were rescued one of the men went raving mad, broke away, and was never seen again. Another solemnly averred that some of the molten lead, as he stood looking up agape at the fire, had run down his throat as it spouted from the roof. He died within twelve days, and actually lodged within his stomach was found a mass of lead weighing nearly eight ounces. How he had lived so long was a marvel.

Twelve months were not suffered to pass before a third lighthouse was commenced—that of Smeaton. This was of stone, dovetailed together. It was commenced in June, 1757, and completed by October, 1759. This lighthouse might have lasted to the present, had it not been that the rocky foundation began to yield under the incessant beat of the waves.

This necessitated a fourth, from the designs of Mr. (now Sir J.) Douglass, which was begun in 1879 and completed in 1882. The total height is 148 feet.

The Breakwater was begun in 1812, but was not completed till 1841.

The neighbourhood of Plymouth abounds in objects of interest and scenes of great beauty. The Hamoaze, the estuary of the Tamar and Tavy combined, is a noble sheet of water. The name (*am-uisge*), Round about the water, describes it as an almost land-locked tract of glittering tide and effluent rivers, with woods and hills sloping down to the surface. Mount Edgcumbe, with its sub-tropical shrubs and trees, shows how warm the air is even in winter, in spots where not exposed to the sea breeze.

Up the creek of the Lynher (*Lyn-hir*, the long creek) boats pass to S. Germans, where is a noble church, on the site of a pre-Saxon monastery founded by S. Germanus of Auxerre. The little disfranchised borough contains many objects to engage the artist's pencil, notably the eminently picturesque alms-houses.

The noble church has been very badly "restored." The Norman work is fine.

Cawsand, with its bay, makes a pleasant excursion. This was at one time a great nest for smugglers. An old woman named Borlase had a cottage with a window looking towards Plymouth, and she kept her eye on the water. When a preventive boat was visible she went down the street giving information. There was another old woman, only lately deceased, who went by the name of Granny Grylls. When a young woman she was wont to walk to the beach and back carrying a baby that was never heard to wail.

One day a customs officer said to her, "Well, Mrs. Grylls, that baby of yours is very quiet."

"Quiet her may be," answered she, "but I reckon her's got a deal o' sperit in her."

And so she had, for the baby was no other than

a jar of brandy. She was wont by this means to remove "run" liquor from its *cache* in the sand. A man named Trist had been a notorious smuggler. At last he was caught and given over to the press-gang to be sent on board a man-of-war. Trist bore his capture quietly enough, but as the vessel lay off Cawsand he suddenly slipped overboard and made for a boat that was at anchor, shipped that, and hoisted sail. His Majesty's vessel at once lowered a boat and made in pursuit. After a hard row the sailing smack was come up with and found to be empty. Trist had gone overboard again and swum to a Cawsand fishing-smack, where he lay hid for some days. As there was quite a fleet of these boats on the water, the men in His Majesty's service did not know which to search. So Trist got off and was never secured again.

Near Cawsand is a rock with a white sparry formation on it, like the figure of a woman. This is called Lady's Rock, and the fishermen on returning always cast an offering of a few mackerels or herrings to the ledge before the figure.

A curious custom on May Day exists at Millbrook, once a rotten borough, of the boatmen carrying a dressed ship about the streets with music.

An excursion up the Tamar may be made by steamer to the Weir Head. The river scenery is very fine, especially at the Morwell Rocks. On the way Cothele is passed, the ancient and unaltered mansion of the Edgcumbes, rich in carved wood, tapestry, and ancient furniture. It is the most perfect and characteristic mansion of the fifteenth century in Cornwall. Lower down the river is S. Dominic.

Early in the eighth century Indract, with his sister Dominica, Irish pilgrims, and attendants arrived there, and settled on the Tamar. A little headland, Halton, marks a spot where Indract had a chapel and a holy well. The latter is in good condition ; the former is represented by an ivy-covered wall. However, the church of Landrake (Llan-Indract) was his main settlement, and his sister Dominica founded that now bearing her name. In the river Indract made a salmon weir and trapped fish for his party. But one of these was a thief and greedy, and carried off fish for his own consumption, regardless of his comrades. There were "ructions," and Indract packed his portmanteau and started for Rome. Whether Dominica accompanied him is not stated, but it is probable that she would not care to be left alone in a strange land, though I am certain she would have met with nothing but kindly courtesy from Cornishmen. The party—all but the thief and those who were in the intrigue with him—reached Rome, and returning through Britain came as far as Skapwith, near Glastonbury, where a Saxon hanger-on upon King Ina's court, hearing that a party of travellers was at hand, basely went to their lodgings and murdered them at night in the hopes of getting loot. Ina, his master, who was then at Glastonbury, came to hear of what had been done, and he had the bodies moved to the abbey. Whether he scolded the man who murdered them, or even proceeded to punish him, we are not told.

Bere Ferrers has a fine church, with some old glass in it and a very singular font, that looks almost as if it had been constructed out of a still earlier capital. Bere Alston was once a borough, returning two members.

On the east side of Plymouth is the interesting Plympton S. Mary, with a noble church; Plympton S. Maurice, with a fine modern screen, and the remains of a castle. Here is the old grammar school where Sir Joshua Reynolds received his instruction, and here also is the house in which he was born. He gave his own portrait to the town hall of the little place—for it also was a borough, and, to the lasting disgrace of Plympton be it recorded, the municipality sold it. The old house of Boringdon has a fine hall. The house has twice been altered, and the last alterations are incongruous. One half of the house has been pulled down. Above it is a well-preserved camp. Ermington Church deserves a visit; it has been well restored. It has a bold post-Reformation screen. Holbeton has also been restored in excellent taste. On Revelstoke a vast amount of money has been lavished unsatisfactorily. Near Cornwood station is Fardell, an old mansion of Sir Walter Raleigh, with a chapel.

The same station serves for the Awns and Dendles cascade, and for a visit to the Stall Moor with its long stone row, also the more than two-mile-long row, leading from the Staldon circle, and the old blowing-houses on the Yealm at Yealm Steps. There the old moulds for the tin lie among the ruins of two of these houses, one above the steps, the other below. A further excursion may be made into the Erme valley, with its numerous prehistoric remains, and to the blowing - house at the junction of the Hook Lake. This is comparatively late, as there is a wheel-pit.

North of Plymouth interesting excursions may be made to the Dewerstone, perhaps the finest bit of rock scenery on Dartmoor, or rather at its edge, where the so - called Plym bursts forth from its moorland cradle. The summit of the Dewerstone has been fortified by a double line of walls. A walk thence up the river will take a visitor into some wild country. He will pass Legis Tor with its hut circles in very fair preservation, Ditsworthy Warren, and at Drizzlecombe, coming in from the north, he will see avenues of stones and menhirs and the Giant's Grave, a large cairn, and a well-preserved kistvaen. By the stream bed below is a blowing-house with its tin moulds. Shavercombe stream comes down on the right, and there may be found traces of the slate that overlay the granite, much altered by heat. From Trowlesworthy Warren a wall, fallen, extends, in connection with numerous hut circles, as far as the Yealm. For what purpose it was erected, unless it were a tribal boundary, it is impossible to discover.

A visitor to the Dewerstone should not fail to descend through the wood to the Meavy river, and follow it down to Shaugh Bridge.

An interesting house is Old Newnham, the ancient seat of the Strode family.

Hard by is Peacock Bridge. Here a fight took

place, according to tradition, between a Parker and a Strode, with their retainers, relative to a peacock, and Strode had his thumb cut off in the fray.

Buckland Monachorum also is within reach, the church converted into a mansion.

Meavy Church contains early and rude carving. Sheepstor stands above an artificial lake, the reservoir that supplies Plymouth with water. This occupies the site of an ancient lake, that had been filled with rubble brought down by the torrents from the moor.

A delightful walk may be taken by branching from the Princetown road to Nosworthy Bridge, passing under Leather Tor and following Deancombe, then ascending Combshead Tor to an interesting group of prehistoric remains, a cairn surrounded by a circle of stones, and a stone row leading to a chambered cairn. By continuing the line north-east Nun's or Siward's Cross will be reached in the midst of utter desolation. Far away east is Childe's Tomb, a kistvaen.

The story is that Childe, a hunter, lost himself on the moor. Snow came on, and he cut open his horse, and crept within the carcass to keep himself warm. But even this did not avail.

> So with his finger dipp'd in blood,
>   He scrabbled on the stones :
> "This is my will, God it fulfil,
>   And buried be my bones.
> Whoe'er he be that findeth me,
>   And brings me to a grave,
> The lands that now to me belong
>   In Plymstock he shall have."

The story goes on to say that while the men of Plymstock were preparing to transport the body thither, the monks of Tavistock whipped it off, threw a bridge of planks, since called Guile Bridge, over the Tavy, and interred the hunter in their cemetery, thereby obtaining possession of his lands.

END OF VOL I.

THE DEVON LIBRARY
NUMBER ONE

A Devon Anthology

Devon has always been set apart from up-country England. With Cornwall it was 'anciently one province', and yet it is as different from that county as from the rest of England. Devon has excited strikingly varied feelings, vividly expressed by many writers.

Charles Kingsley and Gerard Manley Hopkins praised its beauties. Coleridge recalled with nostalgia the bells of Ottery St Mary, where he was born. But Herrick loathed 'dull Devonshire' (though he left some touching epitaphs on Devonians) and Keats thought it a 'slipshod' county of cowards – though he liked the idea of romping with Rantipole Betty of Dawlish. Francis Kilvert draws an appetising picture of the girls wading on the beach at Seaton and Fanny Burney a vigorous one of the tough fisherwomen of Teignmouth. Devon, too, was the cradle of the Forsytes, as it was of their creator.

Professor Simmons has ranged widely and deeply through the literature of his county, and his composite picture is a true likeness. It is also the perfect sampler for other titles in *The Devon Library*. Here, illuminating the unique character of their county, are the people of Devon: their speech, proverbs and customs, their literature and their history – from Roman times to the Plymouth air-raids, from Drake and Raleigh to the Lynmouth floods.

Widecombe Fair

Eden Phillpotts knew Devon, and the Devon character, as well as anyone who came to write about the county. Above all he knew, and loved, Dartmoor. The *Dartmoor Cycle* of novels has come to be remembered and admired above all his other work.

Of the Dartmoor novels none was more popular in its day than *Widecombe Fair.* From its pages came a wildly successful play, *The Farmer's Wife,* and two films. There was something about the author's joyous celebration of the Devon character which caught and held the public imagination.

The story of the farmer in search of a wife is only one of several comedies and tragedies of village life here skilfully woven into a satisfying whole. And throughout the book individual personalities emerge, some good some bad, some delightful others absurd, each shot through with the authentic breath of Devon.

L.A.G. Strong, himself a novelist of Devon, wrote of *Widecombe Fair* 'The whole book is mellow and warm as the sunlight of early October in the coombes and hollows of the moor. This is how the people of Devon spoke, round about the start of the twentieth century, accent for accent, rhythm for rhythm, caught and set down with the skill and faith of an artist in words who knew and loved them.'

Mrs Beer's House

Patricia Beer is well-known as a poet and literary critic of distinction; and more recently, with the publication of *Moon's Ottery,* as a novelist. Perhaps her best-known book *Mrs Beer's House* was published first in 1968 when, among many critical plaudits, it was named by P.N.Furbank in *The Times* as 'favourite book of the year'.

It is the story of her Devon childhood between the wars, divided until the age of fourteen between home in Withycombe Raleigh, outside Exmouth, and long spells in Torquay during the school holidays.

Her life, and that of her sister Sheila, was dominated by the personality of her mother, a member of the Plymouth Brethren, and by the peculiar rigidity of the Saints' code which, among other things, virtually consigned her father's family to oblivion, because they were non-believers.

Much has been made of the extraordinary, almost sinister power which Mrs Beer exercised over the household. Indeed, an unforgettable portrait emerges. But this is also a book, written with great subtlety and wit, about the process of growing-up. There is the sea and the seaside, and expeditions to Exeter. There is the experience of Grammar School. And there are fascinating catalogues of books which influenced the future poet. Deceptively innocent observations tick like benevolent time-bombs and explode later in the mind with delight. For all its strangeness, Patricia Beer's childhood will touch-off a host of recollections and delight everyone who reads it.

THE CORNISH LIBRARY

'Well-chosen works from a literary heritage which is as rich as clotted cream.'
The Times

The aim of *The Cornish Library* is to present, in attractive paperback editions, some of the best and most lasting books on Cornwall and the Cornish, both fiction and non-fiction.

Titles in print, or shortly to be published:

All the books in *The Cornish Library* are numbered to encourage collectors. If you would like more information, or you would care to suggest other books that you think should appear in the series, please write to me at the following address: Anthony Mott, The Cornish Library, 50 Stile Hall Gardens, London W4 3BU.